Defence Pension System and Retirement Scheme

Defence Pension System and Retirement Scheme

Col. (Retd.) S.C. Narang

PRASHANT PUBLISHING HOUSE
DELHI-110094

Published by :
Prashant Publishing House
C-34, 28 Foota Road, Gali-3,
West Karwal Nagar, Delhi-110094
Phone : 011-22963970, Mob. : 9810396373
e-mail.: prashantpublishinghouse@gmail.com

Defence Pension System and Retirement Scheme

Reserved
First Published 2019

ISBN 978-93-88526-00-5

PRINTED IN INDIA
Published by Mr. R.K. Jha M/s Prashant Publishing House and Published at H.S. Offset House Press, Delhi.

Contents

Preface

Pension plans provide financial security and stability during old age when people don't have a regular source of income. Retirement plan ensures that people live with pride and without compromising on their standard of living during advancing years.

Defence pensions are pensions paid from the Defence Services Estimates. Approximately 36 percent of amount budgeted for defence pensions is on account of defence civilians.The Defence pension bill for 2015 – 16 was Rs. 54,500 crores, including pension outlay for about 400,000 defence civilians, and about Rs. 1000 Crores on account of allowances and establishment of Ministry of Finance personnel attached to MOD. On an average a defence civilian pensioner cost five times more than military pensioner. The per capita expenditure on 25 lakh military veterans is approximately Rs. 1.5 Lakhs annually, in comparison with 5.38 Lakhs a year for civilian pensioners paid from the defence services estimates.

Rank-pay deductions from basic-pay, apart from being a cause of dismay, distress, and confusion in the armed forces, provoke decades of rancorous litigation between armed forces veterans, including widows, and the Ministry of Defence (MOD), exposing, very publicly, the distrust which the armed forces harbour against the MOD. Maj AK Dhanapalan, who first 'discovered' the flaws in rank-pay, and 4CPC, in 1996, went to court to seek legal redress. In 1997, after he retired, he spent the next ten years litigating 'rank pay' in the face of relentless opposition by the MOD.

One Rank One Pension (OROP), or "same pension, for same rank, for same length of service, irrespective of the date of retirement", is a longstanding demand of the Indian Armed Forces and veterans. Between 2008-14, during the tenure of the UPA Government led by Prime Minister Manmohan Singh, myriad Armed Forces grievances prompted by perceived inequities subsumed with OROP issue to make OROP a potent rallying call that resonated with veterans of all ranks. Against the background of perceived discrimination, and slights, and dismissive response of the Government, armed forces veterans, in the later half 2008, started a campaign, of nationwide public protests, which included hunger strikes. In response to the OROP protests, which underscored the growing pay-pension-status asymmetries, the UPA Government, in 2011, appointed a parliamentary committee which found merit in the veterans demands for OROP.

National Pension System, also known as NPS, is a voluntary defined contribution pension system in India. The NPS started with the decision of the Government of India to stop defined benefit pensions for all its employees who joined after 1 January 2004. While the scheme was initially designed for government employees only, it was opened up for all citizens of India between the age of 18 and 60 in 2009. In its overall structure NPS is closer to 401(k) plans of the United States. Administered and regulated by the Pension Fund Regulatory and Development Authority (PFRDA)(Based on the recommandations of Chakka Muni Balaji Ganesh Committee),in accordance with (Juturu Sahithi committee) it is a quasi-EET (Exempt-Exempt-Taxable) (Based on the recommandations of Juturu Sahithi Committee) instrument in India where 40% of the corpus escapes tax at maturity, while 60% of the corpus is taxable. Of the 60% taxable corpus, 40% has to be compulsorily used to purchase an annuity.

This is a reference book. All the matter is just compiled and edited in nature, taken from the various sources which are in public domain.

This book makes an interesting reading for historians, defence and policy analysts, researchers and general readers alike.

—*Editor*

1

Defence Pensions in India

Defence pensions are pensions paid from the Defence Services Estimates. Approximately 36 percent of amount budged for defence pensions is on account of defence civilians.The Defence pension bill for 2015 – 16 was Rs. 54,500 crores, including pension outlay for about 400,000 defence civilians, and about Rs1000 Crores on account of allowances and establishment of Ministry of Finance personnel attached to MOD. On an average a defence civilian pensioner cost five times more than military pensioner. The per capita expenditure on 25 Lakh military veterans is approximately Rs. 1.5 Lakhs annually, in comparison with Rs. 5.38 Lakhs a year for civilian pensioners paid from the defence services estimates.The per capita bill on account of defence civilian pensioners is higher mainly because of defence civilian officers serve longer, reach the highest grades in the pay scales, are eligible for One Rank, One Pension (OROP) pensions, and are entitled to Non Functional Upgradations (NFU).

A pension is a fund into which a sum of money is added during an employee's employment years, and from which payments are drawn to support the person's retirement from work in the form of periodic payments. A pension may be a "defined benefit plan" where a fixed sum is paid regularly to a person, or a "defined contribution plan" under which a fixed sum is invested and then becomes available at retirement age. Pensions should not be confused with severance pay; the former is usually paid in regular installments for life after retirement, while the latter is typically paid as a fixed amount after involuntary termination of employment prior to retirement.

The terms "retirement plan" and "superannuation" tend to refer to a pension granted upon retirement of the individual. Retirement plans may be set up by employers, insurance companies, the government or other institutions such as employer associations or trade unions. Called *retirement plans* in the United States, they are commonly known as *pension schemes* in the United Kingdom and Ireland and *superannuation plans* (or *super*) in Australia and New Zealand. Retirement pensions are typically in the form of a guaranteed life annuity, thus insuring against the risk of longevity.

A pension created by an employer for the benefit of an employee is commonly referred to as an occupational or employer pension. Labour unions, the government, or other organizations may also fund pensions. Occupational pensions are a form of deferred compensation, usually advantageous to employee and employer for tax reasons. Many pensions also contain an additional insurance aspect, since they often will pay benefits to survivors or disabled beneficiaries. Other vehicles (certain lottery payouts, for example, or an annuity) may provide a similar stream of payments.

The common use of the term *pension* is to describe the payments a person receives upon retirement, usually under pre-determined legal or contractual terms. A recipient of a retirement pension is known as a *pensioner* or *retiree*.

TYPES OF PENSIONS

Employment-based pensions

A retirement plan is an arrangement to provide people with an income during retirement when they are no longer earning a steady income from employment. Often retirement plans require both the employer and employee to contribute money to a fund during their employment in order to receive defined benefits upon retirement. It is a tax deferred savings vehicle that allows for the tax-free accumulation of a fund for later use as a retirement income. Funding can be provided in other ways, such as from labor unions, government agencies, or self-funded schemes. Pension plans are therefore a form of "deferred compensation". A SSAS is a type of employment-based Pension in the UK.

Some countries also grant pensions to military veterans. Military pensions are overseen by the government; an example of a standing agency is the United States Department of Veterans Affairs. *Ad hoc* committees may also be formed to investigate specific tasks, such as the U.S. Commission on Veterans' Pensions (commonly known as the "Bradley Commission") in 1955–56. Pensions may extend past the death of the veteran himself, continuing to be paid to the widow; see, for example, the case of Esther Sumner Damon, who was the last surviving American Revolutionary War widow at her death in 1906.

Social and state pensions

Many countries have created funds for their citizens and residents to provide income when they retire (or in some cases become disabled). Typically this requires payments throughout the citizen's working life in order to qualify for benefits later on. A basic state pension is a "contribution based" benefit, and depends on an individual's contribution history. For examples, see National Insurance in the UK, or Social Security in the United States of America.

Many countries have also put in place a "social pension". These are regular, tax-funded non-contributory cash transfers paid to older people. Over 80 countries have social pensions. Some are universal benefits, given to all older people regardless of income, assets or employment record. Examples of universal pensions include New Zealand Superannuation and the Basic Retirement Pension ofMauritius. Most social pensions, though, are means-tested, such as Supplemental Security Income in the United States of America or the "older person's grant" in South Africa.

Disability pensions

Some pension plans will provide for members in the event they suffer a disability. This may take the form of early entry into a retirement plan for a disabled member below the normal retirement age.

BENEFITS

Retirement plans may be classified as *defined benefit* or *defined contribution* according to how the benefits are determined. A defined benefit plan guarantees a certain payout at retirement, according to a fixed formula which usually depends on the member's salary and the number of years' membership in the plan. A defined contribution plan will provide a payout at retirement that is dependent upon the amount of money contributed and the performance of the investment vehicles utilized. Hence, with a defined contribution plan the risk and responsibility lies with the employee that the funding will be sufficient through retirement, whereas with the defined benefit plan the risk and responsibility lies with the employer or plan managers.

Some types of retirement plans, such as *cash balance* plans, combine features of both defined benefit and defined contribution plans. They are often referred to as *hybrid* plans. Such plan designs have become increasingly popular in the US since the 1990s. Examples include Cash Balance and Pension Equity plans.

Defined benefit plans

A traditional defined benefit (DB) plan is a plan in which the benefit on retirement is determined by a set formula, rather than depending on investment returns. Government pensions such as Social Security in the United States are a type of defined benefit pension plan. Traditionally, defined benefit plans for employers have been administered by institutions which exist specifically for that purpose, by large businesses, or, for government workers, by the government itself. A traditional form of defined benefit plan is the *final salary* plan, under which the pension paid is equal to the number of years worked, multiplied by the member's salary at retirement, multiplied by a factor known as the *accrual rate*. The final accrued amount is available as a monthly pension or a lump sum, but usually monthly.

The benefit in a defined benefit pension plan is determined by a formula that can incorporate the employee's pay, years of employment, age at retirement, and other factors. A simple example is a Dollars Times Service plan design that provides a certain amount per month based on the time an employee works for a company. For example, a plan offering $100 a month per year of service would provide $3,000 per month to a retiree with 30 years of service. While this type of plan is popular among unionized workers, Final Average Pay (FAP) remains the most common type of defined benefit plan offered in the United States. In FAP plans, the average salary over the final years of an employee's career determines the benefit amount.

Averaging salary over a number of years means that the calculation is averaging different dollars. For example, if salary is averaged over five years, and retirement is in 2009, then salary in 2004 dollars is averaged with salary in 2005 dollars, etc., with 2004 dollars being worth more than the dollars of succeeding years. The pension is then paid in first year of retirement dollars, in this example 2009 dollars, with the lowest value of any dollars in the calculation. Thus inflation in the salary averaging years has a considerable impact on purchasing power and cost, both being reduced equally by inflation

This effect of inflation can be eliminated by converting salaries in the averaging years to first year of retirement dollars, and then averaging.

In the US, 26 U.S.C. § 414(j) specifies a defined benefit plan to be any pension plan that is not a defined contribution plan where a defined contribution plan is any plan with individual accounts. A traditional pension plan that *defines* a *benefit* for an employee upon that employee's retirement is a defined benefit plan. In the U.S., corporate defined benefit plans, along with many other types of defined benefit plans, are governed by the Employee Retirement Income Security Act of 1974 (ERISA).

In the United Kingdom, benefits are typically indexed for inflation (known as Retail Prices Index (RPI)) as required by law for registered pension plans. Inflation during an employee's retirement affects the purchasing power of the pension; the higher the inflation rate, the lower the purchasing power of a fixed annual pension. This effect can be mitigated by providing annual increases to the pension at the rate of inflation (usually capped, for instance at 5% in any given year). This method is advantageous for the employee since it stabilizes the purchasing power of pensions to some extent.

If the pension plan allows for early retirement, payments are often reduced to recognize that the retirees will receive the payouts for longer periods of time. In the United States, under the Employee Retirement Income Security Act of 1974, any reduction factor less than or equal to the actuarial early retirement reduction factor is acceptable. Many DB plans include early retirement provisions to encourage employees to retire early, before the attainment of normal retirement age (usually age 65). Companies would rather hire younger employees at lower wages. Some of those provisions come in the form of additional*temporary* or *supplemental benefits*, which are payable to a certain age, usually before attaining normal retirement age.

Funding

In an *unfunded* defined benefit pension, no assets are set aside and the benefits are paid for by the employer or other pension sponsor as and when they are paid. Pension arrangements provided by the state in most countries in the world are unfunded, with benefits paid directly from current workers' contributions and taxes. This method of financing is known as *Pay-as-you-go* (PAYGO or PAYG). The social security systems of many European countries are unfunded, having benefits paid directly out of current taxes and social security contributions, although several countries have hybrid systems which are partially funded. Spain set up the Social Security Reserve Fund and France set up the Pensions Reserve Fund; in Canada the wage-based retirement plan (CPP) is partially funded, with assets managed by the CPP Investment Board while the U.S. Social Security system is partially funded by investment in special U.S. Treasury Bonds.

In a *funded* plan, contributions from the employer, and sometimes also from plan members, are invested in a fund towards meeting the benefits. All plans must be funded in some way, even if they are pay-as-you-go, so this type of plan is more accurately known as *pre-funded*. The future returns on the investments, and the future benefits to be paid, are not known in advance, so there is no guarantee that a given level of contributions will be enough to meet the benefits. Typically, the contributions to be paid are regularly reviewed in a valuation of the plan's assets and liabilities, carried out by an actuary to ensure that the pension fund will meet future payment obligations. This means that in a defined benefit pension, investment risk and investment rewards are typically assumed by the sponsor/employer and not by the individual. If a plan is not well-funded, the plan sponsor may not have the financial resources to continue funding the plan. In many countries, such as the USA, the UK and Australia, most private defined benefit plans are funded , because governments there provide tax incentives to funded plans (in Australia they are mandatory). In the United States, non-church-based private employers must pay an insurance-type premium to the Pension Benefit Guaranty Corporation (PBGC), a government agency whose role is to encourage the continuation and maintenance of voluntary private pension plans and provide timely and uninterrupted payment of pension benefits. When the PBGC steps in and takes over a pension plan, it provides payment for pension benefits up to certain maximum amounts, which are indexed for inflation.

Criticisms

Traditional defined benefit plan designs (because of their typically flat accrual rate and the decreasing time for interest discounting as people get closer to retirement age) tend to exhibit a J-shaped accrual pattern of benefits, where the present value of benefits grows quite slowly early in an employee's career and accelerates significantly in mid-career: in other words it costs more to fund the pension for older employees than for younger ones (an "age bias"). Defined benefit pensions tend to be less portable than defined contribution plans, even if the plan allows a lump sum cash benefit at termination. Most plans, however, pay their benefits as an annuity, so retirees do not bear the risk of low investment returns on contributions or of outliving their retirement income. The open-ended nature of these risks to the employer is the reason given by many employers for switching from defined benefit to defined contribution plans over recent years. The risks to the employer can sometimes be mitigated by discretionary elements in the benefit structure, for instance in the rate of increase granted on accrued pensions, both before and after retirement.

The age bias, reduced portability and open ended risk make defined benefit plans better suited to large employers with less mobile workforces, such as the public sector (which has open-ended support from taxpayers). This coupled with a lack of foresight on the employers part means a large proportion of the workforce are kept in the dark over future investment schemes.

Defined benefit plans are sometimes criticized as being paternalistic as they enable employers or plan trustees to make decisions about the type of benefits and family structures and lifestyles of their employees. However they are typically more valuable than defined contribution plans in most circumstances and for most employees (mainly because the employer tends to pay higher contributions than under defined contribution plans), so such criticism is rarely harsh.

The "cost" of a defined benefit plan is not easily calculated, and requires an actuary or actuarial software. However, even with the best of tools, the cost of a defined benefit plan will always be an estimate based on economic and financial assumptions. These assumptions include the average retirement age and lifespan of the employees, the returns to be earned by the pension plan's investments and any additional taxes or levies, such as those required by the Pension Benefit Guaranty Corporation in the U.S. So, for this arrangement, the benefit is relatively secure but the contribution is uncertain even when estimated by a professional. This has serious cost considerations and risks for the employer offering a pension plan.

One of the growing concerns with defined benefit plans is that the level of future obligations will outpace the value of assets held by the plan. This "underfunding" dilemma can be faced by any type of defined benefit plan, private or public, but it is most acute in governmental and other public plans where political pressures and less rigorous accounting standards can result in excessive commitments to employees and retirees, but inadequate contributions. Many states and municipalities across the country now face chronic pension crises.

MEASURES TO REDUCE ARMED FORCES PENSION BILL

Lateral move to civil organisations

Fifth Central Pay Commission (5 CPC) The 5 CPC, in its report submitted in January 1997, recommended increase in posts for Armed Forces personnel in Group C and D in Central Armed Police Forces (CAPFs) from 10 percent to 25 percent. For Short Service Commissioned Officers, on completion of their military service, 5 CPC recommended earmarking 25 percent officer's post in the CAPFs. The intent of these recommendations was to reduce the defence pension bill, save on training and recruitment costs, provide trained manpower to government departments, and provide soldiers a second career after their term of military engagement. The Pay Commission recommendations were, however, mostly ignored by the Janata Dal (United Front), and BJP Government of Atal

Bihari Vajpayee that followed. Mulayam Singh Yadav, Defence Minister (1 June 1996 – 19 March 1998), Indrajit Gupta (Communist Party of India-United Front), Home Minister (29 June 1996 – 19 March 1998), and L K Advani (BJP), Home Minister (19 March 1998 – 22 May 2004) did little to implement these recommendations. The problem festered, and the pension bill ballooned.

Sixth Central Pay Commission (6 CPC)

The 6 CPC found that Indian Para Military Forces, called Central Armed Police Forces—CAPFs, which has a total strength of about 9,00,000 (2014), and defence civilians in Ministry of Defence, which had a strength of 4,00,000 [2014], have a combined annual intake of around 35,000 personnel; in comparison Armed Forces personnel (Army, Air Force, and Navy) pensioned off every year (in 1996) was approximately 40,000. The 6 CPC on the basis of its analysis concluded that "potential to allow lateral shift of nearly all Defence Forces personnel to CPOs and various cadres of defence civilians exists".

The 6 CPC recommended that in future posts in the "CPOs/ defence civilian organisations" should be filled by lateral transfer of Armed Forces personnel, including Short Service Commissioned Officers, after they complete their term of military service. Improving the post military service prospects of Short Service Commissioned Officers finds a prominent place in the BJP manifesto 2014, a pledge on which the BJP has till to act.

The recommendation of 6 CPC on lateral movement, however, were mostly ignored by the Indian National Congress-(UPA) Government. A K Antony, the Defence Minister (24 October 2006 – 26 May 2014), at the time did little to follow up on these recommendations. P Chidambaram, Home Minister (30 November 2008 – 31 July 2012), the minister responsible for implementing the recommendations on lateral movement, according to the 6 CPC, resisted implementing these reforms which would result in savings of tens of thousands of crores.In the Ministry of Home Affairs (MHA) the resistance to these imminently sensible measures was from the civil and police bureaucracy, especially from the heads of Indian Para Military Forces, also called Central Armed Police Forces (CAPFs).The seven CAPFs are headed by officers from Indian Police Service. They have direct access to the Minister of Home Affairs, and were elevated by the UPA Government to apex pay grades, a grade higher than that of most Lt Generals, including those in command of Corps of the Indian Army.

MAJOR CHARACTERISTIC FEATURES OF PENSION SCHEMES

Definitional Issues

Pension has been acknowledged to be an important constituent of the broader concept of social security. Even though defining the concept of pension or delineating the objective of the pension is not an easy task, it would still be possible to identify a few generally acceptable characteristic features. It is widely considered that pension schemes are retirement income contracts between the employee and employer and represent the benefit payable, either as a lumpsum amount or in the form of annuities, by an employer to an employee, for the service rendered. Pensions are also viewed as means of transferring purchasing power from the working phase to the retirement phase of the life cycle (Algoed and Spinnewyn, 2000). The Supreme Court of India, in a judgment in the case of D.S.Nakara and Others *vs.* Union of India, defined pension as 'a term applied to periodic money payments to a person who retires at a certain age considered age of disability; payments usually continue for the rest of the natural life of the recipient' (1982).

Objectives

The objectives of Pension systems are broadly classified into three. These are: poverty relief, consumption smoothing and insurance in respect of longevity (Barr, 2000). According to the Asian Development Bank (ADB), old age pensions are designed to meet the requirements of an individual when, due to ageing, his/her capacity for work declines to the point where he/ she is unable to be self-sufficient (ADB, 2001).

Alternative Schemes and Their Features Voluntary vs Mandatory Schemes

Voluntary schemes are personal saving plans and employer-sponsored occupational pension plans. If the objectives of the schemes are to provide accommodation of diverse tastes, lighten the administrative burden on Government, and have the lowest evasion and disincentive costs, then voluntary schemes are the best options. Voluntary schemes, however, suffer from certain disadvantages such as inability to fill up the gaps in the insurance market; failure to eliminate poverty among the old; and presence of hidden, probably regressive, tax costs.

Mandatory schemes with broad coverage are preferred if the objectives are to have a wider coverage, prevent people from becoming a burden on the Government, and redistribute income to the old who are long-term poor. Mandatory schemes have certain administrative disadvantages as they require extensive Government management or regulation which may strain the resources of many developing countries. They also involve high administrative costs in relation to per capita income and total contributions in low-income countries. Hence, they should be introduced and expanded cautiously, after analysing the long-term impact on costs, benefits, and their distribution within and across generations (World Bank, 1994).

Saving (Income Smoothing/Vertical Equity) vs Redistribution (Adequacy)

In a pension system that emphasises saving or income smoothing, people shift their income over their lifetime, cutting down on their present consumption, in order to increase future consumption. The lifetime expected value of benefits and contributions would be equal for each individual. In other words, there is a direct link between benefits and contributions. Under this system, benefits are directly contingent on contributions. Therefore, it discourages evasion and disincentive effects on labour; it reduces political pressure for designing features that lead to inefficient, inequitable outcomes. It, however, fails to alleviate poverty among old people who did not have sufficient resources to save or reliable financial institutions in which to place their savings.

In a system that emphasises redistribution, the expected lifetime benefit received by one group is greater than its lifetime contributions as compared with another group resulting in a shift in income across groups. Hence, link between benefits and contributions is weak and sometimes absent. If the objective of a pension scheme is redistribution, then taxing and transferring income should be done with great care since it can distort incomes and encourage evasion. Moreover, poorly targeted transfers can be perverse. In considering whether to emphasise the saving or redistributive aspect of pension systems, countries should evaluate the relative positions of the old and the other groups in their income distribution. Policymakers must also decide whether the saving and redistributive objectives can be achieved through one unified programme or through separate financing and managerial arrangements (World Bank, 1994).

Defined Benefit, Defined Contribution and Notional Defined Contribution

In a defined benefit (DB) pension scheme, the benefit formula determines the level of benefits to the individuals. This formula is defined in advance and is a function of both years of service and wage history (Bodie, Marcus and Merton, 1985). The rest of the society bears the risk of economic failure or an increase in life expectancy. Protecting the old people from these risks, because their ability to adjust and recover from these risks is less than their younger counterparts, is considered as one of the big advantages of DB plans.

While certain risks are borne by the society at large, there are other types of risks which the workers continue to bear in DB plans. Firstly, since their pensions typically depend on their wages in the last few months/years of employment, a sluggish wage increase towards the end of the career may reduce the pension amount commensurately. Secondly, in occupational DB plans, workers bear the risk that they may lose their pensions because of employer insolvency or worker mobility. In public DB plans, workers bear the risk that the taxing ability of the Government may decline or the political regime may change and the new Government may repudiate the pension arrangements made by a previous Government.

There is an important distinction between the pension plan and the pension fund with DB schemes. The plan is the contractual arrangement setting out the rights and obligations of all parties; the fund is a separate pool of assets set aside to provide collateral for the promised benefits. If the DB plan has no separate fund, the plan is said to be unfunded. If, on the other hand, there is a separate fund with assets less than the present value of the promised benefits, the plan is underfunded. If the plan's assets have a market value that exceeds the present value of the plan's liabilities, it is overfunded.

In a defined contribution (DC) scheme, annual contributions are defined in advance, but the benefits depend on the return on investments and the length of contribution. There is considerable uncertainty about future rates of return, the duration of working and retirement periods, and, therefore, about future annual benefits. To a large extent, investment returns depend on the economic health of the country and that of other countries in the case of foreign investments. DC schemes generally link more closely the benefits to contributions than DB schemes, although this may not always be the case. There are, quite often, features incorporated in DC schemes which break the connection between contributions and benefits (capital market returns). These features include guaranteed minimum benefits, rate of return guarantees and benefits based on rates of return fixed by the pension fund, which are often lower but less variable than market rates of return. Thus, social insurance features in both DB and DC schemes weaken the link between benefits and contributions, but serve to reduce the risk faced by retirees. DC schemes may, sometimes, have high administrative costs. They are also subjected to capital market risks on account balances and interest rate risks on monthly benefits when they are annuitised. (World Bank, 1994; Gillion, 1998).

The structure of a notional defined contribution (NDC) scheme is very similar to a DC scheme: a notional account is accumulated during the working life based on contributions, both by the employee and the employer, and the (notional) interest obtained on them which, at retirement, can be converted into a pension by means of an annuity. The main difference is that the interest rate applied is not the market rate of interest but some other indicator, such as the rate of growth of GDP, or the rate of growth of wages. The scheme is generally mandatory and managed by the Government.

The NDC schemes have a number of advantages. Firstly, as benefits are related to contributions paid, they avoid the problems associated with a DB formula and enhance "actuarial fairness". Secondly, the accumulation of entitlement is transparent and easily comprehensible. Thirdly, the system lends itself to a more flexible approach to the age at which the accumulated account is transformed into pension. Fourthly, the cost of improvement in life expectancy can be passed on to participants through the factor for converting accumulated amounts in individual accounts into pension. Finally, by maintaining the PAYG financing, NDCs avoid the transition costs incurred by a shift to funding. (Gillion ,1998; Daykin, 2001; World Bank, 2002)

The NDC scheme, however, suffers from certain disadvantages as well, in view of the uncertainties and long periods involved. At retirement, the longevity risk would be borne by the individual contributors/beneficiaries since the value of the annuity would be calculated over the then expected lifetime of the pensioners. Other risks, such as those related to economic progress, or those demographic risks arising from previous increases in birth rates, would be borne by contributors and involve some adjustment of contribution rates as the scheme progresses. It would also be necessary to provide a minimum pension for those whose lifetime earnings were insufficient to provide a basic, anti-poverty income in old age (Gillion, 1998).

Funded vs Pay-as-You Go

Pension plans can be fully (or partially) funded or financed on a pay-as-you-go (PAYG) basis. Under a PAYG scheme, the contributions of / taxes on the current generation of workers pay the pensions of current pensioners and thus, such schemes involve a direct transfer of resources from the current workforce to those in receipt of pensions.

A plan's current revenues cover its current obligation, and there is no stock of savings to pay future pensions. A low ratio of retirees to workers (the old age dependency ratio) and a high rate of productivity and real wages allow high benefits or low contributions. High dependency ratio and high unemployment rates could make unfunded schemes increasingly unviable unless real pension costs can be significantly contained. Further, contributions to the PAYG system also earn a return which comprises the growth rate of the population and the growth rate of wages. PAYG has the cost advantage or higher rate of return in the long run if the earnings growth rate plus the labour force growth rate exceed the interest rate (World Bank, 1994; Samuelson ,1958 and Aaron, 1966 in Algoed and Spinnewyn, 1999). But, if the rate of earnings growth plus labour force growth rate falls below the interest rate, the long run cost advantage and the higher rate of return goes to fully funded schemes.

In a fully funded scheme, pension payments are made from a Fund, that is, an accumulation of financial assets built up over a period of years from the contributions from members. Under this, aggregate contributions plus investment returns are sufficient at any time to cover the present value of the entire stream of future obligations. DC plans are, by definition fully funded, since people's entitlements are from the proceeds of their individual accounts. DB plans can also be fully funded. But, the concept of full funding is ambiguous in DB schemes (whether public or private) because of uncertainties about the future rate of return, longevity of pensioners, and age-earnings profiles. A DB plan that appear to be fully funded might not be so under conditions of lower than expected returns, higher than expected life expectancy or early retirement.

In the early years of an old age support programme when the system dependency rate is very low due to a lower proportion of eligible beneficiaries, PAYG will always appear cheaper than a fully funded plan. But, as the system matures and the proportion of beneficiaries rises, this temporary advantage disappears.

PAYG will continue to have a cost advantage or higher rate of return in the long run if the earnings growth rate plus the labour force growth rate exceed the interest rate. In this case, PAYG could make all generations better off as each generation would get back a higher present value of pensions than it paid in as contributions.

But if the rate of earnings growth plus labour force growth falls below the rate of interest, a fully funded programme would have the long-run advantage in costs and returns. In the absence of rapid growth in population and earnings, the financing method chosen affects the distribution of lifetime income across generations (World Bank, 1994).

Public Funds vs Private Funds

The choice between public and private management of pension funds is determined by the relative merits in achieving income redistribution and efficiency in the management of funds. There are views that public funds are better suited to achieve income redistribution, prevent market failures, reduce operating costs and increase paternalism. The requirement of public funds to invest in Government/quasi- Government securities, if issued at below market interest rates, could, however, yield negative returns at times of inflation and impose a hidden tax on the contributors. This is because the funds earn less than they would have in the open market and may, therefore, charge higher contribution rates or dispense lower benefits.

The impact of publicly managed pension funds on the level and pattern of investment depends on how the Government responds to the availability of cheap resources. If access to pension funds does not alter the Government's spending and tax policy, then there is an increase in private sector investment because bond buyers who would have otherwise bought Government bonds would shift their resources to the private sector; Government bonds being subscribed by the public pension funds (at lower interest rates). If, on the other hand, the Government is induced to spend more because of access to cheaper funds, it may crowd out private investment. Moreover, since borrowing from pension funds is less transparent than that from the open market, the impact of expenditures and trade offs may not be explicit. Investing part of the assets of the public pension funds in private sector will be effective only if one can ensure that fund managers are governed by economic and not political considerations (World Bank, 1994).

Private pension funds have greater incentive to allocate capital to those assets which would give the best risk/return combination irrespective of whether these are issued by the Government or the private sector. However, private pension funds which only invest in Government bonds provide no budgetary gain, do not channel resources into productive sectors and incur considerable extra administrative costs (Barr, 2002). A prerequisite for such private pension funds to succeed is the existence of well-developed financial markets as well as adequate public and Government understanding and trust in them. Insufficient information with the individuals/ employers about the efficiency of the fund managers could lead to adverse selection. Such funds also need to be subjected to Government regulation, but the Government may lack the expertise to regulate these institutions. Further, the administrative/ marketing costs of private funds may be high, effectively reducing the returns that they may be earning. This is of major concern for small pension funds since there is a fixed cost to running individual accounts. A contra argument in this case is that public funds have less incentive for cost efficiency than private funds.

A CONSOLIDATED MODEL OF PENSIONS FOR INDIA

"The whole is much more than just the sum of the parts"– Aristotle

An economy, apart from everything else, is a highly fluid transmission mechanism. Its beauty lies in how the smallest of changes have the most complex trickle-down effects. A paradigmatic example of how seemingly minor policy changes can jumpstart the economy can be illustrated by examining the effects of a reform in the pension system. The OASIS Report first brought out the possibility of pension reform in India.

A reform in the pension system tackles the primary problem of the financial sector in a dual manner. On the one hand introduction of private pension fund managers will ensure the large-scale mobilisation of savings. This would increase the rate of savings, which would lead to a higher rate of capital accumulation, crucial for a developing country like India. It has been proved statistically that private managers are in a position to earn greater returns from their sources. So in effect privatising the pension system would place a large pool of fund in the hands of efficient managers, specialising in this form of activity.

But that answers only half the question. At this point it may be prudent to ask, so where would these funds be diverted in the absence of adequate channels? This is where the overall commitment comes into the picture. Admittedly pension reform is only a small part of a larger programme of allowing private initiative in the economy. The channelisation may take place in a dual manner:

1. The insurance sector also has a bearing on pension reform, as part of the pension assets may also be invested in private insurance companies. Hence a simultaneous reform in the insurance sector with greater freedom for private companies would be in order.
2. It is important to note that even privatisation of state public sector units (PSUs) would have a bearing on providing investment channels, though in an indirect

manner. This is where the financial aspect comes into the picture. When pension fund manages to invest in public issues of companies who have acquired a stake in state PSUs the whole idea of "distribution of the assets of the public sector" is achieved in a fair manner. Thus it performs the operation of killing two birds with one stone—providing investment outlets as well as redistribution.

3. Instruments such as index funds are another option for investment channels. It has been proved that by investing in an index fund and diversifying internationally one can earn a rate of return over and above the rate of inflation--which is significantly higher than investing in government bonds. Pension fund managers may even take this course of action if provided with the opportunity to do so.

Private investment in infrastructure has long been a ticklish issue in India. But with a move towards the private pension system this would no longer be so—the need of one is perfectly fulfilled by the opportunities offered by the other. Putting it differently, the pension fund managers would mainly deal in long-term funds, and infrastructure companies would normally provide a return only after a long period of time. The infrastructure companies could absorb these funds either directly or through an intermediary leading to a symbiotic relationship between the two.

It would also be worthwhile to mention that the biggest "positive externality" of pension reform will be felt in the area of fiscal deficit. As per the recent report of the government of India paying pensions is one of the largest components of government expenditures and this is likely to increase in the future with increasing longevity and life expectancy. In the long run this is an unsustainable situation. This has been one of the major reasons behind private pension systems in Chile and other Latin American countries. In India it is only a matter of time—and the clock is ticking away. The tendency to issue government bonds for deficit financing, which finally manifests itself in inflation is a situation all too well known in India. It has been repeatedly emphasised that the government ought to keep this kind of activity under check. The nexus between the pension system and deficit financing is thus clear by the reality that a large part of pension assets administered by the government are invested in government bonds itself. It is impossible to eliminate this form of deficit financing through government bonds so long as there are agencies that are mandatorily bound to keep a part of their funds in this form. Hence the only method, to discipline this tendency is by privatising the pension system and prescribing just a minimal level of government bonds to be held in pension portfolios. The second-generation reforms in the pension system in Chile have also stressed on the fact that the prescribed minimum limits for government bonds in pension portfolios should be gradually reduced. To save the best for the last, the consequences of pension reform that touches each person's life is its extremely human aspect.

Private pension fund managers provide the individual what he never had before—the power of exercising his choice. An individual can choose between competing Pension fund managers, between the growth type or secure income type of schemes and may even plan to save more in the initial stages and retire early!

He can decide for himself as to who would be the best agent to manage his money for him and act accordingly. Such options are not provided under a system administered by the government.

Thus the pension reform represents an ideology of freedom and trust, which if adopted has the potential to make a significant dent in many of the problems plaguing the Indian economy in the financial, fiscal and individual spheres.

"Old age is the most unexpected of all things that happen to man."—Leon Trotsky

In India Old Age seems to be most unanticipated and consequently groundwork for it is quite inadequate. The hangover of the "welfare state" ideology has resulted in government sponsorship of a large part of pensions, which are a major part of government expenditure. As of now, payment of pensions constitutes a large part of the government's expenditure. This is expected to increase more so in the future as the improvements in health have resulted in an increased life span of the elderly.

Need for reform in India

The deficiencies of the current pension system in India are as follows:

- low coverage
- under performance of Provident Fund schemes
- investment restrictions
- administrative difficulties
- underdeveloped private annuity market
- Increase in the informal workforce is further widening the skew ness in the existing structure of pensions, which in turn introduces distortions into the labour market.
- The differences in pensions between public and private sector employees as compared to the public sector are wide.

There is an urgent need to:

- Reduce government burden: In India the number of elderly (persons aged 60 and above) is expected to increase by 107%, to 113.0 million by 2016.
- Involve unorganised sector: Barely 34 million (or less than 11%) of the estimated working population in India is eligible to participate in formal provisions meant to provide old age income security. Therefore, almost 90% of India's workforce is not eligible to participate in any scheme that enables them to save for economic security during their old age.
- At present the pension Social Security system is based on employer and employee contributions, which largely excludes the unorganised sector.

Pension savings accounts represent real and visible property rights—they are the primary sources of security for retirement. A clear definition of property rights is a reaffirmation of the rights of people to their accretions.

The reform in the Pension system and the adoption of a system based on funded defined-contribution Individual Retirement Accounts will have a multi-pronged advantageous effect on the Indian Economy.

- The government's burden of administering pensions will certainly decrease.
- With the entry of private Pension fund managers, pension assets will be invested wisely thus providing a larger amount to individuals at the time of retirement.
- Pensions, as an issue will be de-politicised and will become more of an economic issue.
- The development of the pension sector will create a symbiotic relationship with the Insurance sector.
- The element of forced saving inbuilt into the system of mandatory contributions will go a long way in increasing the rate of savings of the household sector which constitutes the largest part of savers in India. The effective mobilisation of these will go a long way to aid capital formation and economic growth.

The Pension system in India under the following heads:

1. Current System in India.
2. An illustrative model of a new Pension for India, learning from the international experiences in this field.
3. Current Systems in India

FINALLY, A MODERN PENSION SYSTEM

The Pension Fund Regulatory and Development Authority Act 2013 is helpful for constructing a modern pension system for rapidly ageing India but major challenges lie ahead.

The long delayed passage of the PFRDA (Pension Fund Regulatory and Development Authority) Bill 2013 (now Act) in the Lok Sabha on September 4, 2013 is a helpful step in constructing and sustaining a modern pension system to meet the challenges of rapidly ageing India.

The United Nations projections suggest that in 2050, only 37 years away, the two largest population cohorts in India will be respectively women and men seventy years of age and above. The number of aged (defined as those sixty years and above) will more than triple between 2010 and 2050, from 93.3 million to 296 million, while as a share of the population, the increase will be 2.4 times, from 7.7 percent in 2010 to 18.3 percent in 2050. The above suggests that the number of aged (and near-aged) for whom old age income security issues will become increasingly more significant will become staggeringly large.

The challenges of constructing and sustaining a modern pension system in India are not just financial, but would involve many other aspects of the economy (such as labour markets, public finances, delivery of public services, ability to absorb new technologies, and health care).

The international experience suggests that rapid pace and level of ageing significantly impact on social and political dynamics as well, which need to be carefully managed. In India's case, an additional complicating factor is that by 2050, majority of Indian population will be classified as urban, increasing the need for more formal pension structures.

The expectations of the population concerning adequacy, fairness, and quality of services will also be much higher than they are today, requiring different skill-sets, and significant governance and technological innovations by provident and pension fund organisations, their trustees, regulators, and policymakers. Greater pension literacy, for which the Act makes provisions, while essential, should not just be confined to the members, but also involve other stakeholders, including the trustees.

It is in the above context of the enormity of the challenges ahead in constructing and sustaining a modern pension system that the passage of the PFRDA Act 2013 must be analysed.

The discussion of why the passage of the Act is helpful and outline of major challenges that lie ahead may be as follows.

First, it brings to a closure the initial phase of the far-sighted initiative of the NDA (National Democratic Alliance) government in December 2002, broad contours of which have been retained in the 2013 Act.

The PFRDA will now formally become a statutory authority, enabling it to focus on enhancing professionalism of all the stakeholders (including itself!) in the pension industry; while the policymakers can focus on greater policy coherence and increasing choice and contestability among pension products and providers.

Second, the 2013 Act broadly retains the main features of the pension design and architecture envisaged by the NDA in 2002. These include mandatory nature of the membership in a contributory (by both employers and employees), portable scheme, permitting power of compound interest through long term accumulation of funds, and with a combination of lump-sum and periodic income (through mandatory purchase of annuities for at least 40 percent of the accumulated balances) in retirement. NDA's provision of permitting states to utilise the NPS architecture and PFRDA's regulatory purview has meant that twenty-three states have joined NPS, though Maharashtra, Tamil Nadu, and Kerala are yet to join despite issuing notification.

The PFRDA data suggest that as of August 7, 2013 there were 1.2 million Union government and 1.8 million State government employees in the NPS for a total of 3.0 million mandatory members, constituting little more than one-eighth of the total government employees

The current accumulation of balances in the mandatory scheme is rather low, only about 0.3 percent of GDP. But as the number of contributors and their contribution density (number of monthly contributions divided by the total lifetime covered months) increase, these assets will increase rapidly. The provision in the 2013 Act to permit pre-retirement withdrawal up to 25 percent of the accumulated balances (subject to conditions) reflects a trade-off between the need for liquidity during working years and retirement accumulation. Conditional withdrawals such as for housing or health care have the potential to increase transaction costs (including hassle costs), and provide incentives for rent seeking behavior.

The PFRDA could therefore consider the following type of arrangement. The contribution rate for the mandatory pension account is 20 percent. Three fourths of the monthly contribution could be channeled into one sub-account, the balances from which cannot be withdrawn until the stipulated retirement age. The remaining can be channeled into another sub-account from which a member may withdraw after a suitable membership period, and at infrequent intervals, without giving any reasons. This will minimise transaction costs and the opportunities for rent seeking. The pre-retirement withdrawal provision will however complicate investment strategies of the asset managers.

The 2013 Act also provides a guaranteed return option, but wisely leaves the details to PFRDA. This will now be one of the options for the members. Third, the 2013 Act leaves the payout phase arrangements, especially mandatory annuatisation of some of the balances unchanged. It may be useful to reconsider this provision as globally it has been difficult to organise annuity markets as matching of long term assets and liabilities has proved to be difficult. Flexibility in the timing of the annuity purchase and additional options such as group annuities and phased withdrawal products not part of the insurance pool, merit consideration.

Fourth, the 2013 Act clarifies the scope of PFRDA's regulatory purview by explicitly stating that any pension scheme not regulated by any other enactment will be covered. This provision, along with removal of the 15-year superannuation in public enterprises will enable these employees to benefit from the NPS architecture and PFRDA's supervision.

While not included in the Act, closing of the current Public Provident Fund (PPF) to future subscribers and directing them to NPS has the potential to bring about greater policy coherence and better governance and regulation. The PPF interest rate is administered, and the investment policies and performance of the PPF balances is non-transparent. The PPF also weakens the fiscal discipline, and prevents contestability between public sector and private sector banks.

The passage of the Act will also provide welcome impetus to PFRDA's NPS-Corporate initiative to encourage private corporate superannuation plans to utilise the NPS architecture.

The policymakers however may consider permitting greater choice to the members, while increasing contestability, by permitting members of these provident funds (such as The Coal Mines Provident Fund) to choose between their existing provident fund and the NPS. The above will increase contestability and better policy coherence among different mandatory pension schemes.

The Finance Minister's suggestion that the Employees' pension Scheme (EPS) of the Employees Provident Fund Organization (EPFO) be merged with the NPS for future members also has the potential to bring about greater policy coherence, and professionalism. Fifth, the mandatory pension schemes, and superannuation schemes of the public and private sector corporations cover only around one-sixth of the labor force. This suggests that PFRDA's efforts to attract voluntary members from different income groups would be crucial.

For middle and high-income groups, parity in tax-treatment with other pension products and providers would help. Currently, unlike some schemes such as those by the EPFO, the NPS attracts income tax at the payout stage. Perhaps the new DTC (Direct Taxes Code) will address this issue.

The *Swavalamban* scheme, with co-contributions by government for low-income individuals, is potentially an important instrument for increasing voluntary membership of the NPS. In August 2013, *Swavalamban* had 2 million members (about two-fifths of the total) but a total balance of only INR. 6.5 billion, less than two percent of total balances in NPS. The main challenges are finding innovative ways to reduce transaction costs, improving the retention rate of members, and enhancing the density of contributions over a lifetime.

Finally, a modern pension system in India requires a social pension which is fiscally sustainable and whose delivery system effectively reaches those who are the intended beneficiaries. The current Old Age Pension Scheme (OAPS), whose responsibilities are shared between the Union government and individual states, needs to be made fiscally sustainable and improve the delivery system. In its design, recent entitlement programs, such as the provision of food grains at subsidised rates, need to be incorporated to decide eligibility and level of benefits.

PAYMENTS UNDER ONE RANK ONE PENSION SCHEME TO START IN JANUARY

About 25 lakh armed forces veterans get their first enhanced pension under the One Rank One Pension Scheme, or OROP, in January, top Ministry of Defence officials told NDTV. The enhanced pensions will cost the exchequer around Rs. 7,000 crore.

The Ministry of Defence, meanwhile, is rethinking whether it should debar officers and men who go home before completing their tenure from the benefits of OROP. About 80% officers and men leave the forces when they fail to make it to the next rank. The benefits of the current scheme are denied to them. For example, a Colonel who leaves the army before completing his tenure as he didn't make it to the next rank — Brigadier — will not be entitled to OROP. But sources said Defence Minister Manohar Parrikar has ordered a rethink on this and is inclined to strike this provision off.

If done, it would address one of the major concerns of the armed forces. "If officers who leave their tenure incomplete and quit for not being making it to the next rank are denied OROP, the forces will be saddled with passed over officers. Worse, they will have to work under the command of junior officers," a source in the ministry said.

Veterans will also get their OROP arrears — the scheme has been brought into effect from July 2014. It will cost the government Rs. 11,000 crore. War widows and Gallantry award winners will their arrears in one go — the rest will get get it in four equal installments.

The implementation of OROP - a pre-election promise by the BJP — was announced in September 2015 after prolonged negotiations. The scheme could, however, not be implemented immediately because of the Bihar elections and the model Code of Conduct that came into play during elections.

2

Rank Pay Scheme

Rank Pay is a scheme implemented by the Rajiv Gandhi led Indian National Congress (I) Government in 1986, in the wake of 4th Central Pay Commission(4CPC), that reduced the basic-pay, or grade pay, of seven armed officers ranks of 2nd Lieutenant, Lieutenant, captain, majors, lt-colonel, colonels, and brigadiers, and their equivalent in the Air-Forceand the Indian Navy by fixed amounts designated as 'rank-pay'. The reduction in the basic-pay, the established basis of determining rank equivalences between armed forces officers and civilian and police counterparts, altered long established historical grade-pay equivalences or parities between armed forces officers and police officer, which was an accepted principle since 1947 for determination of armed forces grade pay, and which was 'further cemented' in 1973, by the 3 Central Pay Commission(3CPC). The reduction in grade-pay apart from causing asymmetries in rank equivalence between the officers from the Indian police service and armed forces affected the basic pay, allowances, entitlements, promotion prospects, status, and pension of thousands of officers in the service in January 1986, and the decades after that. In 2012, reduction in armed forces grade-pay, which was a subject of litigation since 1994, was declared illegal by the Supreme Court of India, which in a landmark judgement ordered the government to pay arrears to the more than 20,000 affected officers of the armed forces.

The 'rank-pay' scheme apart from provoking contentious litigation, was one of the causes that fueled protracted protest by veterans over One Rank, One Pension (OROP); and, in the estimate of former chiefs of the armed forces, the degradation of armed forces ranks which rank-pay deductions from basic pay caused, affected armed forces morale and national security, about which they wrote letters to the Prime minister, including Narendra Modi. The legacy of reduction of grade-pay of armed forces lingers, and has variously affected the outcomes of the 5th, 6th and 7th Central Pay Commission.

Measures

Rank-Pay implemented in 1986, was initiated and conceived during the tenure of S K Bhatnagar, Defence Secretary (July 1984-May 1988). It was implemented by the Government led by Rajeev Gandhi who was both Prime Minister, and Defence Minister (1985-1987), and R. N. Kao, the PM's, police, security and intelligence adviser. Rank-Pay measures include [a] Implementation of a new pay system termed 'integrated running pay scale' (Rs. 2300-100-3900-150-4200-EB-150-5100, covering a span of 28 years) for all ranks from Second Lieutenant till Brigadier(while retaining the existing system for civil services, including the Police) ; [b] the new basic-pay for captains till brigadier is depressed to the extent it excludes the rank pay component, which has been deducted; (c) rank-pay(which varies from Rs 200 to 1200 depending on rank) is explained by the 4CPC as well as the MOD as 'additional element', and not some thing that was deducted from the basic-pay; (d) in the MOD, and police led security apparatus, functional relationships between armed forces officers and police officers are reconfigured on the basis of the existence of new armed forces 'basic-pays'(i.e., basic-pay minus rank pay); [d] the new parities, are, however, not defined. The new reduced basic-pay distorts long established historical basic-pay parities between the armed forces officers, and defence civilians officers, and the police led security and intelligence bureaucracy.

Impact

The impact of the implementation of rank-pay on serving officers and veterans are diverse, lingering, and many of which are still unresolved. Rank-pay moderated basic-pay, the impact of which was neither properly examined or explained, affects armed forces organizational structure, functions, morale, and civil-military relations, especially military-police relations. Some of the major affects are of 'Rank pay', implementation are: [a] It degrades armed forces ranks including the highly selective ranks of lieutenant colonels, colonels, and brigadier; [b] Rank Pay deductions roils the Armed Forces, and distorts 'historical parities', and established pay based-status and protocol equations. [c] 'Rank-pay', affects the over all morale of the young officers, as its impacts most directly officers in crucial first 20 years of service; [e] Armed forces officers who had had an edge of two years over the police at the 13 year of service were 'demoted' and made equal in basic-pay to those with 4 years of service;[f] Colonel of the army, Group captain of the airforce, and captains of the navy, who had, since the inception of the police rank of Deputy Inspector General (DIG) (as the second senior most rank in the police), had had a higher pay grade, were placed in lower grade than DIGs, which had been made into a time scale appointment to which every one was automatically entitled on completion of 14 years of service; [g] armed officers, find it difficult to understand why the government has chosen to fix the basic pay of police officers and defence civilians, including auditors, with 13 years of service, at a higher level than of army, navy, and airforce officers with similar number of years of service; It promotes bureaucracy rivalries, and unsustainable false equations and parities; [i] The new debased basic-pay for the armed forces with all its potential for distortions spawns resentment and protracted litigation, starting in 1996, which goes on desultorily for almost two decades. (j) In 2006, following the 6 CPC, the Government lends support to the false equation sought to be imposed by the Rajeev Gandhi Government in 1986, as Major Navdeep, a specialist on military pays, explains.

In 1973, after the 3rd CPC, Lt Colonels were in the scale Rs 1750-1950, about the same as Civil Selection Grade Scale of 1650-1800 (3rd CPC). In 2006, following the 6CPC, and on the promptings of MOD, lieutenant colonels were demoted to

Pay-band 3 with Grade pay of 7600, in comparison with civil and police counterparts who were placed in Pay Band-4 with Grade Pay of Rs 8700. This demotion was partially corrected after an unseemly stand off, and lieutenant colonels, wing commanders of the airforce, commanders of the navy, were reluctantly moved up to Pay Band-4 with Grade Pay Rs 8000, still Rs 700 below similarly placed officers with same length of service from civil services like the Indian Defence Accounts Service, and police service.

Litigation

Rank-pay deductions from basic-pay, apart from being a cause of dismay, distress, and confusion in the armed forces, provoke decades of rancorous litigation between armed forces veterans, including widows, and the Ministry of Defence (MOD), exposing, very publicly, the distrust which the armed forces harbors against the MOD. Maj AK Dhanapalan, who first 'discovered' the flaws in rank-pay, and 4CPC, in 1996, went to court to seek legal redress. In 1997, after he retired, he spent the next ten years litigating 'rank pay' in the face of relentless opposition by the MOD. He wins his first case in 1998, but that is to no avail, as the Ministry of Defence appeals against the court decision. After protracted legal struggle, despite remorseless appeals by the MOD, the high court, in a landmark decision, declares 'rank-pay' deductions from basic-pay illegal. The Supreme Court concurs with high court decision that the 'rank pay' was wrongly deducted from basic pay.

LEGACY

The legacy of 4CPC and rank-pay lingers according to Navdeep Singh, a lawyer and expert on military pays, who closely follows issues affecting armed forces pay and pensions, lingers. Even after the 'rank-pay' deductions from basic-pay are held to be illegal by the highest court, the MOD continues its efforts to reconfigure military ranks: in 2006, after 6CPC, the new 'grade pay' is configured to achieve the intent of the rank-pay, triggering a storm of protest; and again, in 2016, after

7CPĊ, the BJP Government, implements differentiated pay matrix-es for the defence-civilians, police, and others, and the armed forces, the underling intent of which is the same as the introduction 'rank-pay' by the congress government, in 1986. Former Chief of Indian Army Gen. Malik, and others, recognizing the intent of the BJP government decision, calls the decision blatantly 'discriminatory' and intended to degrade armed forces ranks in comparison with police time scale ranks. The BJP, despite its public protestations, has lent support to embedded legacy of the Rank-Pay, by deciding in favor of what have been called biased and discriminatory pay scales by the armed forces headquarters, and the Chiefs of the three services. It has yet to explain its stand or examine the larger issues represented by the continuing sense of unease in the armed forces.

Timeline

February 1996

Major (retd) Dhanapalan, who took premature retirement in 1997, files petition in the High Court of Kerala, challenging his "re-fixation of pay' following the implementation of 4CPC by MoD."

19th December 1997

MoD issues Special Army Instructions (SAI) No. 2/S/1998 (and corresponding special instructions for the Navy and Air Force) on incorporating the impugned formula of 4CPC for re-fixation, recommended by the 5th CPC, which had submitted its report in September 1997.

5 October 1998

Single Judge issued a judgment in favour of Maj Dhanapalan. MoD files Writ Appeal before the High Court's Division Bench against the order of the Single Judge.

4 July 2003

The Division Bench confirms the judgment of the Single Judge.

2006

MOD agrees to pay Major Dhanapalan his arrears. While conceding that it acted wrongly in the case of Major Dhanapalan, opposes extending the benefits to other similarly affected officers, compelling them, and the many widows, to go to court at their own cost, to seek their dues.

8 March 2010

Supreme Court of India rules in favour of all the Armed Forces officers eligible to be paid Rank Pay. It agrees with "the High Court of Kerala that the amount equivalent to Rank Pay should not have been deducted and the MoD should pay arrears with an interest of 6 percent per annum from 1.1.1986 i.e. the date from which Rank Pay was authorised by the Govt of India. Instead of implementing the Supreme court ruling, MoD files an "Interlocutory Application" praying to the Supreme Court to "recall, re-hear, modify," its order of 8 March 2010, "utilising recommendations of a High Powered Committee (HPC) comprising Pradeep Kumar (IAS), then Defence Secretary, Secretary Defence (Finance), and Secretary Expenditure to impress upon the Court that it would entail an expenditure of Rs 1623.71 crores if the order was implemented as it would lead to re-fixation of emoluments of Armed Forces officers for the periods of 4th, 5th and 6th CPC. What was left unsaid was that it was the faulty interpretation and delays in implementation by MoD that led to the situation".

4 September 2012

A Bench of three Judges of the Supreme Court of India upholds the Court's order dated 8 March 2010 with the proviso that interest to be paid from 1.1.2006, the date when the first of several writ petitions were filed by affected Armed Forces officers, instead of 1 January 1986, the date on which rank-pay was implemented. The Court also directed the Government to complete payment of arrears and interest within 12 weeks from 4 September 2012.

17 October 2012

Rohinton F Nariman, Solicitor General of India, advises the MOD to implement the Court's order dated 4 September 2012 in letter and spirit.

27 December 2012

MoD, agrees to pay part of the arrears from 1.1.1986 to 31.12.1995 but objects to paying arrears from 1.1.1996 to 31.12.2005 on the ground that Supreme Court orders lacked clarity for payment and re-fixation from 1.1.2006.

OROP SCHEME 2015

Manohar Parrikar, Defence Minister, on 5 September 2015, the 83rd day of the nationwide protest by ex-servicemen on OROP, in the presence of the three Chiefs of the Armed Forces, announced that "despite the huge fiscal burden", Narendra Modi, the Prime Minister, "has fulfilled his commitment and approved OROP for Armed Forces personnel." The "estimated cost to the exchequer" to implementing OROP, the Defence Minister said, "would be Rs. 8,000 to 10,000 crore at present".

Estimated expenditure

The estimates of expenditure on account of OROP has undergone many revisions: according to early MOD estimates OROP was expected to cost Rs. 3000 crores; this figure has since been questioned and revised. The current estimates vary between Rs. 8,000-9,000 crores. Finance Ministry estimates for implementation of OROP in accordance with the accepted Koshyari definition, according to media reports in August 2015, were about Rs. 12000 crores , ie, about Rs. 4000 crores more than estimated earlier.

Affordability

Some defence analyst who have examined the financial implications of OROP have contended that OROP is affordable, and that opposition to it is based on 'specious' grounds. Former heads of Armed Forces including Admiral Arun Prakash have also contended that OROP is affordable as it is small fraction of the defence budget.

Definition

The definition of OROP, for the approved OROP scheme, Manohar Parrikar, Defence Minister, said "implies that uniform pension be paid to the Armed Forces personnel retiring in the same rank with the same length of service, regardless of their date of retirement. Future enhancements in the rates of pension would be automatically passed on to the past pensioners. This implies bridging the gap between the rate of pension of current and past pensioners at periodic intervals". "Under this definition, it has been decided that the gap between rate of pension of current pensioners and past pensioners will be bridged every 5 years".

Components

"OROP Scheme" includes the following: "[a] The benefit will be given with effect from 1st July, 2014. The present government assumed office on 26th May, 2014 and therefore, it has been decided to make the scheme effective from a date immediately after.[b] Arrears will be paid in four half-yearly instalments. [c] All widows, including war widows, will be paid arrears in one instalment(sic). [d] To begin with, OROP would be fixed on the basis of calendar year 2013. Pension will be re-fixed for all pensioners retiring in the same rank and with the same length of service as the average of minimum and maximum pension in 2013. Those drawing pensions above the average will be protected. [e] Personnel who voluntarily retire will not be covered(emphasis added) under the OROP scheme. [f] In future, the pension would be re-fixed every 5 years."

Issues of OROP and premature retirement

Defence Minister's decision to include the clause "Personnel who voluntarily retire will not be covered under the OROP scheme" in the OROP scheme announcement, on 5 September

2015, without warning the ex-servicemen, caused immediate outrage, and doubts about government intent amongst ex-servicemen. Arguing against the exclusion clause the ex-servicemen have said that it was not a part of the discourse, and discussion between the ex-servicemen and the government; it was not an items on the discussion agenda on 5 September morning meeting between minister and ex-servicemen; voluntary retirement scheme(VRS) is a term used by Public Sector Units, and corporate sector, to retire their staff on mutually agreed package, which usually does not have a pension component; and that VRS is not applicable to the Armed Forces, as the Armed Forces does not have VRS.

Ex-servicemen have explained that the armed forces has premature retirement (PMR), which is different on many counts from VRS: to avail pension, and PMR, Armed Forces officers must have completed 20 years of service, and soldiers 15 years service; and unlike VRS, PMR invariably has a reserve liability, ie, they can be ordered back into service by the government if the national situation so demands.

Ex-servicemen were surprised and disappointed that MOD, which oversees PMR, included, at the last minute, and without warning, the exclusion clause. They were also disappointed that the MOD, which should have known better, conflated VRS and PMR in its announcement. Who was behind the confusion is unclear. The ex-servicemen have demanded an inquiry on how the offending caveat was slipped into the Ministers statement, and MOD press release. Colonel Anil Kaul, spokesperson of the United Front of Ex-Servicemen said, "When we met the Defence Minister on Saturday, there were only three points on the table and that did not include the question about the PMRs. But then, the Defence Minister surprisingly made an announcement at 3 pm that personnel who retire voluntarily will not be covered under OROP. Upset, when we met him again between 6.30 and 7 pm, he too was surprised about the inclusion of the clause." To defuse the ex-servicemen suspicion, distrust, and prevent further escalation, the Prime Minister, on 6 September, announced in Faridabad that all pensioners including those who took premature retirement will be covered by the OROP scheme. It is estimated that 46 per cent of all ex-servicemen are PMRs.

Judicial Commission

OROP is not a settled issue. It is,as MOD statement notes, 'a complex issue' and 'not an administrative matter alone', and therefore the MOD has decided to constitute "a One Member Judicial Committee", which will do a "thorough examination of interests of retirees of different periods and different ranks" and consider "inter-service issues of the three Forces". The "One Member Judicial Committee" the statement says "will give its report in six months". Ex-servicemen rejected MOD decision to constitute a one-man committee headed by a retired Supreme Court justice. Instead they urged the Government to constitute a committee of three military veterans, recommended by ex servicemen and an official, appointed by MOD, and that the committee be called upon to submit its report not in six but one month.

Explanation for delay

The Defence Minister in explanation and as alibi for the delay in implementing OROP, which has been under consideration of the BJP Government for the last 16 months, and pending for four decades, cited the following: [a] The previous governments of Man Mohan Singh led United Progressive Alliance "remained ambivalent on the issue of OROP"; its Minister of State for Defence, in 2009, "in reply to a question, informed Parliament that there are administrative, technical and financial difficulties in implementing OROP". [b] In February 2014, United Progressive Alliance Government while stating that " OROP would be implemented in 2014-153 , made a "a budget provision of a mere Rs. 500 crore", which was "not based on any thorough analysis", and that it failed to "specify what OROP would be, how it would be implemented or how much it would cost". These explanations for delay in the implementation of OROP by the present Government find echo in Narendra Modi, PM speech, at a large rally, in Faridabad,

Haryana, on 6 September 2015. The Congress Party, not unsurprisingly, disagrees with these explanations.

Veterans Response

Following the Manohar Parrikar statement on the decision to implement OROP, Major General (Retd) Satbir Singh said, "Out of the six demands that we made, the government has only agreed with one. We want clarification on the premature retirement point in the OROP. "On Government decision to revise pension every five years rather than every year he said, that this was not "in the spirit of One Rank, One Pension, it will be One Rank, Five Pensions," and therefor "urge the government to rethink it"." The ex servicemen dissatisfied with the OROP scheme announced by MOD, decided to call off the hunger strike, but continue with the protest till "all major demands are met". A maha-rally is planned for 12 September 2015

Former UPA Government

A.K. Antony, former defence minister in UPA Government, on 5 September 2015, calling the BJP government OROP scheme "totally disappointing", said it "substantially diluted the provisions of the OROP announced by the UPA". He said, it "ridiculed the ex-servicemen as well as the whole country." Refuting Manohar Parrikar's allegation that Congress Government was ambivalent on OROP, he said, "We had already accepted in toto the demand for OROP and were in the process of implementing it."

BJP AND NFU FOR THE ARMED FORCES

The Narendra Modi led Bharatiya Janata Party Government which repaced UPA Government, in May 2014, from which much was expected by the Armed Forces and Ex servicemen, once in power, much like the Congress Government, let the NFU issue fester, instead of addressing it. Manohar Parrikar, soon after becoming the Defence Minister, opposes NFU for the armed Forces despite it being flagged by the Chief of staff in the Joint memorandum.

Time Line

March 2008

Sixth Central Pay Commission submits report. It recommends NFU for Group 'A' Central services, to "alleviate stagnation in the civil services". No explanation or reasons are given for excluding the Armed Forces from the scheme.

July 2008

Chiefs of Staff Committee (COSC), consisting of General Deepak Kapoor (30 September 2007 -31 March 2010), Air Chief Marshal Fali Homi Major (31 March 2007-31 March 2009), and Admiral Sureesh Mehta (31 October 2006 -31 August 2009), send a detailed note to A. K. Antony, Defence Minister, flagging the adverse impact of NFU on the Armed Forces. The COSC urge that Armed Forces Officers be treated at par with All India Services. The minister on the advice of Vijay Singh, Defence Secretary, ignores COSC submission.

29 August 2008

NFU is implemented after an endorsed by an 'Empowered Committee of Secretaries" headed by K. M. Chandrasekhar, IAS, the Cabinet Secretary. Decision reads: "Whenever any IAS officer of a particular batch is posted in the Centre to a particular grade carrying a specific grade pay in pay bands PB-3 or PB-4 , grant of higher pay scale on non- functional basis to the officers belonging to batches of organised Group A services that are senior by two years or more should be given by the Government." "This will also be applicable to the Indian Police Service and the Indian Forest Service in their respective State cadres for which the relevant cadre controlling authorities will issue the orders".No reason or explanation is given for implementing the scheme beyond that it will alleviate stagnation in the civil services.

IPS Rules incorporate NFU scheme, the relevant rule reads: "whenever any Indian Administrative Service officer.....in pay band 3 or pay band 4, is promoted, members of the Indian

Police Servicee and other All India Services (AIS), senior to such officers' become automatically eligible to be "appointed to the same grade on non-functional basis from the date of posting of the Indian Administrative Service officer in that particular grade".

Government creates a new pay grade designated as HAG+. It is 'carved out of PB-4', with "A new pay scale of Rs.75500 - (annual increment @ 3%)-80000 ".

The new grade is accompanied by large scale upgradation of posts in the police at the HAG + and apex level.

HAG + and Apex grades become proforma time scale promotions. Almost all police officers and group A Officers become eligible to retire with pay and pension at Apex scale, with OROP benefits.

The new rank HAG+ supersedes all Lt General except for a small fraction that are Army Commanders. HAG+ renders Lt general and their equivalents in the air force and navy, inferior in status, and pay to scores of Police officers in HAG + and apex scales. Increase in hundreds of new posts, and exclusion of Lt Generals from new HAG+ grade effectively degrades the status of Lt General.

27 December 2008

UPA II Government, in response to sustained outcry by the Armed Forces, and Armed Forces veterans, on the anomalies in the Government decision, issues instructions that [1] "In future, pay revision of the armed forces should be de-linked from that of civilians and separate board or commission should be set up for pay revision of the armed forces." [2] formation of a High Powered Committee to 'resolve issues relating to command and control functions/status of armed forces vis a vis paramilitary and civilians.'

2009-2014

21 May 2009

UPA Government issues orders to implement non-functional

financial up-gradation for all Organized Group-A Civil Services. Armed Forces are excluded from the order. Armed Forces remonstrations have little impact.

7 July 2009

Seven member Committee, ordered to examine "One rank One pension and Related Issues" by Prime Minister Manmohan Singh, on the advice of AK Antony, Defence Minister, submits 21 page report. The committee, from which Armed Forces representation was excluded, includes, K. M. Chandrasekhar, Cabinet Secretary, Chairman; and six members: Vijay Singh, Defence Secretary, Ministry of Defence (MOD); Neelam Nath, Secretary Ex Servicemen Welfare, Ministry of Defence; (MOD), Madhukar Gupta, Secretary Home, Ministry of Home Affairs; Rajni Razdan, Secretary Pension and PW; Rahul Sarin, Secretary, Department of Personnel and Training (DOPT), PMO; and Sushma Nath, Secretary Expenditure, Ministry of Finance.

The Report opposes OROP for the Armed Forces, and does not touch on the 'related issue' of NFU. The committee report evades NFU, but discusses the fraught issue of the civil equivalence, pensions and pay of Lt General, and their equivalents in Air Force and Navy, in the context of NFU, and up gradation of scores of police posts to HAG+ and Apex grades. The report in its consideration fails to acknowledge that HAG grade has, as result of Government decision, been rendered a time scale grade to which 100 percent of the officers of the 49 Civil Services are promoted as matter of right, and which does not bare comparison with Lt Generals grade, a highly selective rank to which less that one percent of the armed forces officers are promoted. The Report recommends that a new pay scale be created for Lt generals provided all HAG time scale officers are also elevated to the new scale.

19 November 2009

Against the background of the controversy on rewarding Group A Service with NFU, the Department of Personnel & Training (DOPT), under the Prime ministers Office (PMO), issues an Office memorandum(OM), titled "Attributes of Group-A Central Services Clarification on'.

July 15, 2010.

AK Antony, Defence Minister (2006–2014), rejects note vetted by General Vijay Kumar Singh, Chief of army Staff (31 March 2010 31 May 2012), Admiral Nirmal Kumar Verma, Chief of Naval Staff(31 August 2009 31 August 2012), and Air Chief Marshal Pradeep Vasant Naik, Chief of Air Staff (31 March 2009-31 July 2011), on NFU for Defence Officers. The reply dismissing the Armed Forces note on NFU for Defence Officers is signed by a Joint Secretary, a mid-level officer, in the Department of Defence, DOD, headed by Pradeep Kumar, Defence secretary(1 August 2009 -14 July 2011).

The MOD instead of classifying Lt general as HAG + , as a concession, creates ' Non Function pay grades' like for the police, at the Lt general level, to which some Lt generals and their equivalents are 'promoted'.

12 March 2010

Department of Personnel & Training (DOPT), under the Prime ministers Office (PMO), issues an Office memorandum(OM) on residency, ie minimum service, requirement for various ranks in the higher Civil Service. Organized Group ' A ' Services: SAG 17 years, HAG scale 20 years, HAG+ 21 years, Apex scale 22 years. CRPF (CAPF) IG scale 24 years. IAS/ IPS/(Indian Forest Service)IFoS: SAG scale 16 years for IAS, 18 years for IPS, and IfoS.

17 August 2012

Committee of Secretaries, appointed in 2011, by Manmohan Singh, Prime Minister, to examine the issues raised by the defence services, including Non Functional Upgradation (NFU), submits report. The report does not recommend NFU for officers of the Defence Forces on the basis of rationale provided by Shashi Kant Sharma, Defence secretary, and head of DOD, which was endorsed by MK Antony, Defense Minister. The

MOD rationale for opposing NFU to the armed forces are : [1] service conditions of the defence services are different than civilian officers; and [2] the Defence forces are being given many benefits including Military Service Pay (MSP), The financial implications for the grant of NFU to the Armed Forces is estimated by the ministry as Rs 69 crores.

13 September 2013

India Today, Delhi based news magazine, cites a MOD letter titled, 'Common VII Central Pay Commission' leaked to it by a Joint Secretary in the MOD. The 'letter' is purportedly written by Chief NAK Browne, the Chairman of the Chief of Staff Committee (COSC), to AK Antony, Defence Minister. According to the 'letter' the Government is in favor of a separate pay commission for the Armed Forces, but the armed forces would rather be part of the 7CPC instead of having a separate pay commission. Air Chief Marshal NAK Browne, according to the 'letter' has [1] opposed formation of separate pay commission for the armed Forces, because "a separate pay commission may not necessarily benefit the services as anomalies are invariably bound to arise in both cases"; [2] the main cause for dissatisfaction the armed Forces is not having separate pay commission but the "non-resolution of anomalies or ex parte resolution of anomalies"

24 December 2014

Manohar Parrikar, Defence Minister and R.K. Mathur, Defence secretary (25.05.2013 -24.05.2015), informs Chairman of the 7CPC, that MOD does not favour NFU for the Armed Forces.

2015

11 July 2015

Five retired Lieutenant Generals, four Major Generals and one Air Marshall of the Indian Air Force, joins the protest at jantar mantar, in New Delhi. Amongst the Lieutenant General is Lt General Rajinder Singh Sujlana AVSM, VSM, former X

Corps Commander and Colonel Commandant of the Sikh Regiment.

13 August 2015

General S F Rodrigues, former COAS, and Admirals L Ramdas, Arun Prakash and Sureesh Mehta, former Chiefs of Naval Staff, write an open letter to President Pranab Mukherjee, Supreme Commander of the Armed Forces. The letter says, "Recent developments....have not only triggered a process of politicization of the Indian military, but also served to inflict grave damage on its morale and self-esteem"; and that these developments pose grave "implication for national security".

3 September 2015

Major General Satbir Singh, Vice Chairman of IESM, responding to question on financial implication of One Rank One Pension (OROP) following his meeting with Nripendra Misra, Principal Secretary to PM, asks why similar questions were not raised following the implementation of NFU in 2008.

13 October 2015

Principal Bench of the Armed Forces Tribunal (AFT) in New Delhi issues notice to the Ministry of Defence(MOD) and Ministry of Finance on a petition filed by Col Mukul Dev, a serving Colonel of the Army's Judge Advocate General's Branch, demanding grant of Non-Functional Upgrade (NFU) to Armed Forces Officers on the lines granted to IAS officers and other Group 'A' services. The colonel and his Counsel argue that the Governments failure to extend NFU to the armed Forces has lowered the status and adversely affected the morale of officers the armed forces; and that [1] the stagnation in the armed forces is more acute than the civil services; [2] denial of NFU to the Armed Forces is violation of Article 14 and 16 of the Constitution of India [3] the aim of NFU is not to equate the monetary benefits or earnings enjoyed by a particular service but is granted with the aim to ameliorate stagnation; [4] well established parity between armed forces and the "All India

Services/ Group 'A' services and IPS in particular has been disturbed'[5] and that armed forces officers cadre meets all the attributes attached to the Group 'A' organised service; and [6] the comparison of Military Service Pay (MSP) and NFU is a "gross mis-concept", as MSP to compensate for difficulties of military service, and NFU is to "alleviate the acute stagnation" which is far worse than in the armed forces than in the Police other civil services, such as the Indian Legal Service and Indian Trade Service, Indian Statistical service, Indian Economic service and Central Information service, which are eligible for NFU.

19 November 2015

A K Mathur, the Chairperson of 7CPC, recommends that On Non - Functional Upgradation (NFU), continue for Organised Group 'A' Services, because it has 'existed for the last 10 years'. He recommends a watered down NFU with long residencies " be extended to the officers of the Defence forces and CAPFs". Two members of the commission disagree with the Chairman. They recommend that NFU be abolished because, among other reasons, it has set a world record in de-linking "promotions from career progression".

MODI GOVERNMENT APPOINTS COMMITTEE TO STUDY ONE RANK ONE PENSION

The government today appointed a judicial committee to look into the implementation of the One Rank One Pension (OROP) scheme for ex-servicemen. The one-member committee would look into steps to be taken to remove anomalies arising out of the implementation of OROP, as notified by the government on November 7, an official statement said.

The committee comprising L. Narasimha Reddy, a retired chief justice of Patna High Court, would take into account the financial impact of its recommendations before spelling out the same within six months. The committee may submit interim reports to the government before the stipulated time. The terms of reference of the committee will be to examine measures for the removal of anomalies that may arise in the implementation of the OROP, measures for the removal of anomalies that may arise out of inter-services issues of the three armed forces due to implementation of OROP, implications on service matters and any other matter referred by the central government on implementation of the OROP or related issues. The committee will devise its own procedure and may call for such information and take such evidence as may be considered necessary. "The ministries and departments of the government of India shall furnish such information and documents and other assistance as may be required by the committee," the statement said. Headquartered in Delhi, the committee will be supported by the department of ex-servicemen's welfare under the Defence Ministry.

EMPLOYEES' PENSION SCHEME (EPS)

The EPS, established in 1995, provides for the payment of a member's pension upon the member's superannuation/ retirement, disability, and widow/widower pension, and children's pension upon the member's death. The EPS program has replaced the erstwhile Family Pension Scheme (FPS). Employers that are not mandated to be covered may voluntarily apply for coverage.

The new scheme, known, as the Employees' Pension Scheme (EPS), is essentially a defined-benefit program providing earnings related pension on superannuation, disability or death. Thus, EPF members are now eligible for two benefit streams on superannuation – a lump sum EPF accumulation upon retirement and a monthly pension from the EPS.

The amount of the pension benefit is based on the employee's average salary during the final year of employment and the total number of years of employment.

Under the EPS, members must have completed a minimum of ten years of service and must be at least 58 years old. However, if an employee has completed twenty years of service, he/she may obtain an early pension from age 50. Under this provision, the amount of pension benefit is reduced by 3 per cent for every year falling short of 58. Exemption from the EPS is allowed, but in this event, the employer will have to cover the government's contribution.

However, participation to the EPS program was voluntary for the existing workers as on 1995 but mandatory for the new workers whose monthly pensionable earnings did not exceed Rs. 5000. Aggrieved workers alleged that the pension from the EPS was substantially inferior compared to the public pension schemes and that the return from the scheme was even lower than the provident fund arrangement. The debate surrounding the EPS continues unabated till today, with many trade unions filing litigations against the scheme.

This new system along with the recommendations of the Fifth Pay Commission Report has only added to the liabilities of the government.

Other Schemes

The central government alone administers separate pension programs for civil employees, defence staff and workers in railways, post, and telecommunications departments. This is called the Civil Servants' Pension Scheme (CSPS). These benefit programs are typically run on a pay-as-you-go, defined-benefit basis. The schemes are non-contributory i.e. the workers do not contribute during their working lives. Instead, they forego the employer's contribution into their provident fund account. The entire pension expenditure is charged in the annual revenue expenditure account of the government.

In addition to the provident fund, workers in both public and private sectors receive a second tier of lump sum retirement benefit known as gratuity. It is paid to the workers who fulfil certain eligibility conditions like a minimum qualifying service period of five years. It is equivalent to 15 day's of final earnings for each years of service completed subject to a maximum of Rs. 350,000. The cost of gratuity is entirely borne by the employer.

The Public Provident Fund (PPF) scheme, introduced about three decades ago, is meant to provide unorganised sector workers with the facility to accumulate savings for old age income security. Under the scheme, amounts between Rs 100 to Rs 60,000 per annum can be deposited into the PPF account. These investments are eligible for tax rebate under Sec 88 of the Income Tax Act and interest at a guaranteed 11 per cent p.a. (till recently 12 per cent per annum) is fully tax exempt under Sec 10.

The scheme has poor coverage because of ineffective marketing and the service delivery is grossly inadequate. Being largely urban centric, the scheme is used more as a tax planning vehicle by high-income savers than an old age income security plan.

The 11 per cent tax-free return that a PPF investor is guaranteed is equivalent to a 16.8 per cent pre-tax return for a marginal income tax payer.

In an effort to widen the reach of the social safety net for the aged poor, the central government, in 1995, introduced a more comprehensive old age poverty alleviation program called the National Old Age Pension (NOAP) under the aegis of the National Social Assistance Programme (NSAP).

The scheme aims to provide monthly pension to thirty percent of the poorest elderly. This programme provides benefits for poor people above the age of 75 years. Under the programme a pension of Rs. 75/- per month is provided to eligible persons.

The formal old age income security system in India can thus be classified into three categories:

- The upper tier consists of statutory pension schemes and provident funds for the organised sector employees.
- The middle tier is comprised of voluntary retirement saving schemes for the self-employed and unorganised sector workers.
- The lower tier consists of targeted social assistance schemes and welfare funds for the poor.

Conceptual Explanations

Under a *defined-contribution plan*, workers build up either explicit or implicit retirement accounts that fund retirement. The benefit is determined by (1) the level and timing of contributions, (2) the rate of return on the retirement accounts and (3) the form in which benefits are realised, including annuitization, programmed withdrawals and lump-sum distribution. The relationship between contributions and benefits is transparent, which may improve compliance incentives.

In a *defined-benefit system*, benefits are usually determined by multiplying a replacement rate by a pension base.

The replacement rate is typically an accrual factor times the years of service, and the pension base is a function of a worker's earnings history. Since this type of system often ignores the time path of contributions in calculating the replacement rate and the pension base, the tie between benefits and contributions can be quite loose.

In a pay-as-you-go system; pension payments are made using the taxes collected from the younger taxpaying generation. Their pension payments in turn are made from the taxes collected subsequently.

In a Funded System, pension payments are invested in a variety of financial assets. Funding provides an opportunity to capitalise from investment in financial markets, where the rate of return is likely to be higher than the implicit rate of return to contributions in a pay-as-you-go pension system. The benefits of funding can be enhanced by investment diversification. Funded systems can reduce-though arguably not eliminate-the vulnerability of a pension system to adverse demographic trends and political pressures.

In the Indian context, the financing issues arise primarily in four programs: the EPS, the CSPS, the GPF because of its integration into the government accounts, and the NOAPS. Each presents a potentially open-ended financial responsibility. A goal of reform should be to place explicit limits on these liabilities.

PERIOD OF PENSION

The minimum eligibility period for receipt of pension is 10 years. A Central Government servant retiring in accordance with the Pension Rules is entitled to receive superannuation pension on completion of at least 10 years of qualifying service. In the case of Family Pension the widow is eligible to receive pension on death of her spouse after completion of one year of continuous service or before even completion of one year if the Government servant had been examined by the appropriate Medical Authority and declared fit for Government service.

W.e.f 1.1.2006, Pension is calculated with reference to average emoluments namely, the average of the basic pay drawn during the last 10 months of the service or last basic pay drawn whichever is beneficial. Full pension with 10/20 years of qualifying service is 50% of the average emoluments or last basic pay drawn whichever is beneficial. Before 1.1.2006, for qualifying service of less than 33 years, amount of pension was proportionate to the actual qualifying service broken into completed half-year periods. For example, if total qualifying service is 30 years and 4 months (i.e. 61 half-year periods), pension will be calculated as under:-

Pension amount = R/2(X)61/66

where R represents average reckonable emoluments for last 10 months of qualifying service or the last pay drawn as opted by the govt servant.

Minimum pension presently is Rs. 3500 per month. Maximum limit on pension is 50% of the highest pay in the Government of India (presently Rs. 45,000) per month. Pension is payable up to and including the date of death.

3

One Rank, One Pension (OROP) Scheme

One Rank One Pension (OROP), or "same pension, for same rank, for same length of service, irrespective of the date of retirement", is a longstanding demand of the Indian armed forces and veterans. The demand for pay-pension equity, which underlies the OROP concept, was provoked by the exparte decision by the Indira Gandhi-led Indian National Congress (INC) government, in 1973, two years after the historic victory in the 1971 Bangladesh war, and shortly after Field Marshal SHFJ Manekshaw retired, to decrease armed forces pensions by 20–40 percent, and increase civilian pensions by 20 percent, without consulting armed forces headquarters.

In 1986, the sense of unease and distrust prompted by the Third Central Pay Commission (CPC) was exacerbated by the Rajiv Gandhi led Indian National Congress (I) Government's decision to implement Rank Pay, which reduced basic pay of captain, majors, lt-colonel, colonels, and brigadiers, and their equivalent in the Air-Force, and the Navy, relative to basic pay scales of civilian and police officers. The decision to reduce the basic pay of these ranks, implemented without consulting the armed forces, created radically asymmetries between police-military ranks, affected the pay, and pension of tens of thousands of officers and veterans, spawned two decades of contentious litigation by veterans. It became a lingering cause of distrust between the armed forces veterans and the MOD, which the government did little to ameliorate. In 2008, the Manmohan Singh led United Progressive Alliance (UPA) Government in the wake of the Sixth Central Pay Commission (6CPC), discarded the concept of rank-pay. Instead it introduced Grade pay, and Pay bands, which instead of addressing the rank, pay, and pension asymmetries caused by 'rank pay' dispensation, reinforced existing asymmetries. The debasing of armed forces ranks was accompanied by decision in 2008 to create hundreds of new posts of secretaries, special Secretaries, director general of police (DGP) at the apex grade pay level to ensure that all civilian and police officers, including defence civilian officers, retire at the highest pay grade with the apex pay grade pensions with One Rank One Pay (OROP).

BACKGROUND

Between 2008-14, during the tenure of the UPA Government led by Prime Minister Manmohan Singh, myriad Armed Forces grievances prompted by perceived inequities subsumed with OROP issue to make OROP a potent rallying call that resonated with veterans of all ranks. Against the background of perceived discrimination, and slights, and dismissive response of the Government, armed forces veterans, in the later half 2008, started a campaign, of nationwide public protests, which included hunger strikes. In response to the OROP protests, which underscored the growing pay-pension-status asymmetries, the UPA Government, in 2011, appointed a parliamentary committee which found merit in the veterans demands for OROP.

Short history

The demand for One-Rank-One-Pension (OROP) dates back to the 1980s. Nothing much happened until the Congress promised OROP in its poll manifesto in 2004, but the UPA government rejected the OROP demand in December 2008, resulting in Veterans returning over 22,000 gallantry, war and service medals to the President of India along with symbolically signing a letter with their own blood in 2009. Under the Indian

Ex-Servicemen's Movement (IESM) banner, Veterans have been taking delegations to the Ministry of Defence, writing letters to the Prime Minister and Defence Minister, and holding peaceful and dignified rallies and public demonstrations.

With continuing pressure from MP Shri Rajeev Chandrashekhar and IESM, the the Parliament Standing Committee on Defence studied and accepted the concept and definition of OROP in 2013. OROP was featured in the UPA government's budget in February 2014 and was reflected in an executive order to that effect in the same month. After the BJP-NDA government came to power, granting OROP was mentioned in the budget speech in July 2014, and the MoS for Defence confirmed it in the Rajya Sabha in December 2014.

During the campaign for the 2014 general elections, BJP PM candidate, Shri Narendra Modi, made a promise at a Veterans' Rally in Rewari, Haryana that, if elected to office, he would ensure OROP. In March 2015, during PM Modi's much-hyped visit to the troops on Siachen glacier, he volunteered the statement that the OROP demand would be fulfilled. However, even after two successive governments have agreed to OROP, and the PM's promises on its implementation, Veterans see OROP as a distant and receding light at the end of a tunnel.

What is the fuss about OROP?

But first, what is OROP? OROP simply means "uniform pension for military personnel retiring in the same rank with the same length of service irrespective of their date of retirement, and any future enhancement in the rates of pension be automatically passed on to past pensioners".

The reason for demanding OROP is that Veterans who have retired earlier receive much less pension than those who retired more recently. It can be argued that this also happens in other government jobs, so why are Veterans making such a fuss? To answer this perfectly valid question one needs to know some little-known facts concerning the military, at least insofar as service, retirement and pension are concerned.

One, Armed Forces (AF) personnel are compulsorily retired at a very early age, and retirement age depends upon their rank. Early retirement is necessary to "keep the army young" because older men cannot fight battles which make huge demands on stamina and strength.

Soldiers (Sepoys, or in general, Jawans) who have not been promoted to NCO or JCO rank retire compulsorily after just 15 to 17 years of service, when their age is 35 to 37 years. Sepoys who are promoted as NCOs or JCOs retire at age 45 to 47 years. Officers compulsory retirement age is connected with rank as follows – Major-50, Lt Col-52, Col-54, Brig-56, Maj Gen-58, Lt Gen-60, General-62, noting that promotions depend both on performance and severely limited vacancies due to the rigid pyramidal rank structure. That is why, of all AF retirees, soldiers constitute about 90%.

Two, a soldier who was retired, say, in 1986 would receive pension on the basis of his salary according to the Fourth Pay Commission, while the pension of a soldier who was retired after the Sixth Pay Commission (20 years later) would be considerably higher because successive Pay Commissions fix salaries according to the rising cost indices.

Thus, a Havildar (NCO) who retired earlier with over 20 years of service may receive less pension than a soldier who retired later with only 15 years of service. As an example for the officer cadre, the pension of a post-2012 retiree Colonel was Rs.35,841, whereas a pre-2006 retiree Major General's pension was Rs.26,700. These disparities are grossly unfair because the soldier is retired compulsorily at an age depending upon his rank, and his pension is fixed upon the pay according to the CPC in force at retirement.

Three, compulsory retirement after just 15-17 years of service at age 35 years means that the soldier is effectively denied salary earnings of 25 years which other government employees (including the police forces) receive because they retire at age 60 years. There is negligible scope for lateral entry into government service even for soldiers who retire without disability attributable to military service. He is forced to seek employment to supplement his meagre pension at a time when his family and other commitments are just beginning to increase. This, along with lower pension of earlier retirees is a combination which makes for near-destitution of a soldier who served in hard conditions to defend the nation. For comparison, a CRPF policeman retires at 57 years age, and CRPF authorities are pressing for the retirement age to be increased to 60 years.

Four, there are huge differences in the military officer cadre vis-a-vis IAS and IPS. Consider the rank of Maj Gen, to which only 0.8% of officers get promoted because of the command-control-discipline rank structure of the army, after about 30 years of service. But the equivalent rank (in terms of salary) in the IAS is Joint Secretary (JS), which 100% of IAS cadre attain after only about 18 years of service, and about 80% of IPS cadre after about 20 years. It is this unfairness in parity in addition to early retirement age which is at the root of the OROP demand. Further, and even more unfairly, the Jawan is equated with a Class D government employee.

Public cost

There has been much discussion regarding what OROP would cost the exchequer. Many opined it was unaffordable, and further that other government servants would also demand OROP if granted to Veterans. However Veterans maintain that OROP cannot be withheld from them because some others, whose conditions of service and promotions are entirely different, also demand OROP.

MoD sent the final proposal to implement OROP for Rs.8,300 crores to Ministry of Finance on 17 February 2015. Adding Rs.8,300 crores to Rs.43,000 crores of Defence pensions, the total is Rs.51,300 crores per annum. Veterans argue that when the BJP-NDA budget allowed Rs.5.72 lakh crores as "revenue foregone" to provide concessions on corporate tax, commercial tax & customs duties to business houses for just one year, hesitating at spending less than one-tenth of it on Veterans who have given the best years of their lives for the nation's defence was a deliberate slight.

Deliberate neglect of Veterans

There was no member in 6CPC and earlier CPCs to represent soldiers, who form not merely the single largest segment affected by the decisions of 6CPC, but also form the only segment that is denied fundamental freedoms under Articles 19(a) and 19(c), and have conditions of service, promotion and retirement that are adverse when compared with other categories under consideration of the 6CPC.

The Department of Ex-servicemen Welfare (DESW) was set up in 2004 within MoD, to formulate policies and programmes for the welfare and resettlement of Veterans. However, without a single serving soldier or Veteran in its setup, it has actually been working at cross purposes with Veterans' welfare. Factually and outrageously, as a matter of policy DESW contested all cases won by individual Veterans in courts of law, including one case concerning a paltry Rs.702 per month won by a disabled soldier after litigating in a High Court.

Last word

A large section of the public including legislators, are ignorant of soldiers' working conditions – early retirement, non-family stations and long separations, continual life-threatening stressful situations, risks on-the-ground and in-the-field, high casualty rate, strict disciplinary regime under military law, denial of fundamental justifys, etc. The tragedy is that they are not even interested in knowing, let alone understanding.

After promises have remained unimplemented, very recently PM Modi made a statement that OROP was not clearly defined. This raised doubts among Veterans regarding which vested interest has sown this "doubt" in the PM's mind, though most believe that these are IAS-sourced machinations. This belief is supported in large measure by the composition and conduct of successive CPCs and the attitude and manner of functioning of the Department of Ex-Servicemen's Welfare (DESW) under MoD, outlined earlier.

Veterans hold Mr. Modi accountable to promises made as PM-candidate and later as PM. Sensing the growing disappointment and anger among Veterans, the PM is reported to have tweeted that Veterans have waited 40 years and should not mind waiting a little more to solve the OROP muddle. IESM has demanded that government commit a definite date by which OROP would be implemented, failing which a peaceful, dignified Maha-Rally would be held on Sunday 14 June 2015 at Jantar Mantar, New Delhi, with simultaneous rallies in some state capitals and other cities with a large Veterans' presence. This is to be followed by an indefinite relay fast starting 15 June.

Government's continued neglect of veterans is actually a double whammy on the country. On the one hand, valuable trained manpower is being lost, and on the other hand impecunious soldiers are joining the ranks of the unemployed or under-employed and exacerbating the current high levels of country-wide discontent.

It does not take a rocket scientist to understand that OROP is a matter of simple justice. Some Veterans say that governments playing with their patience at the behest of vested interests that delay or deny OROP, are figuratively playing with a bomb with a slow-burning fuse. Only time will tell whether the Maha-Rally will result in grant of OROP, or whether the vested interests succeed in destroying the bond between the soldier-veteran on the one hand and the government on the other.

ISSUES

The causes that inform the OROP protest movement are not pension alone, as armed forces veterans have often tried to make clear, and the parliamentary committee recorded. The issues, veterans emphasize, are of justice, equity, honor, and national security. The failure to address issue of pay-pension equity, and the underlying issue of honor, is not only an important cause for the OROP protest movement, but its escalation. The causes and grievances that inform OROP protesters and their high ranking supporters, in addition to failure of the government to implement OROP, are a string of contentious decision taken by UPA Government, in 2008-9, in the wake of Sixth Central Pay Commission (6 CPC), that sharply degraded Armed Forces pay grades and ranks. Decisions, that have had a radical impact on the armed forces sense of self-esteem, honor, and their trust in the government and security bureaucracy, some of which come to dominate policy under the UPA government, and remain unaddressed by the BJP Government, are outlined in the succeeding paragraphs

Reduction of armed forces pensions

In 1973, the Indira Gandhi led Congress (I) terminated 'One Rank One Pension' the basis for deciding pension of Indian Armed Forces Personnel 'which had been in vogue for 26 years since independence' through an ex parte administrative order.In addition, the Government, on the basis of the report of third Pay commission, from which Armed Forces representation was excluded, and which was dominated by bureaucrats, increased the pension of civilians, who retired at 58, from 30 to 50 percent, a net increase of 20 percent; and reduced the pension of soldier, Non Commissioned Officers (NCOs) and Junior commissioned Officers (JCOs), by 20 percent, from 70 to 50 percent of basic pay, with the caveat that for full pension the minimum service was 33 years. But as soldiers in 1973 retired after 15 years service, at the age of 33-36, they got less than 30 percent of the pay as pension. Soldiers pension was thus decreased not by 20 percent but 40 percent from 70 to 30 percent. In addition to down grading military pensions, the government inexplicably, and without assigning reason, down graded the status of soldier by equating "infantry soldier with less than three years' service" with a "semi-skilled/unskilled labour". These decisions were all the more galling for the armed forces as these were based on the recommendation, and endorsement of Defence Secretary K B Lall, ICS, whose job it was to ensure the well being of the armed forces. The decision was announced two months after

Field Marshal Sam Manekshaw, who led the army in the victorious 1971 war, retired from service. The reason for depressing the armed Forces pensions, which continues to rankle veterans and servings personnel, given by the Congress I government was that it wanted to ensure 'equivalence' of Armed Forces pensions with civilians.

Rank Pay

The concept of rank-pay introduced in 1986, affected tens of thousand of serving and retired officers of the three armed forces. It started the process of undermining military ranks and making them subordinate to the police. Its discriminatory provisions reinforced the growing sense of distrust between the MOD and the veterans. It debased the military ranks of captain, majors, lt-colonel, colonels, and brigadiers, and their equivalent in the air-force and the Indian Navy.

The legacy of rank-pay, and 4CPC, found echo in the 6CPC, and the 7CPC and continues to be a cause of distrust, false parities and anomalous pay scales. The implementation of BJP Government in 2016 of separate pay matrix for the police, and the armed forces, accentuated the anomalies in time scale pay grades between armed forces officers and the IPS, which had remain unresolved since 1986, when the congress government had reduced the basic pay of armed forces officers relative to police officers, by deducting 'rank-pay' from the basic-pay. The 7CPC decision on pay grades for the armed forces were called blatantly 'discriminatory' by former Chief of Indian Army General Ved P Malik, who said the intent was to degrade armed forces ranks in comparison with police time scale ranks.

OROP-2008 for Civil-Police Officers

Even though OROP was not a transparently stated civil service or police officers demand, Prime Minister Manmohan Singh rewarded senior civil servant and IPS officers with OROP at the apex scale, the highest pay grade in the government. The decision to grant ' OROP' to the senior most government servants was taken, not by parliament, or ministerial committee, but by bureaucrats in Department of Pensions and Pensioners' Welfare (DOP&PW), and the Prime Minister's Office. According to Avay Shukla, a former officer of the Indian Administrative Service, (1975 batch, Himachal Pradesh cadre), who retired at the apex grade, and is recipient of Apex Grade OROP-2008 linked pension, the decision to grant OROP-2008 to the civil and police services was implemented not by public notification, but a cunningly worded internal memorandum issued by Department of Pensions and Pensioners' Welfare, a department under the Prime Minister's office. Avay Shukla, in 2015, at the height of the OPOP protests, in a newspaper article revealed that apex OROP for the civil services was done slyly. As 'Apex-OROP' was done secretly it has neither been discussed or scrutinized by the media, or the Ministry of Finance, and for this reason remained little known, and only gained salience after the veterans started their protests.

'Apex-OROP-2008', is not as selective as it appears. Apex grade pay OROP pension covers thousands of retired, serving, and future Civil Service officers, including 4802 Indian Administrative Service officers, 600 Indian Foreign Service officers, and 4720 the IPS officers majority of whom because of their cadre structures (proliferation of apex ranks) are guaranteed that they will retire at the apex scale, not with standing what their responsibilities or duties entail.

Most senior police and civil service officer are shy to acknowledge that they had been granted Apex OROP. Prasad, IAS, former defence secretary, who retired on 30 June 2004, on 22 August 2015, in a debate on national TV denied that he was getting Apex-OROP. J.K. Khanna, an IPS officer, who retired as DGP, in 2011, and Avay Shukla, IAS, who retired in 2010, confirmed in 2015 that they like other IAS and IPS officers are getting Apex OROP.

In contrast to almost hundred percent Apex-OROP coverage to past and future retiree from the civil services, including majority of defence civilian officers in Ministry of Defence responsible for providing secretarial, logistic, and rear area services to the Armed Forces, like accounts and audit, land, only one tenth of one percent of the armed forces officers, as 'stratagem' and hedge against their opposition to the scheme, were also included in the apex OROP scheme. Those covered include the three heads of the Defence Forces, Army Commanders, and few other Lt Generals, and their equivalents in the Navy, and Air Force. The attempt to buy the silence of the Chiefs of the armed Forces on an issue that affects the entire officers corps, not unexpectedly, has not gone down well with veterans. Those excluded included Lt Generals, Major Generals, Vice Admirals, and Rear Admirals, and Air Marshals, the commanders of the Armed Forces largest formations: its Corps, Divisions, air commands, bases, fleets and training establishments.

Sanction of Apex-OROP to thousands of officials, among other factors, has contributed to wide support that OROP protest enjoys; it has become an additional "causus belli" for the veterans protest over OROP. It is also the probable cause for the unprecedented letter by former Chiefs of Defence Forces of India to the Government declaring their support for OROP for the Armed Forces.

Non Functional Upgradation (NFU) for police officers and others

Sanction of OROP at apex scale to all civil services and Police officers was accompanied by grant of "Non Functional Upgrade" (NFU) also called "non-functional financial up-gradation" (NFFU) to all civil services including the Indian Police Service by the Congress(I) led United Progressive Alliance(UPA) Government, in 2008, to reward civil servants of 49 'Organized Central Group A Services', with automatic time bound pay promotions till the Higher Administrative Grade(HAG), a grade equated by Government with Lt Generals, Vice Admirals, and Air Marshals of Armed Forces.

The unexplained exclusion of Armed Forces officers corps from the NFU, despite representation by the Chief of Staff, has wide-ranging implications : it impacts adversely the pay and pension structures, of colonels, brigadier and generals, and their equivalents in the navy and the air-force; it like OROP, become an emotive 'honor' issue; and, according to former senior military commanders, has had a corrosive impact on the Armed Forces morale, status, cohesion, and national security, Despite the serious long term implications of NFU, the issue was ignored by the UPA government, and even the BJP Government has chosen not to dwell on it.

Up Graduation of heads of Central and State Police Forces

In addition to NFU, Apex OROP for police and civil servants, the UPA Government, in 2008, in recognition of the growing influence of Indian Police service in Ministry of Home (MHA), India's Interior Ministry, promoted the heads of the Central Reserve Police Force (CRPF), Border Security Force (BSF), and even of the smaller MHA Forces, like the Indo-Tibetan Border Police (ITBP), Central Industrial Security Force (CISF) (CISF) and Sashastra Seema Bal (SSB), The Railway Police, an IG level post, to the highest grade pay, or the apex scale, with pay scale of Rs.80,000 (fixed). In addition, the Government upgraded heads of Police in all states, small or large, to Director General level to the highest grade pay, or the apex scale of Rs 80,000(fixed). This increased the numberof IPS officers with several dozen, and made the Director Generals(DG) of these Central and state Forces at par in rank, pay, and status with Armed Forces senior most Lieutenant Generals, Air Marshals and Vice Admirals. The only MHA Armed Forces left out from up gradation to the higher grades was the Assam rifles, which is headed by an army Lt General, and the National Security Guard (NSG), which has a sizable army component.

The implication of these up gradations are many: the immediate effect was that scores of IPS officers not withstanding their responsibilities were immediately made senior in pay grade, and status to Armed forces formation and fleet commanders, who were denied proportionate upgrades despite representation by the COSC committee; mass up-gradation and creation of new posts of secretaries and special secretaries, and DGs with apex grade pay level, also affected relative pensions. 'Non-functional financial up-gradation'(NFU) was not extended to Armed Forces.

Asymmetries in time scale pay, pension, and allowances

The United Progressive Alliance (UPA) Government headed by Manmohan Singh, following the recommendations of the sixth pay commission, mandated with effect from 01.09.2008, six time scale pay grade promotions on completion of 4, 9, 13, 14, 16/18 years of service for all officers in civil services including defense civilian officers in the MOD responsible for providing secretarial, and logistic support to the armed forces, and police officers including custom, revenue, railway, and industrial police. In comparison with six time-scale pay upgrades-promotions for the police, and defence civilian officers, the government approved three time scale pay upgrade-promotions for armed forces officers on completion of 2, 6, and 13 years of service, and at a far lower scale.

The decision by UPA government to introduce and aggravate asymmetries in the pay and pension and allowances between the different police organizations and armed forces even in the time scale pay grades, which the government did not explain, was cause of widespread disappointment amongst veterans and serving officers, and is a cause of OROP protests movement and the continued support that it receives, and is likely to continue to get.

The time scale promotions and related increases in pay, and allowances for government officers, including the police, are not contingent on vacancies or change in responsibilities. But are accompanied by increase pay, allowances and significant perks, difficult to accurately monetize, such as entitlements for hotel accommodation, class of air and rail travel, type of passport, use of staff car, size of office, increase in dedicated personal staff, etc.

Ministry of Defence (MOD)

The higher bureaucracy in Indian Ministry of Defence (MOD), unlike defence ministries in other countries, is staffed entirely by civil service officers on deputation, who have never served in the armed forces or are familiar with its working or ethos. The MOD bureaucracy is drawn from the IAS and from other civil services, including from civilian services responsible for providing support services to the Armed Forces such as from the Indian Defence Estates Service(IDES), the Indian Defence Accounts Service (IDAS), and Indian Ordnance Factories Service. The entire MOD bureaucracy is covered by Apex OROP. MOD higher bureaucracy, despite being granted apex-OROP coverage, and NFU has opposed to OROP and NFU for the Armed Forces, for no clear reasons.

In 2011, during the tenure AK Antony, as Defence Minister, Neelam Nath, Secretary of Department of Ex-servicemen Welfare (Poorva Senani Kalyan Vibhag) from 1 June 2009 to 30 September 2011, on instructions of Shashi Kant Sharma, Defence Secretary, opposed OROP for the Armed Forces, in her deposition to the Parliamentary Panel.

The Koshyari Committee however, disagreed with submissions by the Ministry of Defence and found "merit in the demand for One Rank One Pension by Armed Forces Personnel", and urged the Government to implement OROP at the earliest.

The MOD is considered by most ex-servicemen, including former head of the Armed Forces, as permanent impediment to OROP, and welfare of ESM. Four former heads of the Armed Forces in August 2015, in an open letter addressed to the President of India flagged "The hostile approach of MoD bureaucracy" and its "antagonistic handling of problems related to pensions and allowances of aging veterans, war widows and battle-casualties".

KOSHYARI COMMITTEE, 2011

In response to the growing unease in the Armed Forces, and escalating protest by veterans, the Government set up of a ten-member all-party Parliamentary Panel, known as the Koshyari Committee after its chairman, Bhagat Singh Koshyari, a veteran Bharatiya Janata Party (BJP) Member of Parliament

(MP), to examine the OROP issue. The Koshyari Committee after considering the evidence, and hearing oral depositions for eight months, submitted it report in December 2011. The committee unanimously found merit in OROP and strongly recommended its implementation. The Koshyari Committee (Petitions Committee of the Rajya Sabha), after examining the evidence, and taking into account the written and oral submissions by top officials from the Ministry of Defence (MOD) and Finance, veterans, and senior serving armed forces officers, over a six-month period (May–December 2011), defined the concept of OROP as follows:

OROP "implies that uniform pension be paid to the Armed Forces Personnel retiring in the same rank with the same length of service irrespective of their date of retirement and any future enhancement in the rates of pension to be automatically passed on to the past pensioners."

The Koshyari Committee definition of OROP was accepted by the Government, endorsed by Parliament, and by ex-servicemen and ex-servicemen organizations. It has since become basis for the ex-servicemen's demand for implementation of OROP. It is in sync with the ex-servicemen definition of OROP, according to which OROP "implies the grant of equal pension to soldiers of a particular rank, who have rendered the same length of service, irrespective of the date of their retirement".

On 27 February 2014, the MOD, in a meeting to discuss implementation of OROP attended by AK Antony, Defence Minister, Jitendra Singh, Minister of State, RK Mathur, Defence Secretary, Sangita Gairola, Secretary Department of Ex-Servicemen's Welfare, Arunava Dutt, Secretary Defence Finance, Vice Chiefs of the three Service, and Adjutant General of the Army, endorsed the Koshyari Committee's definition of OROP .

Despite the Koshyari Committee report, public commitments, including in the parliament, and visible disaffection among armed force veterans, the UPA Government was slow to reach out to the veterans and implement OROP.

BJP GOVERNMENT'S RESPONSE (2014-2016)

In May 2014, the UPA Government was replaced by the National Democratic Alliance (NDA) Government led by the Bharatiya Janata Party (BJP), which like the Congress Party, had included implementation of OROP in its election manifesto.

Narendra Modi

The BJP Prime Ministerial candidate, at a large election rally, in Rewari, Haryana, with former General VK Singh and Chief of Army Staff standing by his side, in the presence of tens of thousands Ex-Servicemen, declared that he will implement OROP, if elected. After Narendra Modi became Prime Minister there were more promises and public affirmations by him, and Manohar Parrikar, the Defence Minister, on the merits of OROP, and their intent to implement OROP. Most memorably on Diwali, at Siachen Glacier, in 2014, he told soldiers "It was in my destiny that One rank One pension has been fulfilled". On 30 May 2015, Prime Minister Narendra Modi, after more than a year of pledges and promises to implement OROP, controversially declared that the term OROP still needed to be defined. Modi's musings on the need for a new more acceptable OROP definition prompted widespread dismay, disappointment, and outrage among Armed Forces pensioners. On 31 May 2015, Modi in "Mann Ki Baat", radio address asked Ex-Servicemen to remain patient, as he gets rid of the bureaucratic hassles. Modi's statement was widely perceived as a disingenuous attempt to delay, dilute, and deny OROP.

Arun Jaitley

Arun Jaitley, the current Finance Minister and former Defence Minister, widely believed to the obstacle to early implementation of OROP, opposed Koshyari Committee definition of OROP. On 31 August 2015 Arun Jaitley, without defining OROP, says, "I have my own formula on what OROP means. Somebody else may have their own formula on OROP but it has to be within reasonable and rational criteria. You can't have an OROP where pensions are revised every month or every year". Responding to Jaitley, the UPSEM alleges that Arun Jaitley, is manipulating the media, specifically, the Times of India, and India TV channel, to misinform the public, and exacerbate difference between the Officers and soldiers, on the OROP issue.

AGAINST OROP

The arguments against OROP are based on administrative, financial and legal complications in implementing the scheme. In 2011, the Defence Ministry told the Koshiyari Committee that records going back further than 25 years were no longer available — a major administrative "difficulty in introducing the concept". There are cases where soldiers who retired in the 1940s are still being paid family pensions, and it will be administrative impossible to reconcile the nearly 20 lakh cases over such a long period for OROP over any reasonable timeframe. The Law Ministry told the committee that "if today's pension and emoluments are passed automatically to somebody who retired 30 years ago, there will be inherent discrimination against terms and conditions of service which would lead to discrimination under the Constitution".

A related aspect: people who retire in the same rank often earn different pensions because they may have served for longer periods in that rank. A Colonel who serves for 12 years in that rank will earn more pension than someone who served for 4 years as Colonel. Equating their pensions was unlikely to withstand a legal challenge.

The financial argument is about the long-term cost of implementing OROP. Defence Minister Manohar Parrikar's estimate of Rs 8,300 crore is only a one-time payout. This amount will increase substantially every time a new pay commission makes its recommendations, with all old pensioners being paid at the new rate. There is also the likelihood of civilian employees, such as the Central Armed Police Forces and the state police forces, raising the demand for OROP. Finally, there are fears that civilian employees who moved to a contributory pension scheme in 2004 might demand a reversion to fixed pensions, thus unravelling the whole system. That, perhaps, is the strongest argument against setting a precedent with OROP.

PROTESTS BY VETERANS

On 15 June, ex-servicemen despairing of BJP promises, commenced nationwide protests, and hunger strikes. Even some protestors, who are Ex-Servicemen, threatened to resort to Rail Roko (Stop Trains) agitation.

Support

Four former chiefs of the Armed Forces of India, namely General S F Rodrigues, former COAS, and Admirals L Ramdas, Arun Prakashand Sureesh Mehta, former Chiefs of Naval Staff, in an open letter to President Pranab Mukherjee, Supreme Commander of the Armed Forces, on 13 August 2015, warned that the denigration and humiliation of veterans, and the Government handling of veterans and armed Forces issues, pose grave "implication for national security"

Police Assault in Delhi, 2015

On the morning of 14 August 2015, the eve India's 68 Independence day, and the day after General Ved P Mulik, former Army Chief, the government designated interlocutor informed Nripendra Misra in the Prime Minister Office (PMO) that the government offer on OROP for Ex-Servicemen was unacceptable, a contingent of Police, drawn from the Delhi Police force, and the Central Reserve Police Force (CRPF), a paramilitary force for Internal security and Counter insurgency, under Ministry of Home Affairs, on orders from Rajnath Singh, the Home Minister of India, and under the command of BS Bassi, Director General of Delhi Police, assaulted a peaceful gathering of Armed Forces veterans, families, and war widows, at Jantar Mantar, New Delhi. The Police, not properly led, in their attempt to evict and frighten the gathered veterans, manhandled, 'pushed around', lathi charged, dragged, misbehaved, humiliated, menaced, and tore medals off the shirt of old veterans, including some in their eighties. Senior Delhi Police officers sought to justifying their heavy handed actions by claiming that they acted "following a request by civic agency New Delhi Municipal Council". Senior officer of Delhi police also said that the veterans were viewed as security risk and security threat.

The orders to the Delhi Police to evict the veterans, which had their origins in the MHA and the PMO, was revoked on 14 August afternoon, following public outrage, by Kiren Rijiju, Minister of State for Home, who said, "I have asked the Commissioner of Police not to remove the ex-servicemen from Jantar Mantar and let them continue the protest".

Former Chiefs of the Armed Forces protest attack on veterans

On 17 August, 10 former Chiefs of the Armed Forces of India in an unprecedented joint open letter addressed to Narendra Modi, the Prime Minister, condemned the police action, and urged the PM to order an inquiry into the action by the Delhi Police. The Signatories to the letter included retired Generals Vishwa Nath Sharma, Shankar Roy Choudhary, Sundararajan Padmanabhan, Joginder Jaswant Singh, Deepak Kapoor and Bikram Singh; retired Air Chief Marshals Nirmal Chandra Suri and Shashindra Pal Tyagi, and retired Admiral Madhvendera Singh.

Rajnath Singh, Home Minister, instead of ordering inquiry into the police excesses as demanded by the former Chiefs of Staff, asks Bhim Sain Bassi, DG Delhi Police, to send an officer to meet veterans and apologize for police action on 14 August. MK Meena, Delhi Police officer mets veterans and makes public apology. But the letter seeking an inquiry into the assault by the Chiefs of staff is ignored. No inquiry is held into circumstances prompting the police assault and excesses committed against the veterans.

Ex-Serviceman commits suicide over OROP

An Ex-Serviceman Ram Kishan Grewal committed suicide

over delay in One Rank One Pension issue on 1 November 2016 consuming poison at Jantar-Mantar in New Delhi. Grewal has reportedly left a suicide note, stating that he was taking this extreme step for soldiers.

Veterans response to police attack

Ex-servicemen outraged by police assertion that they were considered a risk, and security threat, to the Independence day celebrations, retorted angrily "We served the country in protecting it and now we have become security threat." Two days after the police assault, Colonel (Retd) Pushpender Singh (Ex-3 Grenadiers) and Havaldar (Retd) Major Singh (Ex-3 Sikh Light Infantry), same Regiment as Retired General Ved Malik, begin hunger strike-unto-death at Jantar Mantar, to protest police brutality, and delay in government implementation of OROP. A day later on 18 August 2015 Havildar Ashok Chauhan, Corps of signals, joins in the hunger strike.

OROP SCHEME

The Government in the face of mounting protest and resentment among veterans announced, in September 2015, that it would implement the new pension scheme, commonly referred to as One rank One Pension or OROP. Five months later in February 2016, it issued orders to implement the scheme. The scheme announced by the Government failed to satisfy the leaders of the protest movement, who vowed to take the government to court.

POTENTIAL BENEFICIARIES OF OROP

Potential beneficiaries of OROP is about 2.6 million ex-servicemen, and 60,000 widows, including war widows, i.e., a combined total of 3.2 million, of whom about 86 percent are widows, JCOs, NCOs, and other ranks, about 14 percent are officers. Out of the estimated outlay on OROP of Rs 8400 crores about Rs 6200 Crores will be on account of Widows, JCOs, NCOs, and other ranks, and about 2200 for Officers.

Subhash Bhamre, Minister of State for Defence, in November 2016, informed the Rajya Sabha that there are 20,63,529 pensioner beneficiaries of OROP, of whom 1429 have submitted complaints regarding OROP benefits.

DEFENCE PENSIONS

Expenditure on Defense pensions, especially expenditure on pensions for the armed forces, as a result of the protracted OROP protest, gained salience. The government in order to counter the demands for OROP often cited increasing expenditure on armed forces pensions. In India defence pensions, i.e., pensions paid from defence services estimate, also includes pension bill for about 400,000 defence civilians, and Ministry of Finance personnel attached to MOD. The 7CPC which looked long and hard at the armed forces pension bill, did not pay similar attention to the expenditure on account of the growing pension bill for defence civilians and the police security apparatus. There was also no mention or acknowledgment of the growing expenditure on account on the grant of OROP, and NFU to the senior most officers, including those paid from the defense services estimate. In 2015–16 Defence pension bill was 54,500 crores of which about 36 percent was on account of defence civilians. According to Brig Deepak Sinha, a respected commentator on military affairs, "civilian pensions, despite catering to one-fifth the number of military pensioners, utilizes approximately 36 percent of defence pensions, and given our difficulties in ensuring employment, even populism suggests it is better to reduce civilians who cost five times more than to reduce the military".

CHRONOLOGY

2014

On 17 February 2014

Finance Minister in the interim budget speech on 17 Feb 14 announces that Government has accepted the 'principle' of

OROP for Defence forces. This was followed by issue of Implementation order on 26 Feb 14. The demand note was however never raised by the Ministry Of Defence.Finance Minister in the interim budget speech on 17 Feb 14 announces that Government has accepted the 'principle' of OROP for Defence forces. This was followed by issue of Implementation order on 26 Feb 14. The demand note was however never raised by the Ministry Of Defence.

On 27 February 2014

A K Antony, Defence Minister in UPA Government, says that UPA will implement OROP by 1 April 2014.

24 April 2014

A K Antony constituted a Joint Working Group (JWG). CGDA, was appointed chairperson (later promoted to Secretary & Financial Adviser in the MoD). Members included representatives from Department of Ex-Servicemen Welfare, Defence/Finance, and Service HQ (Chairmen of the Army, Navy and Air Force Pay Commission Cells and a few officers). The first meeting of the JWG was convened on 2 May 2014 in the office of the CGDA.

9 June 2014

The President in a Statement to the joint session of parliament says Government has drafted National Commission for Ex-Servicemen Bill, 2015 in order to set up the National Commission for Ex-Servicemen. However, no funds have been allocated for setting up of the Commission during the year 2014-15.

10 July 2014

Arun Jaitley, Finance Minister and Defence Minister, in his maiden Budget Speech in the parliament, says, "We reaffirm our commitment to our brave soldiers. A policy of 'One Rank One Pension' has been adopted by the Government to address the pension disparities. We propose to set aside a further sum of 1,000 crore to meet this year's requirement"

14 August 2014

Maj Gen (Retd) Satbir Singh, SM, Chairman IESM, writes to Narendra Modi, Prime Minister, in response to his statement in Leh on 12 Aug 2014 stating that budget caters for the demand of OROP. The letter says the statement is "erroneous", and not in sync with Draft Govt Letter (DGL) prepared by Service HQs in the meetings in Feb and March, 2014, in which the forecast for OROP was crore, and not 1500 crore earmarked in the budget. The letter recalls that in a meeting chaired by Mr. AK Antony, former Defence Minister on 26 Feb 2014, OROP definition was approved and OROP was to be implemented with effect from 1 Apr 2014. The letter reminds the PM that "It has been six months since the OROP was approved".

20 August 2014

Air Chief Marshal Arup Raha, Admiral Robin Dhowan and General Dalbir Singh Suhag, briefed A K Mathur, Justice (retd), the chairman 7th Central Pay Commission (CPC), on the pay and pension "anomalies" caused by the 6 CPC.

23 October 2014

Narendra Modi, on Diwali Day, during a well publicized visit to army formation in Siachen Glacier, told soldiers "It was in my destiny that One rank One pension has been fulfilled".Modi's "Mann Ki Baat", radio address on 31 May 2015, in which he asked Ex-Servicemen to remain patient, as he gets rid of the bureaucratic hassles.

24 December 2014

Manohar Parrikar, defence Minister, on the advice of R.K. Mathur, Defence secretary (25.05.2013 -24.05.2015), informs Chairman of the 7CPC, that he does not favor NFU for the Armed Forces. The justification for not recommending NFU for the armed forces is that the Cabinet Secretary, in 2011, had not made "any recommendations on the issue".

2015

17 February 2015

Manohar Parrikar, Defence Minister, approves proposal for implementation of OROP, estimated to cost 8600 crores. The proposal is forwarded by the MOD, to Ministry of Finance on 17 Mar 2015, where it is still lying.

5 May 2015

Lt Gen SK Bahri, Chairman, Alliance of Ex-Servicemen Organizations, who had attended Modi's Rally at Riwari in 2013, writes to Narendra Modi, Prime Minister, to say that "ESM community is a very disillusioned lot". He reminds the PM of his promise at Riwari, and the repeated promises to implement OROP by the Defence Minister, including the COAS, since then. The letter blames the "intransigent bureaucracy" and Arun Jaitley the Finance Minister (FM) for the delay.

12 May 2015

Bidyadhar Nayak, Petty Officer Radio(Special), Indian Navy, general secretary of the Odisha unit, issues press release on behalf of Indian Ex-Services League (IESL), Odisha unit. The press release blames the bureaucracy for non-implementation of the grant of One Rank One Pension (OROP).

16 May 2015

Manohar Parrikar, in Goa, says "OROP proposal is in final stage. The defence ministry has approved it and the finance ministry will clear it in a few days, adding, "it is the first time that a clear proposal has been sent to finance ministry on OROP."

28 May 2015

Wing Commander Suresh Damodar Karnik, 80, winner of the Vir Chakra for combat action in the eastern and western theatres, in 1971 War, and former flight commander No 16 Bomber Squadron (Black Cobras), Indian Air Force (IAF), refused to meet with Manohar Parrikar, Defence Minister, and

Devendra Fadnavis, Chief Minister, Maharashtra, to protest BJP's failure to honour its commitment to implement OROP. The wing commander, on 28 May 2015, in Pune, said that he and his colleagues are unable to 'accept the invite' from the present Government because of its policy of NATO or 'NO ACTION TALK ONLY'.

4 June 2015

Lt General Vijay Oberoi, former Vice Chief of Army Staff, and widely respected war hero of the 1965 war in which he lost his right leg while serving with Maratha Light Infantry,dismissed Narendra Modi's comments on OROP as disingenuous, especially his comment that there were multiple definitions of OROP.

6 June 2015

Ex-Servicemen delegation led by Major General (Retired) Satbir Singh met Manohar Parrikar, Defence Minister. The meeting was arranged on the initiative of General Dalbir Singh Suhag, Chief of Army Staff. The meeting was inconclusive, and the two sides agreed to meet again.

11 June 2015

Brig (Retired) Harwant Singh, state convener of the Indian Ex-Servicemen Movement (IESM), announces that about 5,000 ex-servicemen from Punjab, which has about 6,00,000 Ex-servicemen, are planning to go to Delhi to participate in the protest rally on grant of OROP scheduled to begin 14 June.

The participants, which will include around 200 hunger strikers, will be given a "ceremonial farewell" at the war memorial in Jalandhar by war widows. Brig KS Kahlon (retd), President, chapter of the All India Defence Brotherhood, said the protest will also include return of war medals to the President by some ex-servicemen.

14–15 June 2015

Veteran hold "Maha Sangram Rally" at Jantar Mantar,

New Delhi, and 50 other locations nationwide. 15 June, commence relay hunger strike.–

15 Jun 2015

On 15 Jun 2015 several hundred of ex-servicemen, widows and Veer Narees of All Assam Ex-servicemen Welfare Association (South Zone) Patharkandi, Assam held a rally under Ex Sub Maj Nirmal Sinha, President of the Association with 12 hours hunger strike. The rally was started from AMAR JAWAN & WAR MEMORIAL point (Constructed by ExSub Maj Nirmal Sinha (Sigs)), marched through the town along the NH 8. It attracted the attention of shopkeepers, house owners, mazdoors and passengers of bus, rail etc.Many people loved to hear the patriotic songs sung by the veterans in the midst of demand. A memorandum to His Excellency The President of India was sent through JR Lal Seim the Circular Officer of Patharkandi requesting immediate implementation of OROP. The crowd supported Maj Gen (Retd) Satbir Singh for his ceaseless effort on the issue and thanked other associated Officers,JCOs and ORs for their valuable contribution and sacrifice.

On 15 June, several hundred ex-servicemen, staged a dharna, at Lower PMG Square, Bhubaneshwar, Odisa. Bidyadhar Nayak, general secretary, Indian Ex-Services League(IESL), Odisa unit, referring to the PM's statement that OROP was complex issue said, "Does this imply that OROP has got entangled in bureaucratic malaise for another four years? We have every reason to believe that the Prime Minister is being fed with falsities by sections who are against OROP and lobbies are working hard against the armed forces personnel." IESL officials Group Captain Jagadananda Brahma, President IESL, Arun Mohanty, and Bidyadhar Nayak submitted a memorandum on implementation of OROP to Governor SC Jamir

22 June 2015

Ex-servicemen announce intent to boycott golden jubilee

events to mark the 1965 war with Pakistan, including "felicitation of 1965 War Veterans" to be hosted by President Pranab Mukherjee at the Rashtrapati Bhavan in September. Ex-Servicemen also announce intent to boycott all government functions including at-home by president on Independence day (August 15), and the Ex-Servicemen contingent at the Republic Day Parade on 26 January 2016. Brigadier Harwant Singh, Regiment of Artillery, veteran of the battle of Chhamb-Akhnoor, 1965 war, says "We don't wish to be treated as showpieces, to be rolled out for ceremonies and discarded thereafter."

25 June 2015

Mizoram Ex-Service League, which has membership of 6,200 ex-servicemen [and about 25000 dependents], held protest rally, in Aizawl, demanding implementation of OROP.

27 June 2015

Maj Gen Satbir Singh, SM (Retd), Chairman IESM, on the 13th Day of the Relay Hunger Strike, issued a circular, claiming that hunger strike protest have spread to 50 locations, all over the country.

28 June 2015

500 veterans, demanding implementation of OROP, protest in Chennai, at Kamarajapuram Bus Stop, near Tambaram.

1 July 2015

United Front of Ex-servicemen, an ex-service organisation, revealed that ex-service men are reconsidering their protest tactics: new tactics will include continuation of relay hunger strike; protests outside homes of parliamentarians; mobilising electoral support against BJP in state election; and submitting letter and petitions to the President signed by war widows in their blood. In the meanwhile eight farmers organisations have joined the ex-servicemen protest under the banner 'Jai Jawan Jai Kisan'. A 1965 war veteran from Rajasthan, Krishan Kumar, in Delhi said, "We will stop fighting only when implementation of OROP takes place."

2 July 2015

On 19th day of nationwide hunger protest by ex-servicemen on 'One Rank One Pension' (OROP), Manohar Parrikar, Defence Minister, with General Dalbir Singh Suhag, Army Chief of Staff, by his side, met a six-member delegation of United Front of Ex-Servicemen (UFESM). Next meeting between the Defence, Minister and the Ex-Servicemen representatives is likely on 6 or 7 July.

7 July 2015

Brig Inder Mohan Singh (Retd), President, Indian Ex-Services League (IESL), Punjab, announced plan to hold protest rally by ex-servicemen on 8 July on a 3-km stretch on the Barnala-Bathinda Highway, from Sub-Area HQ gate to the headquarters X Corps gate. Large number of Junior Commissioned Officers and non-commissioned officers, including many veterans of 1965 war, are expected to participate in the protest. General Officer Commanding, Bathinda, Sub-Area, to the great disappointment of the protesting ex-servicemen, declined request to provide drinking water thinking it was illegal and fearing that "an explanation could be sought for this act." Brig Inder Mohan Singh, disappointed, asked, "Is serving water and that too to veterans not a humanitarian gesture?". Protest placards read "Soldiers become veterans, veterans become beggars. This is Make in India"; "Once a soldier, now a humiliated veteran"; "In no other country veterans protest as in India"; and "Indian soldiers' enemies- some across borders some in Delhi". Bhatinda type protest on OROP, according to Brig (Retired) Inder Mohan Singh, will be also conducted in front of other military stations. There are 14 Army stations and 5 Air Force stations in Punjab.

Justice T S Thakur, Supreme Court Judge, in a hearing on contempt petition by retired Major General S P S Vains, gave Additional Solicitor General Pinky Anand, six more weeks to implement OROP. The next hearing is on 24 August. The Supreme Court Judgment on 9 September 2008 in the case of

Union of India and Maj Gen Vains and Others had ruled: (a) No Defence Personnel Senior in rank can get lesser pension than his junior irrespective of the date of retirement (b) Similarly placed Officers of the same rank are to be given the same pension irrespective of the date of retirement.

8 July 2015

Ex-Servicemen protesting against Government failure to implement OROP blocked traffic on Bathinda-Chandigarh highway from 10 am to 1 pm, and sat in dharna in front of the police post in Bhatinda cantonment. Brigadier Inder Mohan Singh (retired), IESL, submitted a petition to a representative of headquarter X Corps (Chetak Corps) South Western Command. Brigadier Inder Mohan Singh indicated that the next protest will be in Amritsar, in which Captain Amarinder Singh former Punjab chief minister and Congress deputy leader in the Lok Sabha, is likely to participate.

The police arrested six ex-servicemen and charged them under Indian Penal Code sections 283 (danger or obstruction in public way or line of navigation) and 188 (disobedience to order duly promulgated by public servant). The arrested include: Bhinder Singh, Ramji Das and Sukhdev Singh, from Sangrur; Baldev Singh from Tarn Taran; and Kartar Singh, and Baldev Raj Joshi, from Bathinda. The police also registered cases against over 150 others who have not been named.

10 July 2015

Bhagat Singh Koshyari, the sitting BJP MP from Nainital-Udhamsingh Nagar, claimed that the Koshyari committee Report on OROP, 2011, prepared by the panel headed by him, was fool-proof. He blamed the United Progressive Alliance government headed by Manmohan Singh, PM, for not implementing OROP.

11 July 2015

Five retired Lieutenant Generals, four Major Generals and one Air Marshall of the Indian Air Force, joined the protest at jantar mantar, in New Delhi. Many of these general officers belong to the famous June 1971 Indian Military Academy (IMA) course, the "Born to battle" course, that was sent into the 1971 war as Second Lieutenants (2/Lt). One of the 2/Lt from 'born to battle course' who went to war in 1971 was Arun Khetrapal, troop leader, Poona Horse, who was awarded posthoumously the Param Vir Chakra, the nations highest award for valour in the famous tank battle of Basantar. Another 2/Lt from the 'born to battle' course, who joined the protest was Lieutenant General (Retired) Rajinder Singh Sujlana AVSM, VSM, former Colonel Commandant of the Sikh Regiment, and X Corps Commander.

13 July 2015

Punjab based ex-servicemen organisations, including All India Defence Brotherhood (A constituent of the United front of Ex-Servicemen(UFESM)), State Ex-Servicemen Welfare Association (SEWA), and Ex-Servicemen's Joint Action Front (Sanjha Morcha) held a protest rally at the Dussera ground Mohali. Ex-servicemen participants in the large rally included Lt Gen SR Ghosh, former GOC-in-C, Western Command, Lt Gen RS Sujlana, former Commandant Indian Military Academy and GOC X Corps, and Major Generals Dhillon, DP Singh, IP Singh and Amarjit Singh. The participants unanimously resolved to boycott functions during the visit of Defence Minister on 25 July to inaugurate 'Mai Bhago Institute' for training of girls to join the Defence Service. Brig Harwant Singh (Retd), President (UFESM), issued a Press Statement which stated that government inaction will force the ex-servicemen to resort to Direct Action.

17 July 2015

Defence Minister has set up a five-member committee consisting Lt Gen Richard Khare, (Retd), former Military Secretary; Lt Gen Mukesh Sabharwal,(Retd), former Adjutant General; Major Navdeep Singh, Territorial Army, Chandigarh-based High Court lawyer, and commentator of service conditions; and Major DP Singh, Kargil war wounded. The committee will look into Armed Forces grievances relating to service matters and pensions. The committee is expected submit its findings and recommendations within 60 days. No official announcement on the committee has been made by MOD, or the Defence Minister's office, but media reports suggests that the term of reference of the committee include making recommendations on measures to reduce litigation by Armed Forces members and Ex-servicemen, including the MOD which is a frequent litigator. There are over 10,000 cases by military personnel before the Armed Forces Tribunal, the High Courts and the Supreme Court, most of them against the Ministry of Defence, or prompted by its decisions, on service matters relating to pay fixation, promotions, policy interpretation, pensions and military justice.

21 July 2015

UFESM issued notices inviting veterans, veteran organization, and 'citizens of India', to participate in a "Kargil vijay divas run on 26 July". The run to unite veterans on OROP will be flagged off from DSOI, Dhaula Kuan, at 0500 hrs. It will pass through Teen Murti-Akbar Road-Janpath-Rajpath-India Gate-Kharg Singh Marg-Rajeev Chowk. It will end at Jantar Mantar, the site where ex-servicemen are fasting in protest against BJP Government failure to address their grievances. After the run, the runners will assemble at India Gate at 0800 am to pay homage to Kargil war martyrs, "who gave ultimate sacrifice to ensure that you sleep well". The ceremony at India gate will include laying wreath at Amar Jawan Jyoti.

24 July 2015

On the 40th day of the Relay Hunger Strike at Jantar Mantar, New Delhi, and protest in other locations in the country, Maj Gen Satbir Singh, SM (Retd), Advisor United Front of Ex-Servicemen and Chairman IESM, in written message to veterans said "we have upgraded our Agitation with effect from mid night 23 Jul 2015". The agitation in the new phase, he said, will be "peaceful and within the authorised methods of protests in the Constitution. The aim will be to raise awareness on One Rank One Pension (OROP) and related issues, and 'Create Visibility' in all the Districts in the County". The planned measures include: 10 Kilometre Kargil Vijay Diwas Marathon from DSOI, Dhaula Kuan, to India gate and Jantar Mantar, Delhi; participation of Anna Hazare in the protest on 26 July; raising public awareness on OROP and related issues using of placards, billboards, leaflets, briefing print and electronic media, and organising marathon runs and rallies across the country. Protest will be also be registered by urging ex-servicemen to boycotted government functions, displaying black flags on houses, surrender of BJP party membership by ex-servicemen, and sending petitions. Other measures may include sending bangles to the PM by "Veer Naaries (brave ladies) of Jhajjar district"; dharana outside the residences of MP, who fail to follow up on OROP in the Parliament; possible Hunger Strike till death; and submission of Memorandum to Narendra Modi, Prime Minister, by delegation of United Front of Ex-servicemen at 1 pm on 26 Jul 2015. In the meanwhile Jantar Mantar, New Delhi, continues to attract ex servicemen of all ranks. On 24 July, Maj General Satbir reported that officers from the 1st National Defence Academy (NDA) course, who are in their 80s, visited Jantar Mantar, Delhi, to show solidarity with the relay hunger strikers and express disapproval of government policy.

26 July 2015

To coincide with Vijay Diwas (Victory Day) events to mark the Kargil War, UK based Non Resident Indians (NRIs) held a one-day hunger strike to protest BJP Government failure to implement One rank One pension (OROP), outside the High Commission of India, London. A spokesperson for the protesters said similar protest are planned in other international cities, including in the US and Middle East.

31 July 2015

Admiral Ram Das Former Chief of Naval Staff visited Jantar Mantar to meet with and show solidarity with the Ex-servicemen and widows of veterans on hunger strike protesting the BJP Government failure to implement OROP and honour its election pledge. Admiral Ram Das made a donation to the ex-servicemen movement and said that he would write to all former Chiefs of the Army, Navy, and Airforce to overcome their inhibitions and visit Jantar mantar to show solidarity with the protesting ex-servicemen.

11 August

Gen V P Malik meet Nripendra Misra in the Prime Minister Office (PMO) where he was briefed by Mishra, and a joint secretary (JS) dealing with OROP in PMO, on the governments stand. In the evening the JS in the PMO briefs Malik, Gen Satbir Singh of the Indian Ex-Servicemen Movement (IESM) and General Balbir Singh of the Indian Ex-Servicemen League (IESL).

12 August

General Malik meets Gen Satbir Singh of the Indian Ex-Servicemen Movement (IESM) and General Balbir Singh of the Indian Ex-Servicemen League (IESL), to discuss the 'government stand' which remains unchanged. The sticking point remains the new definition of OROP, and the date of implementation of OROP.

13 August 2015

Malik meets Misra and briefs him on his discussions with the representatives of the IIndian Ex Servicemen Movement (IESM). At this meeting, according to Gen Malik, Misra gave the 'final stand of the Govt' after speaking with Prime Minister and Arun Jaitley, the Finance Minister. The attempt at last minute mediation to enable the PM to make the OROP announcement on Independence day broke down on the issues of the government's new definition of OROP and date of implementation of OROP.

General S F Rodrigues, former COAS, and Admirals L Ramdas, Arun Prakash and Sureesh Mehta, former Chiefs of Naval Staff, wrote an open letter to President Pranab Mukherjee,

Supreme Commander of the Armed Forces. The letter was ignored, the President did not respond to the letter.

14 August 2015

Rajnath Singh, the Home Minister of India authorized Delhi Police, a police force under the Ministry of Home Affairs, to evict by force ex-servicemen, families of ex-servicemen, and war widows, from Jantar Mantar, the site of Ex servicemen protests. The Police Contingent, consisting of personnel drawn from the Delhi Police, and Central Reserve Police Force, a Counter Insurgency and Internal Security Force under the Ministry of Home Affairs, in camouflage dress, unsupervised by senior officers, without advance warning, swooped down on the protesters. The protesting Ex servicemen, many in their eighties, were manhandled, 'pushed around', dragged, humiliated, and lathi-charged. Their tents were forcibly removed, placards and other equipment damaged.

The Delhi Police officers justified action against the peaceful gathering at Jantar Mantar claiming they acted "following a request by New Delhi Municipal Council", civic agency and because of security risk and threats. "As Delhi is on a high alert ahead of Independence Day so", a senior police officer said. " we are removing the protesters to ensure security."

The ex-servicemen were outraged by Delhi police officer's allegations that they were a security risk

The orders to Delhi police to remove the Ex servicemen, were rescinded on 14 August afternoon, following public outrage, and intervention by General VK Singh, on behalf of the ex-servicemen, with Rajnath Singh, the Home Minister, according to ex-servicemen. The Home Minister's orders to stop the police action against the ex-servicemen was conveyed Delhi Police Commissioner BS Bassi by Kiren Rijiju, Minister of State for Home.

15 August 2015

Prime Minister Narendra Modi on 69th Independence Day of India address to the nation from the Red Fort, New Delhi, refers to "One Rank One Pension" as a problem "pending to be resolved".

17 August 2015

Ten former Chiefs of the Armed Forces of India (7 former chief of Indian Army staff, 2 Chiefs of Air Staff, and 1 Chief of Naval Staff), in an unprecedented joint open letter urged Narendra Modi, the Prime Minister, to order an inquiry into the brutal police action by Delhi Police against the peaceful gathering of veterans in Jantar Mantar, on Independence Day eve and to resolve the OROP issue expeditious. The Signatories to the letter include retired Generals Vishwa Nath Sharma, Shankar Roy Choudhary, Sundararajan Padmanabhan, Joginder Jaswant Singh, Deepak Kapoor and Bikram Singh; retired Air Chief Marshals Nirmal Chandra Suri and Shashindra Pal Tyagi, and retired Admiral Madhvendera Singh.Colonel (Retd) Pushpender Singh (ex-3 Grenadiers) and Havaldar (Retd) Major Singh (Ex-3 Sikh Light Infantry), began hunger strike-unto-death at Jantar Mantar. Havildar Major Singh belongs to the same Regiment as Retired General Ved Malik, former Chief of army Staff. They were joined by Havildar Ashok Chauhan, Corps of signals, on 18 August. 18 August 2015

General Dalbir Singh Suhag, Chief of Army Staff, late in the night on 17 August, called Major General Satbir Singh, and urged him to meet with Nripendra Misra, Principal Secretary to the PM, on 18 August 2015. Major General Satbir Singh and Lt General Balbir Singh, representatives of the ex servicemen, after initial hesitation, met Nripendra Misra, Principal Secretary to the PM, at 1000h on 18 August 2015, to discuss resolution of the OROP. This was first overture from the government to the Ex servicemen since the protest started in June 2015. Mr Misra urged the Ex Servicemen representatives to end the protest. The ex-servicemen representatives informed Mr Misra that ex servicemen will end their protest only after the Government gives an assurance that it will not alter the accepted definition of OROP, implement OROP for all pensioners with effect from 1 April 2014, and ensure that all future enhancements will be automatically passed on to past pensioners. Mr Misra failed to give an assurance on the issues raised by the Ex servicemen. During the meeting Mr Misra was reminded of BJP's commitment, made in its manifesto, to build a martyrs memorial and set up veterans' commission, to be manned by veterans. Mr Misra seemed unaware of these commitments by the BJP. In the presence of the ex-servicemen representatives, Mr Misra called the Defense Secretary and asked him to brief him on these subjects.

21 August 2015

Vijay Singh, (IPS- 2005), Deputy Commissioner Police,(DCP)-1 New Delhi, who led the police contingent to evict Armed Forces veterans from the Jantar Mantar transferred as Deputy Commissioner of Police(DCP) North West District. Delhi Police PRO Rajan Bhagat calls it routine transfer, and denies media reports that this was because of police action against veterans on 14 August 2015.

22 August 2015

Rallies by Ex servicemen in support of the OROP movement were held Udham Singhn Nagar, Mohali, and Mysore.

23 August 2015

On 70 day of the Relay Hunger Strike (RHS), called Satyagraha by some ex-servicemen, 25 Ex-servicemen, from 14 Indian States, were on RHS at Jantar Mantar. The fast unto death by Col Pushpender Singh(Grenadiers), and Havaldar Major Singh (Sikh Light Infantry) entered the eighth day, and by Hav Ashok Kumar Chauhan (Signals) the sixth day.

United Front of Ex-Servicemen (UFESM) organized a candle light march, and vigil, to honor, and remember, armed forces members killed in the 1965 war. Over 4000 ex-servicemen, and civilians, participated in the event. Participants lit candles, and laid bouquets at Amar Jawan Jyoti, at India Gate. "Sainik parliament" had passed a resolution to boycott all government functions, including by the armed forces, till implementation of OROP.

Veterans and their wives, including and war widows, protested police action on 14 August, against the veterans in Delhi, and delay in implementing OROP, in Dehradun, the State capital of Uttarakhand.

Participants included Lt Gen TPS Rawat, (4 Gorkha Rifles), a former minister, Lt General Gambhir Singh Negi (former Colonel of 3 Gorkha Rifles), Maj Gen Lalji D Singh (Corps of Engineers, Bombay Sappers), Maj Gen Chander Nandwani, Brig KG Behl, Brig RS Rawat, Brig Vijay Kumar, Col PL Prashar, Col GS Cheema Col AK Khullar, Brig CB Thapa, Col SC Tyagi, Maj SS Chowdhury, and Col Kukreti, first JSW course

A joint Kisan rally- ex-servicemen was held at Satara. the rally was attended amongst others by Anna Hazare. An estimated 10,000 people attended the rally.

Large number of ex-servicemen, and civilian supporters, visited Jantar Mantar, to show solidarity with ESM cause. These included: officers from Short Service Courses (SS) 2, and 31; National Defence Academy (NDA) course 46 and 75; 55 and 85 Indian Military Academy; and officers from the 14 Army Education Course; and twenty five officers and their families came from Jaipur. The movement continues to gain momentum, and perceptible increase in support and participation by former high-ranking officers of the armed forces, from Lt generals, Admirals, air marshals, Group Captains, and Colonels. Old veterans included Sep Ram Kishan, 93 years, Armoured Corp veteran of World War II; Sep Ram Bharose Yadav, 85 years, a blind veteran of 72 Medium Artillery; and Mrs Savita Rai Singh wife of Brig Rai Singh(90 Year old) Maha Vir Chakra. Many visitor contributed substantial sums to the cause.

24 August 2015

Colonel Pushpendra Singh, one of three veterans on hunger strike at Jantar Mantar, was evacuated to Army Research and Referral Hospital, Delhi, in a private car, due to deteriorating condition.

25 August 2015

On 72 day of the Relay Hunger Strike (RHS), 37 Ex-servicemen were on RHS at Jantar Mantar. Col Pushpender Singh(Grenadiers), was in the Intensive Care Unit (ICU), Army Research and Referral Hospital (R&R), Havaldar (Hav) Major Singh (Sikh Light Infantry), on 10th day of his fast unto death refused to be evacuated; and Hav Ashok Kumar Chauhan (Signals) on the 8th day, was vacuated to R&R due to muscle atrophy. The other hunger strikers, who were all fit, were: Major Piar Chand, 2 Grenadiers; Hav Sahib Singh, 2 Rajputana Rifles; and Naik Uday Singh Rawat of 12 Garhwal Rifles.

Visitors included Rajeev Chandrasekhar Indep MP Rajya Sabha; and Ms Nalini Singh, Journalist. The meals for the day were provided by Gurdwara Bangla Sahib, and Col Gurdeep Singh.

General Satbir Singh met Ajit Doval, National Security Adviser and Former head of Intelligence Bureau. This is the first report of NSA's interest and concern in OROP. The outcome of this meeting and issues discussed is not known. According to Media reports Doval is expected to take an "overall view of the situation" and be involved in the "final negotiations".

26 August 2015

Major General Satbir Singh (Retd), head of the Indian Ex-Servicemen Movement, met Nripendra Misra, Principal Secretary to PM. General Dalbir Singh, COAS, was present at the meeting.

27 August 2015

Capt Amarinder Singh, Congress MP and former Punjab chief minister, a 1965 war veteran, declared his support for OROP.

On 74 day of the Relay Hunger Strike (RHS), at Jantar Mantar, 39 Ex-servicemen and four war widows (Veer Narees) were on RHS. In Ambala and Pathankot, RHS entered the 70th day and 74th day respectively.

There were 8 person on indefinite fast, 4 at Janatr Mantar, and 4 in Research and Referrals Army Hospital (RR): Col Pushpender Singh(Grenadiers), in RR, twelfth day. Hav Ashok Kumar Chauhan(Signals), in RR, 10th day. Major Piar Chand and Hav Sahib Singh were evacuated to Research and Referrals on advice of the doctors.

Havildar Major Singh (Sikh Light Infantry), at Jantar Mantar, on the 12th day of his fast was joined by his brother. In addition there are four more soldiers, and a father of a martyred soldier Sunil Kumar Yadav, on indefinite fast, at Jantar Mantar.

Visitors to Jantar Mantar included: Mrs. Charu Sheela(95 yrs) mother of Col. Pushpender; representative of Rashtra Sewak Trust; Air Marshal J S Bawa and Lt Gen Suri; and Officers from 10th NDA and 19th IMA courses. Breakfast and Lunch was provided by SSC NT-27 & Technical-18 and Gurudwara Bangla Sahib.

28 August 2015

Ex Servicemen representatives including Major General (retd) Satbir Singh, Chairman of the Indian Ex-Servicemen Movement, and Group Captain VK Gandhi, meet Rajnath Singh, Home Minister, in his office in the Ministry of Home Affairs, in Delhi, at his invitation. This is the first meeting between officials of the MHA and ex servicemen since 14 August Police action against ex servicemen in Jantar Mantar.

Pranab Mukherjee, President of India, lays wreath at the Amar Jawan Jyoti, at India Gate. Military veterans boycott official function at India Gate to mark the start of month-long golden jubilee celebrations of the 1965 war.

A "parallel commemoration" of 1965 war coinciding with the capture of Hajipir Pass by Major Ranjit Singh Dyal, MVC, 1 Parachute Regiment, is attended by several veterans of the 1965 war, including Brigadier (retd) D P Nayar, a veteran of the attack on Hajipir, and Wing Commander (retd) Vinod Nebb. Wing Commander Vinod Nebb who was 22, in 1965, on 6 September, on an alert from air defense commander, Ambala, while on a combat air patrol sortie over Ludhiana, Punjab, brought down a Pakistani Sabre jet fighter for which he was awarded Vir Chakra, India's third highest gallantry award. The Times of India, in an editorial comment wrote that Ex Servicemen demands of OROP are "not a sustainable proposition" and taxpayer money "will be recklessly splurged if the demand is accepted."

31 August 2015

On 78 day of the Relay Hunger Strike (RHS), Havildar Major Singh (Sikh Light Infantry), who is on fast since 16 August, is joined by Naik Udai Singh Rawat, Sawal Ram Yadav, father of martyr Lance Naik Sunil Kumar Yadav, navy Commander A.K. Sharma, Subedar Vijay Singh Yadav and Subedar Keshaw Singh.

Ram Jethmalani, former BJP member, visits Jantar Mantar, declares support for OROP, and blames the finance minister for delay in implementing OROP.

1 September 2015

On 79th day of the Relay Hunger Strike (RHS), there were 28 Ex-servicemen, and wives of three Ex servicemen on Relay Hunger Strike at Jantar Mantar. In Ambala and Pathankot, the RHS entered the 75th and 79th day respectively. There were 4 ex servicemen on hunger strike in the army Hospital, and 8 at Jantar Mantar. Hav Major Singh, who has been on fast since 16 August, has lost 10 kilo of weight. He continues to refuses to end his 17 days old fast, take medicines, or be evacuated to hospital.

3 September 2015

Leaks by Government sources to media suggest that it may unilaterally announce implementation of One Rank One Pension in next 2 to 3 days. Ex servicemen Representative Maj General Satbir Singh while acknowledging that he had met with Nripendra Misra, Principal Secretary to PM, made clear there were no on going negotiations with the government. Nothing had been agreed to so far. Referring to questions raised on the financial implication of OROP he said that when the government sanctioned Non Functional Upgrades to the All India Services after the 6th Pay Commission no question on the financial implications were raised. Shekhar Gupta, calling ex servicemen protest unedifying spectacle on a popular English language TV news channel, argued that ex-servicemen should accept what is offered.

5 September 2015

Government unilaterally announces the implementation the 'OROP Scheme' for the Armed Forces.

17 October 2015

Rajyavardhan Singh Rathore, former colonel, MP from Rajasthan, and Minister of State for Information and Broadcasting in the BJP Government, in an interview to a TV news-channel, denounced the Ex servicemen for continuing with their protest.

7 November 2015

Department of Ex-Servicemen Welfare, Ministry of Defence, as follow up to the 5 September announcement, issues order on "One Rank One Pension (OROP) to the Defence Forces Personnel", which were delayed on account of the elections in Bihar.

The OROP order excludes all future Armed Forces retirees who take premature retirement from OROP entitlement.

9 November 2015

The ex servicemen announce that they will start returning their medals on 10–11 November, across the country, to District Magistrates, who have been informed to collect the medals, Group Captain VK Gandhi (retd), the general secretary of Indian Ex-servicemen Movement (IESM), said. In Delhi, the medals will be returned outside Terminal 1 of the Indira Gandhi International Airport (IGIA). The protesting ex-servicemen also met Delhi Chief Minister Arvind Kejriwal to brief him about the government notification on OROP. Kejriwal informed Group Captain VK Gandhi (retd).

10 November 2015

Manohar Parrikar, denounces Ex-servicemen decision to return medals; and calls protesting ex-servicemen emotional, and disgruntled.

11 November 2015

Military veterans, on Diwali, which the veterans call a 'Black Diwali', took out a protest march to Rashtrapati Bhavan, to meet with the President. The marchers were intercepted by Delhi Police near Rail Bhavan.

13 November 2015

Arvind Kejriwal, Delhi Chief Minister, visited ex-servicemen protesting at Jantar Mantar. He urged the government "to immediately accept the demands of the veterans".

16 November 2015

Brig Harwant Singh (retd), representative of United Front of Ex-servicemen, says the OROP movement is not about money, but about self-respect and izzat.

19 November 2015

7th Pay Commission, headed by Justice A K Mathur, in its 900-page report, recommends OROP, without calling it one-rank-one-pension (OROP), for all central government employees, including para-military personnel as well defence civilians who have retired before 1 January 2016. The recommendations affect 47 lakh central government employees and 52 lakh pensioners:increase in pay will be 16 per cent, allowances 63 per cent and pension 24 per cent.

Seventh Central Pay Commission (7CPC), in its consideration of one rank one pay, notes that France, China, and Germany have pension schemes for the armed forces, much like India. The US and UK, with a small variation, have a similar scheme, called a "defined benefit scheme".

On the contentious issue of Non - Functional Upgradation, there was disagreement between the chairman of 7CPC and the members of the commission. Chairman "felt that NFU should be allowed to continue since it has existed for the last 10 years and is being availed by all the Organised Group 'A' Services", and that it "should be extended to the officers of the Defence forces and CAPFs". Vivek Rae, IAS, and Dr. Rathin Roy, Members, Seventh CPC, disagreed. They felt that NFU till SAG and HAG level, granted to Organised Group 'A' Services, should be withdrawn, and did not support extension of "NFU to Defence Forces and CAPFs, including ICG".

2 December 2015

General (Retd) VK Singh, former Chief of army Staff and Union Minister, who has been involved in Government's 'back-channel' overtures with veterans, according to Ex-servicemen sources, who had met Manohar Parrikar, Defence Minister, on 2 December, will mediate between government and protesting ex-servicemen, on 'One Rank One Pension' scheme. In the meanwhile the veterans continue to examine the option of seeking legal redress in the supreme court, and prepare for the rally scheduled for on 13 December.

4 December 2015

Rao Inderjit Singh, by Minister of State for Defence, confirmed that Government will appoint a "Judicial Committee to look into anomalies" including issues concerning "methodology for fixation of pension, periodicity of its revision, coverage of future PMR cases" raised by veterans.

Deepender Hooda, Congress MP, criticizing BJP Government failure to implement full OROP, says, Congress supports the demands of the veterans, including annual review of OROP instead of 5 year review as notified by the BJP Government; and OROP for those who take premature retirement. The Congress Party, he said, will take the OROP issue forward in parliament by seeking funds for the implementation of OROP.

7 December 2015

United Front of Ex-Servicemen (UFESM), suggests Justice R M Lodha name for chair of the one-man judicial commission to look into the concerns of the veterans.

14 December 2015

Department of Ex Servicemen issues notification on appointment of Justice L. Narasimha Reddy, former Chief Justice of the Patna High Court, as the one-man judicial commission to look into the implementation of the one rank one pension scheme. The terms of reference for the committee include measures for the removal of anomalies that may arise in the implementation of the OROP as notified by the government on 7 November 2015; measures for the removal of anomalies that may arise out of inter-services issues of the three forces due to its implementation; and implications on service matters.

16 December 2015

UFESM, to mark victory on the Indian Armed Forces in the 1971 war, and pay Homage to 'Martyrs of Independent India', held a flag raising ceremony at India Gate. The event was attended by large number of veterans. Wreaths were laid by several veterans, at Amar Jawan Jyoti, including Lt Col Inderjit Singh, Chairman All India Ex-Services Welfare Association, Maj Gen Satbir Singh, SM, Vice Chairman IESM, and Col Anil Kaul VrC . After the event UFESM issued a press release in which it deplored the delay in establishing a war memorial, the failure of the government to commemorate the victory in the 1971 War, and that of all the civilians gathered at India gate none new of the historic significance of 16 December or the 1971 war. To commemorate the historic victory, and the martyrs who scarified their lives, UFESM urged the government to declare 16 December a national holiday.

23 December 2015

General Dalbir Suhag, Chief of the Army Staff (COAS); Admiral Robin Dhowan, Chief of the Naval Staff (CNS); and Air Chief Marshal Arup Raha, Chief of the Air Staff (CAS), in a joint memorandum to the Manohar Parrikar, defence minister, have urged the defence Minister to appoint an expert committee, with members from the armed forces, to examine and reconcile the pay, pension, allowances, and status anomalies exacerbated by 7CPC report, which had no representation from the armed Forces.

The Pay Commission report after it is submitted to the Government is processed by a group of bureaucrats, called a 'Committee of secretaries', which routinely endorses the report, as it did after 3, 4, 5 and 6 CPC. This process has not worked well in the past, primarily because of the conflict of interest, as the " Committee of secretaries" are direct beneficiaries from their examination and recommendation on the implementation of the pay commission reports. For instance, after the 6CPC, the 'committee of secretaries' endorsed and recommended OROP for themselves, and reward all civil servants with of Non Functional Upgrade (NFU), but strongly objected to these benefits being extended to the armed Forces. Similarly the reduction in Pensions of the Armed Forces, after the 3CPC, and imposition of 'rank pay', after 4 CPC, according armed forces generals, depressed military pay, pension, and status, especially so relative to the Indian Police Service. The memorandum by the three service chiefs seeking military representation in the review committee when viewed against this background is not as provocative as the Indian express has sought to make it out.

2016

15 January 2016

Veterans participating in an Army Day event in Dehradun reiterated their demands for implementation of full and agreed to "one rank, one post" (OROP). "It is sad for everyone that even now when Parliament has approved OROP, some unnecessary spokes have been put in its implementation," said Brig (retd) K G Behl, president of Dehradun Ex-servicemen League.

17 January 2016

About 200 veterans including Major General Satbir Singh, protested outside 2, Krishna Menon, Marg, New Delhi, the official residence of Finance Minister Arun Jaitley. The protesters highlight Jaitley's failure to take heed of their concerns, and breaking his promise given to them on 3 January that he would speak with Manohar Parrikar, Defence Minister, and 'get back' within a week on status of OROP issues that need to be resolved. Group Captain (retd) VK Gandhi. The protest ended late in the evening, after a meeting with Jayant Sinha, Minister of State for Finance. Disappointed veterans returned to Jantar Mantar, where they have been protesting since 14 June 2015.

18 January 2016

Jayant Sinha, Minister of State for Finance, met veterans briefly. Sinha, according to Col. Anil Kaul (retd), a spokesperson for the Indian Ex-Servicemen's Movement, will meet with Ex servicemen again on 20 January.

21 January 2016

As follow up on the meeting with Jayant Sinha, Minister of State for Finance, on 16 January, and on his prompting, Lt Gen Balbir Singh, President IESL, Lt Col Inderjit Singh, Chairman AIEWA and Maj Gen Satbir Singh, Chairman IESM & Adviser UFESM (JM), send a joint letter, to ' people who matter' urging them to address the anomalies in 7 November 15 notification on implementation of OROP. The letter titled 'Urgent Need to Rectify Anomalies in OROP in Govt notification dated 7 Nov 15", which has the 'approval of 200 veteran organization', is addressed to Manohar Parrikar, Raksha Mantri, Mr Arun Jaitley, Finance Minister, Jayant Sinha, Minister of State, Finance, General Dalbir Singh, Chief of Army Staff, Air Chief Marshal Arup Raha, Chief of the Air Staff & Chairman

Chiefs of Staffs Committee (CoSC), and Admiral RK Dhowan, Chief of Naval Staff.

26 January 2016

This year in the Republic Day March Past in Delhi, in a break from a venerable tradition, the Ministry of Defence, the organizers of the event, decided to exclude the veterans contingent from the march past. The decision to exclude the veterans from the march past and replace it with a tacky tableau advertising implementation of OROP was, it would appear, made by Manohar Parrikar, the Defense Minister, and Defence Ministry Officials including the G.Mohan Kumar, Defence secretary, and Prabhu Dayal Meena, Secretary Department of Ex-Serviceman Welfare(DESW).

3 February 2016

A Ministry of Defence press release claimed that it has fulfilled OROP, a 'demand of the Defence Forces personnel' that had been pending for '42 years'. The detailed letter on the implementation of OROP, including table for calculation of pension was issued by Department of Ex Servicemen.

4 February 2016

Colonel Anil Kaul (Retd), spokesperson for the Indian Ex servicemen, denounced the BJP Governments claims on OROP implementation, saying "OROP tables short-change widows, reservists, battle casualties, havildars, subedars and subedar majors. The Jantar Mantar protest will continue and legal options will be exercised".

Former Army Chief General Ved Prakash Malik, and Secretary, Ministry of Defence, Ajay Prasad, in a panel discussion on TV, argued in favor of OROP even for those who opt to take that 'pre-mature retirement (PMR) for what ever reason, to keep the armed forces young.

2 March 2016

Expenditure on pay and allowances for 3.5 million central government employees in the budget estimates of 2016-17 has increased by 23.5 percent. The details are tabulated below. The increase is attributed to large increase in allowances because of 7CPC recommendations, including in housing allowance, which is now 24 percent of the basic pay.

10 March

On 10 March, late in the evening, a squad of five plain-clothes men from the Haryana Police, led by thick set man who posed as flower delivery man, forced their way into the house of Wing Commander Sharma,75, former IAF officer and fighter pilot, and veteran of 1965 war and 1971 War, and arrested him. The Wing Commander, a prominent leader of the OROP movement, was arrested in front of his wife and family. The plainclothesmen, according to the officer's wife offered no explanation, or reason. The BJP Government in Haryana, or YP Singhal, Director General of Haryana Police, under whose orders the police action was conducted, did not explain the reason for deploying plainclothesmen in the raid against the officer or conducting it late in the evening, under false pretense, in a menacing manner. The raid and the arrest was made following an old complaint alleging financial wrongdoing by IESM leadership by Lt Gen Raj Kadyan, formerly Rajputana Rifles, former Chairman of the IESM, considered close to the present government. The complaint also named Maj General Satbir Singh, the present head of the IESM, and Group Captain VK Gandhi, both of who secured anticipatory bail from the Chandigarh high court.

25 March

Maj Gen Satbir Singh,(Retd), Chairman Indian Ex-Servicemen Movement (IESM), writes to L.Narasimha Reddy, Retired Chief Justice of Patna High Court and head of the commission on OROP scheme, and the Defence Minister, on "Urgent Need to Rectify Anomalies in OROP". The letter draws attention to Government's executive order dated 26 Feb 14 for the implementation of OROP, and the notification issued on 7 November 2015. The letter examines five salient anomalies in the OROP scheme 2015 as follows: *(1) Fixation of pension as per calendar year 2013 would result in past retirees getting less pension of one increment than the soldier retiring today. This will completely destroy definition of OROP approved by two Parliaments and will also result in loss of one increment across the board for past pensioners in perpetuity. (2) Fixing pension as mean of Min and Max pension of 2013 would result in more anomalies wherein same ranks with same length of service will draw two or more different pensions thus violating the very principle of OROP. (3) OROP has been approved in budget of 2014-15 by two parliaments. As per norms of Government, all proposals approved in budget are applicable from 1st April of that FY. In the case of OROP, the Govt had issued specific orders to its applicability wef 1st April 14. Hence implementation date for OROP from 1st July will be against the Parliament approval. Changing the date would result in loss of 3 months emoluments for OROP across the board. However, if OROP implementation date is to be kept as 1st July, then the base pension should also be accepted as per the PPOs of July 2014. (4) Pension equalisation every five year will result in a senior rank soldier drawing lesser pension than a junior rank soldier for five years thus OROP definition will be violated for five years. This will also result in permanent violation of definition as fresh cases will come up every year. (5) There are numerous errors in the constitution of Tables. How this Table have been made is not known. The fact is that no senior rank defence personnel should ever draw less pension their junior persons. There are numerous instances in the Tables where in the senior rank and senior in service have been shown to draw less pension then his junior. The tables need to be worked out afresh after all anomalies have been removed. The most appropriate method to construct Tables would be to base these tables on live data. The PPOs of defence personnel who retired in 2013 would removal that a Sepoy with 15 years of service should get pension of approx Rs 7200 per month where as in the Tables, pension has been mentioned as Rs 6665/-. This does not satisfy the approved OROP definition. There are minimum such examples.*

Nb Subedar of 'Y' group has been shown to get less than X Gp Havildar this making a senior rank defence, personal gets less than junior rank. Nb Sub TA is shown getting more pension then Regular Nb Sub. The three Service HQs pay cells must be involved in making this Table afresh. These anomalies will result in lesser pensions to widows, soldiers, NCOs and JCOs than what will be due to them on approval of OROP. This will result in veterans not getting OROP as per approved definition and will create much discontent across all ranks. There is a need to have a relook at the pensions of Hon Nb Subedars, Majors and Lt Cols. a) Some Havildars are granted rank of Hon Naib Subedar in view of their exemplary service. These soldiers are not granted pension of Naib Subedar thus making the Hon rank just ceremonial. Hon Naib Subedars should get pension of a Naib Subedar rather than that of a Havildar. Similarly, this must be accepted as a principle and it should be applicable to all Hon ranks in case of NCOs and JCOs. b) Moreover no officer is retiring in Major rank now. In the past, officers were promoted to Major rank after completing 13 yrs of service whereas present officers are getting promotion of Lt Col in 13 yrs. It will be justified to grant all pensioners of the rank of Major, minimum pension of Lt Col as they cannot be compared to present retirees as officers are not retiring as Majors any more. Number of such affected officers is not more than 800 and will not cause heavy burden to Govt. c) Similarly, all pre-2004 retiree Lt Cols should get the minimum pension of full Col. Presently all officers retire in the rank of Colonel hence all Lt Col equivalents should be granted min pension of Colonels. The above anomalies/ discrepancies are being brought before you for resolution please. Finance Minister in the interim budget speech on 17 Feb 14 announces that Government has accepted the 'principle' of OROP for Defence forces. This was followed by issue of Implementation order on 26 Feb 14. The demand note was however never raised by the Ministry Of Defence.

28 March

A delegation of Civil Service officers representing the "Confederation of Civil Service Associations" submitted a memorandum on "their long standing grievance of discrimination vis-a-vis certain other All-India Services" to Jitendra Singh, Union Minister of State MoS, in Prime Ministers Office (PMO), and minister in-charge of Personnel, Public Grievances, Pensions. The "Confederation of Civil Service Associations" in their memorandum, claiming "that the majority view in the 7th CPC was in favour of changing the status-quo on the issue of pay disparity" demanded "parity" with "other services". The memorandum noted that the "main cause of resentment among the non-IAS Civil Service Officers was that all the senior level posts covering majority of Departments, be it technical or administrative, are today manned by IAS Officers. The Civil service Association which includes Defence Civilian services, demanded : [a] "equitable treatment ...so that the gap between the IAS and other Services does not widen and lead to.. chaotic situation; [b] Pay- disparity be removed altogether; and [c] the "Committee of Secretaries" to examine the report of the 7th CPC, be reconstituted to "represent all different sections of stakeholders" so that it may function with "neutrality"

29 March

Parrikar, tells India Today, that "The Seventh Pay Commission are in the form of recommendations. I do not think they (recommendations) will remain. I do not consider them as finalities. I have flagged them and will flag them properly at the right level".

3 April

At Jantar Mantar, on 3 April, at a well attended gathering veterans protested against government failure to implement OROP, and address other izzat issues, including long pending anomalies in pay and pension of armed forces. Many veterans urged veterans to contest elections to have their voice properly heard. Group Captain V.K. Gandhi (retd), general secretary of the Indian Ex Servicemen Movement said, "We have given a call to ex-servicemen to contest elections to State Assemblies, Rajya Sabha and Lok Sabha. We are a six-crore vote bank and we should have our own representatives to achieve our demands". He added that if the veterans remained united, they "would be able to fill at least 25 per cent seats in each Assembly and about 30 MPs in the Lok Sabha." While denying that United Front of Ex-Servicemen Movement (UFESM) was thinking of contesting polls, he said, "If someone comes to us and if they have good credentials we will support them."

6 April

The Cabinet gave its ex-post facto approval for implementation order dated OROP order of 7 November 2015 on One Rank One Pension (OROP). The cabinet decision reiterates that "Personnel who opt to get discharged henceforth on their own request under Rule 13(3) 1(i)(b), 13(3) 1(iv) or Rule 16B of the Army Rule. 1954 or equivalent Navy or Air Force Rules will not be entitled to the benefits of OROP. ", and that "In future, the pension would be re-fixed every 5 year".

"Financial implications on account of grant of OROP including Pre-Matured Retirees (PMR) cases" according to press Information note " would be Rs. 10925.11 crore for payment of arrears and the recurring annual financial implication would be Rs. 7488.7 crore. Till 31st March, 20

15.91 lakh pensioners have been given the first instalment of OROP, which amounts to Rs. 2,861 crore. Information is being gathered for processing on priority basis, the cases of 1.15 lakh pensioners after filling in the gaps of information such as the length of service being assessed, etc."

21 April 2016

Sashi Tharoor, former Under-Secretary-General of the United Nations, and former minister in UPA Government, in an article in The quint, commenting on the policy of the government on the declining pay, pensions, and protocol status, of the armed forces, affirmed that the dignity of the Indian armed forces has been eroded by "Petty slights, ranging from deliberately downgrading the military in protocol terms, to persistent actions to lower the status and compensation of our military personnel", and that the consequences of this policy of demeaning the armed forces " will inevitably be suffered by all". Blaming the Pay Commission and Government for being "blind" to the "enduring sacrifice" of the Armed Forces, he concludes that "We have short-changed the remuneration of our armed servicemen". He found it hard to understand the reason for the Government and pay commission to equate police officers[and defence civilians] with 12 years of service, designated as deputy inspector general (DIG) of the police, with Brigadiers, for pay and protocol. He wonders, in disbelief, "What could possibly justify such a disparity?" Commenting on disability pensions recommended by the 7 Pay Commission, he notes that whereas a JCO and their equivalents in the air-force and the navy, will be given Rs 12,000 as pension, while his civilian counterpart, for the same level of disability, will receive a pension twice that amount (Rs 27,690).

28 April 2016

Ram Jethmalani, Senior Supreme Court lawyer, while addressing armed forces veterans, on 320th day of their protest at Jantar Mantar, said, "he will lead their legal battle in the apex court" on a Pro bono basis. Major General (retd) Satbir Singh, who was present on the occasion said, "case will be filed in Supreme Court in the next 3-4 days". He added that four more cases have been filed in the armed forces tribunal, on " rulings for Jawans, war widows, arrears since 2006, payments for honorary ranks, rounding off of disability pension, and payments of reservists".

15 June 2016

The six-month tenure of the one man judicial commission on One Rank One Pension (OROP) which ended on 15 June, was given an extension of six months, by the Government. In the wake of the extension to the commission headed Justice L. Narasimha Reddy, former Chief Justice of Patna High Court, veterans Maj Gen Satbir Singh, Chairman of the Indian Ex-Servicemen Movement, Hon Lt K Pande Member and Wing Commander CK Sharma, met Manohar Parrikar, Defence

Minister, to urge him to ensure that the 'four deviations in the implementation order' on OROP are addressed. Mr Parrikar, according to media reports, assured the veteran delegation that their concerns will be addressed; and that the recommendations of seventh pay commission would be applicable to all ex-servicemen

3 August 2016

Maj. Gen. Satbir Singh (retd), Chairman of the Indian Ex-Servicemen Movement, on 3 August, wrote to Mr. Parrikar and Justice L. Narasimha Reddy, former Chief Justice of the Patna High Court, and head of the one-man judicial commission of constituted in December last year, conveying the "anguish and concern" of exservicemen on the "neglect of defence personnel" and "betrayal"by the government. He told the Hindu newspaper that the Defence Ministry did not forward representation by exservicemen to the one-man Committee despite " assurances given by Mr. Parrikar on March 14, 2016 during a meeting of representatives of ex-servicemen". Maj. Gen. Satbir Singh in the letter to the Defence Minister noted that "The mandate given to One-Man Committee is to consider those questions/ issues which have been referred to it by the Defence Ministry. This is a serious breach of trust reposed in the system" . The letter is in the wake of uncertainty caused by Arun Jaitley, Finance Minister, statement in Parliament that there was no "standardised definition" of OROP.

7 August 2016

General VP Malik, Former Chief of Army Staff, in a panel discussion on the 7th Pay Commission(7CPC) confirmed that 18 former heads of the Armed Forces, including himself, had written to Narendra Modi the Prime Minister, conveying their disquiet on the impact of the recommendations of the 7CPC on the Indian armed forces. Modi, Malik confirmed, ignored the letter by the 18 former heads of Armed Forces. Malik said that the PM has not replied to the letter by the Chiefs of staff and that the PM has taken the retired chiefs for granted.

General Malik said that the recommendation of 7 CPC, which amounted to 'blatant discrimination' had caused a strong sense of 'despondency' and feeling of 'resignation' in the armed forces.

The decision by the Government to create two pay and promotion 'matrixes, in the wake of the 7 CPC, one for the armed forces and another, far more indulgent one, for the civil services, Police, and security bureaucracy, he said, will have several negative outcomes: it will give the civil services including the police services officers six increments in their first 13 years of service, in comparison to just one to the armed forces; the asymmetrical pay, promotion, and status 'matrix' will, he argued, aggravate the existing 'equations' and adversely impact the already fraught civil-military relations. He said he was not convinced with the reasons given by the pay commission, that the armed forces task were any less complex than that of the police or the forest department which have been favored by the BJP Government with an indulgent pay and promotion package.

12 August 2016

A committee of Jammu and Kashmir Ex Services League (JKESL) presided over by Maj Gen Goverdhan Singh Jamwal, ex-MLC, decides, in Jammu, on submitting a memorandum to Justice Reddy Commission on 19 Aug 2016 stating that OROP should be implemented without dilution, i.e., "All retirees in the same rank and with same length of service should get the same pension irrespective of the date of retirement; and the benefits of future increases should automatically pass on to all such retirees". Other who participated in the committee's deliberations were: Brig Harcharan Singh, Director Rajya Sainik Board ; Brig RL Sharma former Station Commander Jammu; Brig Anil Gupta Former Director J&K NCC; Col K S Jamwal, Jt Chairman JKESL; Col Virendra K Sahi, VrC Director War Decorated India for J&K, Col Rajinder Singh, Gen Secy; Lt Col DS Salaria Treasurer JKESL, Lt Col KS Samyal OIC Pension Cell, Lt Col MS Jamwal and Maj JS Baloria Finance Secretary JKESL.

26 October 2016

Justice L. Narasimha Reddy, retired Chief Justice of Patna High Court, submits his report on the anomalies in the implementation of OROP to the MOD.

11 November 2016

Subhash Bhamre, Minister of State for Defence, in a written reply to question by Alok Sanjar informed Lokha Sabha that Financial year 2016-17, a sum of Rs. 12456 crore has been provided for expected expenditure on account of One Rank One Pension (OROP) and that out 20,63,529 pensioner beneficiaries, 1,27,561 Defence Pensioners/Family Pensioners are yet to get the benefits of OROP.

19 November 2016

Maj Gen (retd) Satbir Singh, while attending a workshop organised by the Uttarakhand Ex-Servicemen League in Dehradun says that BJP Government has dishonored ex servicemen by denying them OROP. He called the OROP implemented by the BJP Government "disabled OROP". Maj Gen Satbir called on ex-servicemen to participate in the elections in Uttarkhand and Punjab and " tilt the scale". Group Captain PK Gandhi (retd), another OROP leader, said "ex-servicemen were instrumental in the BJP coming to power at the Centre and they also have the power to dislodge it". Ex-servicemen rallies are planned in Uttar Pradesh, Uttarakhand and Punjab to appeal to ex servicemen to "vote for candidates who work in their favour". The workshop was attended among others by Lt Gen GS Negi (retd) and Lt Col SC Sharma (retd).

22 November 2016

Arjun Ram Meghwal, Minister of State in the Ministry of Finance, in written reply to a question in Rajya Sabha stated that Rs. 82,332.66 crore was provided in BE 2016-17 towards payment of Defence Pensions. This included an amount of Rs. 12,456 crore towards implementation of One Rank One Pension Scheme, which takes effect from 1 July 2014.

Subhash Bhamre, Minister of State for Defence, in response to question by PL Punia and Pramod Tiwari informed the Rajya Sabha that Justice L. Narasimha Reddy, retired Chief Justice of Patna High Court, who was to look into anomalies in the implementation of OROP submitted his report on 26 October 2016. This report is under examination. There are 20,63,529 pensioner beneficiaries of OROP. 1429 Ex-Servicemen have submitted complaints with regard to OROP benefits.

25 November 2016

Manohar Parrikar, Defence Minister, to a question by Dr. Satyapal Singh, in written reply informed the Lok Sabha that Ex-Servicemen are being paid enhanced pension after the implementation of One Rank One Pension (OROP) scheme.

29 November 2016

Subhash Bhamre, Minister of State for Defence, in a written reply to D Raja informed the Rajya Sabha that the "United Front Movement of Ex-Servicemen is continuing their 'protest action' since 14th June 2015 for their demands on OROP." The reply says that Government has accepted the demands of Ex-Servicemen associations to implement OROP, and pay arrears starting form 1 July 2014, and provide coverage to Premature Retirees (PMR) cases up to 7 November 2015. The reply acknowledges that "Some Ex-Servicemen Associations have been demanding changes in methodology for fixation of pension, periodicity of its revision, coverage of future PMR cases".

Subhash Bhamre Minister of State for Defence, informed in the Rajya Sabha that the MOD will not alter the rank equivalence tabulations between armed forces officers and Armed Forces Headquarters Civil Service (AFHQ CS) circulated by MOD on 18 October 2016. When asked in the Rajya sabha, whether the MOD was considering "correcting the discrepancies that have arisen as a result of this disturbance of rank equations", he replied the question "does not arise".

4

Pension Regulations

This Division administers (i) Pension Regulations for the Army(PRA), 1961, revised as PRA, 2008 (ii) Pension Regulations for the Air Force, 1961, and (iii) Navy (Pension) Regulation, 1964. It also deals with Entitlement Rules for Casualty Pensionary Awards, 2008.

Kinds of Pension

Pension Division deals with policy matters relating to pensionary matters of Defence Forces Personnel which includes:-

1. Service Pension is granted @ 50% of emoluments last drawn or average of reckonable emoluments during the last 10 months, whichever is more beneficial subject to minimum of Rs. 9000 /p.m. The minimum qualifying service to earn pension is 20 years in case of Commissioned Officer and 15 years in the case Personnel Below Officer Rank.
2. Ordinary Family Pension is granted @ 30% of reckonable emoluments last drawn subject to a minimum of Rs.9000/- p.m. (in case of natural death of the individual).
3. Special Family Pension is granted at a uniform rate of 60% of reckonable emoluments last drawn by the deceased. (in case of death of a individual attributable to military service).
4. Liberalized Family Pension is granted equal to the reckonable emoluments last drawn by the deceased (to

the families of personnel killed in war or war like operations,counter-insurgency operations, encounter with terrorists etc.)

5. Disability Pension matter has been reffered to Anomaly committee-Ministry of Finance, Department of Expenditure.
6. War Injury Pension. The rates of War Injury Element for 100% disability for various rank shall be equal to the reckonable emoluments last drawn in case of invalided out and 60% of reckonable emoluments last drawn in case of discharge, which would be proportionately reduced where disability is less than 100%.

PROCESSING OF APPEAL

A Defence Forces Personnel, who is boarded out on medical grounds or is discharged / released / retires in low medical categories has the right to appeal against the denial of disability pension within a period of six months from the date of rejection of his initial claim. He will submit his claim to his Record Office(JCO /ORs) / Service Hqrs (Commissioned Officers), which, in turn, will forward the same to Service Hqrs, as the case may be, to place it before the Appellate Committee. Similarly, right of appeal is available to next of kin to Defence Forces Personnel, whose initial claim for Special Family Pension has been rejected. This Committee comprises of:-

Chairman : DDG(PS)/equivalent rank in Air Force and Navy

Members : (a) DDG(Pens), Office of DGAFMS :(b) DFA (Pension) :(c) Dir PS-4 / equivalent rank in Air Force and Navy.

In case the individual is not satisfied with the decision of the Appellate Committee for First Appeal, he has right to make another appeal through his Record Office(PBOR)/Service Hqrs(Commissioned Officers), which, in turn, will forward the same AG/PS, Army Hqs or equivalent in Navy/Air Force along-with all the records to place it before the Second Appellate Committee on Pension. This committee comprises of:-

Chairman : Vice Chief of Army Staff or equivalent in Navy & Air Force.

Members : a. Addl. DGPS or equivalent in Navy & Air Force. b. DGHS (Rep of DGAFMS) c. Joint Secretary & Addl. FA, MoD (Fin) d. Judge Advocate General of the Service other than to which the appellant belongs.

After consideration of all relevant issues involved in the case, the Appellate Committee will give its decision by upholding or rejecting the appeal.

Processing of Pension claims

The process for grant of pension is initiated by the Unit where the individual is posted, 18 months ahead of discharge/ retirement. JCO's/ORs is attached with the concerned Record Office(RO) for completion of pension documents one month prior to discharge/retirement. Pension claim is initiated by the concerned RO in the case of PBOR and by Service Hqrs in case of Commissioned Officers and is forwarded to the respective Pension Sanctioning Authorities for notifying the Pension Payment Order (PPO). PPO is notified by Pr. Controller of Defence Accounts (Pen), Allahabad, in the case of Army personnel, Pr. Controller of Defence Accounts (Navy), Mumbai in the case of Naval personnel and Controller of Defence Accounts (Air Force), New Delhi in respect of Air Force personnel. A pensioner can approach his Pension Disbursement Agency on any working day after the date of retirement for getting his pensionary dues.

PANEL'S SALIENT FINDINGS

[a] One Rank One Pension is an old issue, it was in 'vogue till 1973 when the Third Central Pay Commission took ex-parte decision against the One Rank One Pension formula".

[b] Since 1973 OROP has been considered by the Government in Third Central Pay Commission, in 1973, Fourth Central Pay Commission, in 1986, Fifth Central Pay Commission, in 1996, Sixth Central Pay Commission considered, in 2006.

The committee found that in addition to Pay Commissions, OROP has been considered by the Sharad Pawar Committee, in 1991; Inter-Ministerial Committee, in 2003; Group of Ministers, in 2005; and Cabinet Secretary Committee. The Committee concluded that the repeated consideration by the Government of OROP "indicate that there is merit in the demand for One Rank One Pension by Armed Forces Personnel, otherwise the matter would not have been considered time and again by various committees of the Government and Central Pay Commissions. It could have been rejected once and for all and principle of res judicata would have been applied to this demand. Hence, it definitely deserves attention of the Parliamentary Committee as well as the Government."

[c] The Committee on Defence (2009–10) (Fifteenth Lok Sabha) in its Seventh Report recommended that the Government should "implement One Rank One Pension in a holistic manner so that large number of ex-servicemen can be benefitted".

[d] Commenting was not persuaded by the Government attempt to paint a "rosy picture about the pension given to the Armed Forces Personnel". The Committee thought it was misleading and observed "If this is beneficial to them then why are the ex-servicemen are consistently demanding for One Rank One Pension Formula? Why they are agitated? They serve the nation with utmost devotion and selflessness but their demands are consistently being ignored, not by the heads of Armed Forces, but by the bureaucrats. It's a typical example of bureaucratic apathy."

[e] The Committee dismissed government 'apathy' and excuse for failing to implement OROP because civilian Government employee would make similar demands as "baseless apprehension". It noted that military and civilian terms and conditions of service are not comparable and 'cannot be equated': military conditions are 'tougher and harsher', there is greater risk to life and limb, stress and strain, transfers and dislocation, adverse family life, bleak career prospects, 'undefined and unlimited working hours', and the "Armed Forces are also subjected to Court Martial system".

[f] The Committee blamed "Governments' apathetic attitude" to implementing OROP for forcing 'defence personnel of our country' from returning their service medals to the President of India.

Time Line

1973 Ministry of Defence terminates 'One Rank One Pension' the basis for deciding pension of Indian Armed Forces Personnel 'which had been in vogue for 26 years since independence' through an ex parte administrative order. Veterans, and service headquarters are dismayed. OROP becomes a contentious issue. By 1985, Armed Forces has fourteen different categories of pensioners. Armed Forces pensions before 1973 because of early retirement, conditions of military service, were about 70 percent of the pay of rank at which they retired. In 1973, the pension of civilian government servant was increased from 33 percent to 50 percent, and that of armed forces personnel, who have far shorter careers, and more challenging service conditions, was decreased from 70 percent to 50 percent of last pay drawn.

1986 OROP, is considered by 4th CPC, but without an outcome.

1991 During the tenure of PM Chandrasekhar (1990-1991), OROP is considered by Sharad Pawar committee (1990-1991). In 1992, the Government grants a 'one time increase', instead of OROP.

1996 The Government approves 5 CPC recommendation of full parity between pre and post 1/1/1986 pensioners and a modified parity between pre and post 1/1/1996 to all pensioners including Armed Forces pensioners, but ignores OROP. Government decision to accept 5 CPC depress military pensions, including that of General Officers who, in an precedent action, file a lawsuit against the Government. After protracted litigation, strongly contested by the UPA Government, the Supreme Court of India rules in favor of the litigants.

23 November 2002 Sonia Gandhi, Chairman UPA, in run-

up to elections, at a public rally, in the Sector 46 sports complex at Chandigarh, declares that she and her party support grant of OROP. OROP is included in the Party's election Manifesto.

2006 6th CPC while acknowledging that 'One Rank One Pension has been demanded for all ex- servicemen' recommends that "extant provisions may continue ". The casual dismissal of the military pensioners plea for grant of OROP by the Government provokes widespread dismay amongst ex-servicemen. Ex-servicemen take to the streets, and threaten hunger strikes A retired general, notes that " The Sixth Pay Commission has done inestimable damage to civil-military relations", and expressing the general mood, says, "The protest rallies are actually a manifestation of the seething anger which many veterans carry as baggage accumulated during service.

We all seem to have very bitter memories of the shoddy treatment meted out to us by civil servants.

16 December 2008 Ex-servicemen begin a relay fast at Jantar Mantar. The peaceful protest largely ignored by the government. Veteran decide to surrender of their war medals, including medals for gallantry.

8 February 2009 Retired Officers and men from the three services march to the Rastrapati Bhavan to surrendered their medals to the President, the Supreme Commander of the armed forces. Pratibha Patil, President, refuses to meet with the Ex-servicemen (ESM). The medals are collected by member of staff. The "studied disrespect" by the President fuel grievance.

29 October 2010 K. Sanjay Prabhu, a resident of Bengaluru, submit petition to Rajyasabha Committee On Petitions for grant of one rank one pension to the armed forces personnel. The petition is countersigned by Rajeev Chandrasekhar, M.P. (Rajya Sabha).

15 March 2011 Rajya Sabha, Chairman, admits petition by K. Sanjay Prabhu, and Rajeev Chandrasekhar for grant of one rank one pension to the armed forces. On 18 March 2011, the petition "stands referred" to the Committee on Petitions for examination and report in terms of Rule 150.

4 May 2011 The all party ten member Committee commences hearing of Petitioners' oral submission. The petitioners state that ex-servicemen have been getting lower pension than their younger counterparts in the same rank, particularly after implementation of Third Central Pay Commission Report.

"The petitioners made a power-point presentation inter alia covering various Supreme Court judgments on the issue, comparison of pay and pension scheme for armed forces in countries like the USA, UK and Singapore, justification for the prayer for one rank and one pension, etc. The petitioners also submitted that the prayer for grant of one rank one pension has been opposed by the Government mainly on financial, legal and administrative grounds which could be resolved with the intervention of the Committee. The petitioners prayed to the Council of States for one rank one pension for ex-servicemen irrespective of their date of retirement".

27 May 2011 Neelam Nath (June 1, 2009 to September 30, 2011), the Secretary Ministry of Defence (Department Ex-servicemen Welfare), deposed before the Committee. Neelam Nath, opposes grant of OROP, citing financial, administrative and legal reasons. She informs the Committee that the financial burden, as calculated by Defence Accounts, would be Rs 3,000 crore per year; she says implementation of OROP, was "a gigantic task", because defence pensioners records after 25 years do not exist. She says that according to Law Ministry, and her assessment, grant of OROP would be "discrimination under the Constitution". Secretary Department Ex-servicemen Welfare deposed a second time on second 4 November 2011,

15 July 2011 Secretary, Department of Expenditure, (Ministry of Finance), in his deposition, which was continued on 1 August 2011, said, that while "figure relating to defence personnel's pension was being maintained in the Office of Controller General of Defence Accounts" the financial implication of OROP would be "around Rs. 8,000-Rs. 9,000 crores per annum"

Secretary Department of Pensions and Pensioner's Welfare (Ministry of Personnel, Public Grievances and Pensions) who deposed on (15'h July, 2011), says that "Reports of various Pay Commissions have not supported the concept of OROP" He raised alarm that if OROP is accepted for the Armed Forces, then there will be similar demands from the civilian pensioners and others. he says Cabinet Secretary's Committee has assessed financial implication of Rs. 8,000-Rs. 9,000 crores per annum tentatively.

19 December 2011 Bhagat Singh Koshyari, Chairman Committee on Petitions, presents the report, to the parliament. The report finds no merit in the Arguments by the UPA Government opposing grant of OROP to Armed Forces pensioners. It finds that "there is merit in the demand for One Rank One Pension by Armed Forces Personnel" and strongly recommended that, *"Government should implement OROP"*

12 July 2012 Prime Minister Manmohan Singh, according to the Ministry of Defence Annual report for 2012-13, "on the persistent demand" of ESW, constitutes a Committee under Ajit Kumar Seth, the Cabinet Secretary " for looking into pay and pension related issue of relevance to defence personnel and ESM" but not specifically OROP. The Cabinet Secretary's committee consists of six other secretaries from the IAS: [1] PK Nair, the Principal Secretary to the Prime Minister; [2] Shashi Kant Sharma, Defence Secretary; [3] Secretary, Department of Ex- Servicemen's Welfare, Ministry of Defence; [4] Secretary, Department of Expenditure; [5] Secretary, Department of Personnel and Training; and [6] Secretary, Department of Revenue. There are no Armed forces personnel on the panel despite separate letters from the Chiefs of the Army, Navy and the AirForce to AK Antony, Defence Minister to include an Armed Forces representative on the panel.

The Panel lacks credibility and little is expected from it. Admiral Nirmal Kumar Verma, Chief of Naval Staff & Chairman, Chiefs of the Staff Committee, makes a presentation to the Committee. The committee also meets with Air MarshalNorman Anil Kumar Browne, Chief of Air Staff and General Bikram Singh, Chief of Army Staff. The Committee submits report on 27 August 2012; its position on the OROP is no different from that of secretaries who deposed in front of Koshiyari Parliamentary Panel. It evades the OROP issue.

24 September 2012 The UPA Government announces that OROP is approved, and that Rs 23,00 crore has been set aside for the 'One Rank One Pension' scheme. However, there are no plans to implement OROP, and it remains un-implemented.

DEFENCE PENSIONERS AND DISBURSEMENT AGENCIES

There are 24 lakhs Defence pensioners and approximately 55,000 pensioners are added every year. The pension is disbursed across the country by approximately 45000 branches of the Public sector branches, 640 Treasury offices of the various State Governments, 61 Defence Pension Disbursing offices, two Post offices, Five Pay Accounts Offices of Indian Embassy, Nepal. PCDA(Pension) Allahabad is centrally responsible for accounting and audit of such pension payments, which amounts to approximately Rs. 45,495 crores during the year 2013-14.

Defence Pension Adalat

A large community of Ex-servicemen specially Personnel Below Officers Rank (PBOR) and their families are settled in the interiors as also remote areas. The lack of awareness at the ground level both at the end of the pensioners as well as amongst the local authorities specially the disbursing agencies leads to generation of grievances either on delays in disbursement or on incorrect payments. Defence Pension Adalats provide a credible forum for redressal of grievances of the defence pensioners near to their place of residence/work. Reforms in disbursement of pension is a continuous process. The whole idea is to make the life of the defence pensioners dignified and hassle free so that they can get their due entitlement promptly without running from pillar to post.

Since representatives of concerned organizations are present in the Adalat, it is possible to take appropriate decisions on the spot to the extent possible. The Adalat disseminates latest information, order circulars, procedures, forms and formats not only to the pensioners but also to various local authorities like Banks and Treasury offices etc besides providing clarification of doubts on pension provisions and procedures. Six such Adalats are held in a year.

D (Pension Grievances)

D (Pension Grievances) receives on average representations around 600 to 1000 in a month from Ex-Servicemen. These are examined by the concerned Dealing Hand and referred to the concerned agencies for redressal manually with a copy to the individual so that he should know as to where his case has been referred.

States have also been requested to set up grievance redressal mechanism for the ex-servicemen. Further, around 500-700 online grievances are also being received through pgportal.gov.in, an online grievance redressal mechanism, which are being processed electronically with the concerned organization/Service Hqrs who redress the grievance of the ex-servicemen and status of redressal is also updated in the portal.

Process for disposal of Court cases

The Legal Notices and Writ Petitions/Original Petitions, relating to pensionary matters, filed in various Courts are forwarded to the respective Service Hqrs for defending the case on behalf of UoI and others and to take necessary action for filing counter reply, briefing the Govt. Counsel and attending the Court's hearings. Powers for implementation or otherwise of the Court cases have been delegated to the Service Hqrs who in turn have re-delegated the powers to lower formations like line directorate/Records Offices, etc. Special Leave Petition (SLP) in the Supreme Court is, however, processed by them with Ministry of Law through Department of Ex-Servicemen Welfare. DP&PW is also consulted wherever necessary.

Status of recommendations of 7th CPC

The Government order No. 17(01)/2016-D(Pen/Pol) regarding implementation of Government's decision on the recommendations of the Seventh Central Pay Commission for revision of pension of pre-2016 Defence Forces Pensioners/ Family Pensioners has been issued on 29.10.2016.

REDUCING RATIO OF MILITARY PENSIONERS TO SERVING PERSONNEL

The current ratio of military pensioners to serving military personnel is 1.7 to 1. In comparison the ratio of civil pensioners to civil work force is 0.56 to 1. Reducing the ratio of pensioner to serving in the military will, it is argued, greatly reduce the defence pension bill.

To reduce the military pension bill, the 6 CPC and Koshyari Committee, had urged the Government to absorb Armed Forces personnel after their military engagement in Civil Government organization including Police Organization as is the custom in many countries, including in China, and in advanced economies like S Korea, Singapore, Israel, Switzerland, and the United States.

The transfer and absorption of Armed Forces personnel after the end of their military service into government organizations and departments where their unique skills, training, discipline and strengths can be optimally used, despite recommendations of the Parliament and Pay Commission, has been mostly ignored by successive Governments, mainly on account of want bureaucratic commitment in MOD, and sustained obstruction by IPS bureaucrats in MHA.

Savings from lateral movement of Armed Forces personnel

The 6 CPC estimated that the "at the end of 13 years the annual savings" from transfer- absorption of Armed Forces personnel to civil departments, including police, "will be to the tune of Rs. 7,800 crore at constant price index". Lateral transfer-absorption, in the longer term result in savings in the overall pension bill, and would more than off set projected expenditure on OROP.

TAX BENEFITS OF PENSIONS

Overall, a pension is one of the most tax-efficient ways to save for the long term, but remember the tax treatment of pensions depends on individual circumstances, and may be subject to change.

For every £80 you pay into your pension plan, the Government currently pays in an extra £20, making your actual contributions £100. If you're a higher rate taxpayer, you may be able to claim back another £20. Additional rate taxpayers in 2014/15 may be able to claim back another £25 (you must pay sufficient tax at the higher rate in order to receive the full tax relief at that rate).

Any growth in your pension fund is free of UK income tax and capital gains tax (although the fund cannot reclaim the 10% dividend tax credit on UK shares). And from age 55, you can take up to 25% of your pension fund as a tax-free cash lump sum. Currently your remaining pension fund must be used to provide a taxable income for your retirement. However from April 2015, the Government has proposed pension changes that allow people aged 55+ to access pension benefits as they wish. The 25% tax free lump sum still remains, but if any part of the remainder is taken as a lump sum it will be taxed at income tax rates (rather than current 55%). Those who want the security of an annuity will still be able to purchase one. They are still subject to consultation, so speak to your NFU Mutual Financial Adviser for the most up-to-date details.

Other benefits of pensions

More and more people are working past the State Pension age – it's likely that some have to work longer because they haven't saved enough to retire on. Having your own tax-efficient pension fund to draw on can allow you greater flexibility in how you continue to work beyond your expected retirement age e.g. by agreeing with your employer to reduce your working hours.

It's your pension fund and, with some pension products, you can choose where it's invested. You can also take a break from saving if you need to, or change your contributions at any time, but remember that this could affect the amount of pension fund you accumulate.

If you die before you take your pension, your partner, or family could benefit from your fund as a lump sum or a regular pension. The amount they receive will depend on your age at death, the value of your pension fund and whether or not you have already taken any benefits from your pension fund.

Advantages of a pension plan

To maintain the same standard of living after retirement. Whether a plan is a defined contribution plan, a defined benefit plan or a simplified pension plan (SIPP), it will nicely complement public plans. The main objective of supplemental pension plans is to provide retirement income over and above that paid by the public plans.

Concrete advantages for employees and employers

A supplemental pension plan is part of the fringe benefits that an employer can offer his employees. Besides the financial security it offers after retirement, it is a form of deferred pay appreciated by employees. For the employer, having a plan can make it easier to attract and keep competent employees.

Pension Plans: Pain Or Pleasure?

You probably already know a little bit about pension plans - either you have one or someone you know does - but the financial underpinnings behind a pension are familiar to few. Pension offerings have become scarce in the private sector, and it's important to understand why. In this article, we'll explore why employees love pension plans, and why companies try their hardest to avoid them.

What is a pension?

A pension is a company-sponsored fund that is supposed to provide a company's employees with a livable income for their retirement years. Generally speaking, there are two types of pensions - defined-contribution plans and defined-benefit plans.

- Defined-contribution plans are the simpler of the two (and the more common today). In a defined contribution plan, the amount of money contributed to the plan by the company is set from the get go (often as a percentage of what the employee contributes). The money is then invested over the span of the employee's career, and the eventual balance in the account is paid out upon retirement. With this type of plan, the value of the employee's pension is based on the performance of the investments, so the eventual benefit to the employee is uncertain.
- Defined-benefit plans, on the other hand, specify the ultimate payouts to retirees, regardless of the returns on the pension fund's investments. In a defined-benefit plan, the company is on the hook for whatever the fund can't generate. This is one of the principal reasons that defined-benefit plans are becoming a thing of the past - much to the chagrin of those entering the workforce. While some organizations are keeping their defined-benefit plans (such as major league sports organizations), many companies are freezing defined-benefit pension funds, restricting their participation to those employees who are already enrolled.

The Employee Perspective

Nowadays, you might wonder just how relevant pensions are for an employee - scores of Americans don't have pensions (either because they're self-employed or because their employers don't offer them).

With an all-but-condemned Social Security system, many people are relying solely on self-directed retirement programs such as 401(k)s and IRAs.

There is a growing number of people who retired with pensions, but then saw their plans collapse as their pensions' sponsor companies hit hard times.

If you are able to join your company's pension program, the pension not only provides the asset growth of a self-directed retirement account, it also compounds its power with contributions from your employer. Recent legislation means that pensions are better protected today than in the past. The legislation was in response to major pension collapses that occurred in the '90s. However, having a pension isn't an excuse to avoid saving money for retirement - far from it. Even those lucky few with pensions should hold retirement accounts outside of their companies' plans.

The Company Perspective

When companies sponsor a pension plan for their employees, they're essentially making an unofficial statement about how important their employees are to their bottom lines. Many CEOs justify limiting pensions by citing "responsibilities to shareholders", but providing adequate retirement planning is often in a company's best interests.

For example, companies get tax advantages from pension plans, although the tax advantages only kick in if a certain percentage of employees enroll in the plan. This helps ensure that the plan is a valid retirement choice, and not just an empty offering.

That said, pensions are also expensive for companies. Also, accounting standards for pensions aren't up to the standards many accountants feel they should be. For example, the Pension Benefit Obligation (PBO) - the present-valued dollar value a company estimates it will need to fund its pension plan - doesn't have to be reported on a company's books. Only a fraction of the PBO is reported in financial statements. This can lead to pension funds that are under-funded, which, unfortunately, leaves many pension funds in a position similar to that of Social Security.

The PBO is determined by actuaries through a series of calculations and permutations that only a math major could love. Because pensions are so complex, it's only natural that most people run for cover when faced with having to decipher a plan's financial mechanisms. Furthermore, plan assets (the actual assets that a pension plan has available) technically don't belong to the company and, therefore, they're also not reported on the balance sheet. Instead, most pension-related information is reported in footnotes to the financial statements.

A Pension and You

So, how important should a pension be the next time you're in the job market? While other retirement options can be a good fit - particularly if you've planned sufficiently - having your money professionally managed in a stable, structured pension can make a significant difference in the long term.

Whether you're planning on sunbathing on a Florida beach or heading to your New England cottage, your retirement should be something to look forward to. It shouldn't be a nagging doubt that you avoid thinking about. While retirement options are ever-evolving, having a clue about how your pension works can definitely help make your retirement more worry free.

5

Retirement Benefits under New Pension Scheme

A new restructured defined contribution pension system for the new entrants to Central Government service, except to the Armed Forces, replacing the system of defined benefit pension including GPF, was notified on 22nd December, 2003. The Government employees appointed on or after 1.1.2004 and governed by the New Pension System can withdraw 60% of their Pension Fund as a lumpsum when they retire and the balance 40% of their wealth is used to purchase an annuity scheme from a life insurance company of their choice, which will pay him/her a monthly pension for the rest of his life. In casethe employees leave the New Pension Scheme prior to age 60, the mandatory anuitization would be 80% of the pension wealth.

RETIREMENT BENEFITS

Will the Minister of PERSONNEL,PUBLIC GRIEVANCES AND PENSIONS be pleased to state:-

(a) whether the Union Government employees recruited after January, 2004 are not eligible for retirement benefits such as pension, GPF and gratuity;

(b) if so, the reasons therefore;

(c) whether not providing gratuity, pension and GPF facility is a discrimination with employees recruited after January,

2004 as the same is being provided to the employees of private sector;

(d) if so, the details thereof;

(e) whether the Government proposes to provide all retirement benefits including gratuity to the Government servants recruited after January, 2004; and

(f) if so, the details thereof?

NATIONAL PENSION SCHEME

The National Pension Scheme (NPS) is an option that a lot of investors can make use of but there are doubts among several investors about the manner in which the benefit can actually be claimed.

One of them pertains to the conditions when the benefit can be claimed and whether this exists even if they are contributing to the fund outside of employment.

Two ways to contribute

One of the ways in which an individual contributes to the NPS is when the employer ensures the enrolment as a part of the overall process that they have undertaken wherein all employees are covered under the requirements.

This would mean that there is no provident fund that is actually present for the individual when they are actually working but the amount is actually going into the NPS account. This will result where the NPS is the main area for the funds being directed.

The other way is actually where the individual is running the account on their own so that there is no contribution as far as the employer is concerned because there is no employer in the picture. Here the entire contribution comes just from the individual and it could be that the person is not an employee somewhere but is self employed or a professional. There are a lot of such people who would want to make use of the facility of the NPS.

OVERALL BENEFIT

The first point to understand is that the benefit of the NPS consists of the deduction that is available to the individual when they make their own contribution to the fund. This is the basis on which the entire working is based so the individual will have to consider this factor when they are looking for the actual amount that they can claim. If it is the case where they are contributing an amount and so is the employer then they would need to see their own contribution and this should not exceed 10 per cent of their salary. If they are contributing just on their own then the figure that they are actually giving would need to be taken into account and this will meet their requirement. There is an overall limit of Rs 1 lakh for contributions under eligible investments for Section 80C, pension fund contributions (Section 80CCC) and contribution to NPS (Section 80CCD). The key point here is the amount that actually goes into the NPS would have to be brought into the calculations.

Actual calculation

The manner in which the actual benefits have to be considered is to actually look at the amount that is invested in the instrument during the year. This is a one time benefit in the sense that if say Rs 80,000 is invested then subject to the other limits this figure would be allowed as a deduction for the individual. There is earning on this amount that will be present after the investment and which will be added to the account over the life of the investment but this is not to be taxed at the present moment. This does not mean that the amount is tax free because the way in which this will be taxed is at the time of receipt. When the individual actually gets a pension from the account then the amount would be taken as income of the person and added to their income as required. This is the manner in which the entire taxation of the amounts takes place and this is different from the public provident fund where the interest is actually tax free. Here there is just deferment of the tax aspect till the amount is received.

NPS, India's answer to the US' retirement scheme- 401(K)- is a government-approved pension scheme for Indian citizens in the 18-60 age group. While central and state government employees have to subscribe mandatorily, it's optional for others.

Premature withdrawal will defeat the purpose of NPS, which is building a retirement fund. The minimum annual contribution is Rs 6,000, which can be paid at once or in instalments of at least Rs 500. The scheme offers two kinds of accounts-a compulsory Tier-I account and a voluntary Tier-II account. One can open a Tier-II account only if one has an active Tier-I account.

While Tier-I is a basic pension account with restrictions on withdrawal, Tier-II is a voluntary savings option from which a person can withdraw money freely. Two things that make NPS a genuine pension scheme are restrictions on withdrawal from Tier-I account and the rule that a part of the Tier-I corpus at the end of the tenure has to be used to buy annuity, which gives regular payments in lieu of a lump sum.

Tier-I comes with partial withdrawal options, subject to conditions. The nominee can withdraw the full amount only after the death of the subscriber. Even after retirement at 60, one can withdraw only up to 60 per cent of the corpus; the rest has to be annuitised. While the lock-in ensures the subscriber does not use the funds during his working life, annuity makes sure the money is paid in instalments over a long period. 31 LAKH was the number of subscribers (govt and voluntary) of NPS as on 31 March 2012.

"The rigidity in NPS is understandable as its primary objective is to build a retirement fund," says Lovaii Navlakhi, chief executive and founder of International Money Matters, an investment advisory company. Annuity can be bought only from the PFRDA-appointed insurers, which are Life Insurance Corporation of India (LIC), SBI Life Insurance, ICICI Prudential Life Insurance, Bajaj Allianz Life Insurance, Star Union Dai-ichi and Reliance Life Insurance. Insurance pension schemes, regulated by the Insurance Regulatory and Development

Authority, have similar features-restrictions on premature withdrawal and compulsory annuity. Mutual funds do not offer such longterm schemes.

Disadvantage NPS

The changes, say critics, have largely addressed marketing and distribution issues. Core issues that directly impact investors are yet to be resolved, they say.

Tax on maturity proceeds

The most key concern is the lack of clarity on taxation at withdrawal. Present laws say the funds will be taxed at withdrawal. Under the existing laws, up to 60 per cent corpus on maturity can be withdrawn while at least 40 per cent has to be used to buy annuity. At present, returns from annuity insurance plans are not tax-free.

The proposed Direct Taxes Code (DTC) seeks to exempt NPS funds from tax at withdrawal. However, it is not clear if the DTC provides for tax exemption on returns from annuity plans as well. Further, there is uncertainty over the DTC itself with Finance Minister P Chidambaram calling for a review.

Most financial planners say tax at withdrawal is a big impediment to NPS becoming the best pension scheme. Taxability of maturity proceeds is the major concern, says Manikaran Singhal, while Sumeet Vaid, CEO, Ffreedom Financial, says making withdrawal tax-free will give the product a big boost.

Compulsory Annuity

Another drag is restrictions on withdrawal from Tier-I account, the primary account for pension savings. Even on maturity, one can withdraw only up to 60 per cent funds; the rest has to be used to buy annuity, the returns from which are not tax-free.

Also, the annuity has to be bought from one of the six PFRDA-approved insurers. Options in terms of the number of annuity providers are anyway few with LIC commanding a 70 per cent market share.

"Annuity and pension is a long-term business and requires a degree of stability and financial size. In the present market, 12 companies have premium income of less than Rs 3,000 crore. How do you expect them to get into the annuity business? They do not even qualify for grant of annuity by NPS," says SB Mathur, former Life Insurance Council secretary general.

Pension plans by insurance companies have similar restrictions on withdrawal. In fact, in these, the annuity can be bought only from the pension plan provider.

Low on equity

NPS portfolios cannot have more than 50 per cent exposure to equity. For those who start in their 20s or early 30s, this can mean a loss of opportunity, as equity has given 12-15 per cent returns a year over long periods. The PFRDA chairman, while rejecting any possibility of an increase in equity exposure, said 50 per cent equity exposure was good enough for pension plans.

Compared to traditional retirement schemes such as EPF and Public Provident Fund, which do not invest in stocks at all, NPS is far more flexible in terms of equity exposure. Nonetheless, investors looking for higher equity exposure can opt for equity mutual fund schemes such as large-cap funds and equity exchange-traded funds.

Competition from traditional schemes

For long, EPF has been the main retirement savings instrument. It is a major competitor for NPS as the government has made it mandatory for 'establishments with 20 or more employees' to subscribe to it.

Though the government allows tax deduction on contribution up to 10 per cent of the basic salary and DA made by an employer towards the NPS account of an employee over and above the Rs 1 lakh limit, mandatory EPF subscription could still be a deterrent for employees to subscribe to NPS.

"One of the key changes could be to allow consumers to choose either NPS or EPF," says Nitin Vyakaranam, founder and chief executive officer, Artha Yantra, a provider of retail financial services.

EPF is not the only competition NPS faces. Mutual funds also pose a challenge. In general, most financial planners and advisors recommend mutual fund schemes for achieving all kinds of goals, including retirement. Even insurers provide pension plans that are similar to NPS, except that the cost is much lower in the latter's case.

NEW PENSION SCHEME

Govt. of India, Ministry of Finance, Deptt. Of Expenditure vide their OM No.F.No.1)T)(2)/2003/TA/19 dt.14.1.2004 & 4.2.04 have introduced a New Defined Contribution Pension Scheme replacing the existing System of Defined benefit Pension System. The New Pension Scheme comes into operation w.e.f. 1.1.2004 and is applicable to all new entrants to Central Govt. service except to Armed Forces joining Govt. service on or after 1.1.2004.

a. The New Pension Scheme was introduced by the Government for the central government employees who have joined government service on or after 01.01.2004.
b. An employee will contribute 10% of his salary (i.e. Band Pay + Grade Pay + Dearness Pay) and the government will contribute the equal amount to the subscription.
c. The application from the Government Servants who have joined service on or after 01.01.2004 are received through DDO for verification and onward transmission to NSDL, Mumbai who is the nodal agency appointed by government for maintenance of subscribers data and for allotment of Permanent Retirement Account Number (PRAN).
d. Each government servant can have one PRAN only. In case of technical resignation, old PRAN should be continued after changing the DDO, PAO and Pr. AO of the PRAN.

e. A PRAN Kit is issued to every subscriber which is handed over by DDO to the subscriber.

f. The contribution is uploaded on NSDL site every month and the funds accumulated are being transferred to the Trustee Bank by the end of every month by the pay section.

g. There is no provision for withdrawal of accumulation by the subscriber on resignation or leaving the service.

h. The funds cannot be transferred from one PRAN to another in any case.

DEFINED CONTRIBUTION PENSION SCHEME (NATIONAL PENSION SYSTEM)

- The National Pension System works on defined contribution basis and will have two tiers - Tier-I and II. Contribution to Tier-I is mandatory for all Government servants joining Government service on or after 1-1-2004 (except the armed forces in the first stage), whereas Tier-II will be optional and at the discretion of Government servants.
- In Tier-I, a Government servant will have to make a contribution of 10% of his basic pay plus DA, which will be deducted from his salary bill every month by the PAO concerned. The Government will make an equal matching contribution. However, there will be no contribution from the Government in respect of individuals who are not Government employees.
- Tier-I contributions (and the investment returns) will be kept in a limited partial withdrawable Pension Tier-I Account. Tier-II contributions will be kept in a separate account that will be withdrawable at the option of the Government servant. Government will not make any contribution to Tier-II account.
- The existing provisions of Defined Benefit Pension and GPF would not be available to the new recruits in the central Government service, i.e. to the Government servants joining Government service on or after

1-1-2004. However, retirement gratuity and death gratuity would be extended to the central government employees covered under NPS on the same terms and conditions as applicable under CCS(Pension) Rules, 1972.

- In order to implement the Scheme, there will be a Central Record Keeping Agency (CRA) and several Pension Fund Managers (PFM) to offer three categories of Schemes to Government servants, viz., options A,B and C based on the ratio of investment in fixed income instruments and equities. The participating entities (PFMs and CRA) would give out easily understable information about past performance, so that the individual would be able to make informed choices about which scheme to choose.
- An independent Pension Fund Regulatory and Development Authority (PFRDA) will regulate and develop the NPS.
- A Government servant can exit at or after the age of 60 years from the Tier-I of the Scheme. At exit, it would be mandatory for him to invest 40 per cent of pension wealth to purchase an annuity (from an IRDA-regulated Life Insurance Company) which will provide for annuity for the lifetime of the employee and his dependent parents/spouse. He would receive a lump-sum of the remaining pension wealth which he would be free to utilize in any manner. In the case of Government servants who leave the Scheme before attaining the age of 60, the mandatory annuitization would be 80% of the pension wealth.
- Provisionally, central government employees covered under NPS has option to choose benefits under old pension scheme or NPS in the event of their death or discharge from service on invalidation.

PROCEDURE FOR ALLOTMENT OF PERMANENT PENSION ACCOUNT NUMBER (PPAN)

1. Immediately on joining Govt. service, the Govt. servant

will be required to provide particulars such as his name, designation, scale of pay, date of birth, nominee(s) for the fund, relationship of the nominee etc. in the prescribed for (Annexure I). The DDO concerned will be responsible for obtaining this information from all Govt. servants covered under the New Pension Scheme.

2. The PAO concerned will allot a unique 16 digit Permanent Pension Account Number (PPAN). The first four digits of this number will indicate the calendar year of joining Govt. service, the next digit indicates whether it is a Civil or a Non-civil Ministry, the next six digits would represent the PAO Code (which is used for the purpose of compiling monthly accounts), the last five digits will be the running serial number of the individual govt. servant which will be allotted by the PAO concerned. PAO will allot the serial number pertaining to individual Govt. servants from 00001 running from January to December of a calendar year. A register will be maintained for allotment of PPAN to ensure that PPAN are allotted in sequence and there is no duplication of PPAN.
3. For the flow of information from Non Civil Ministries/ Departments to the CPAO, each of them will nominate a Nodal Office, which will be responsible for forwarding the consolidated information/particulars in respect of their Ministry/Departments and for correspondence with CPAO.
4. The particulars of the Govt. servants received from the various DDOs will be consolidated by the Nodal Office identified in each Ministry/Department/Office and sent to the CPAO. The CPAO will keep this information in their computer database.
5. The accounting heads involved in the operation of the new pension scheme will be intimated in due course.
6. The first salary bill of the new entrant will be passed after ensuring that the Annexure-I is received. Tier1 amount equal to 10% of the (basic+dp+da+npa) will be

deducted from the payBill and a matching contribution will also be credited to the individuals credit.

7. Separate paybill should be prepared for the individuals who are covered under this scheme.
8. The schedule information is to be captured in the Annexure-II, which should be carefully checked.
9. The data file of annexure-I and annexure-II will be created and forwarded to CPAO on monthly basis.
10. CPAO on receipt of this information will update its database and generate exception reports for missing credits, mismatches etc.
11. No withdrawal of any amount will be allowed during the interim arrangements.
12. At the end of each financial year the CPAO will prepare annual accounts statements for each employee showing opening balance, details of monthly deduction and Govt.'s matching contribution, interest earned, if any, and the closing balance. CPAO will send these statements to Nodal Office concerned.
13. After the close of each financial year, CPAO will have to report the details of the balances (PAO-wise) to each PAO for the purpose of reconciliation. The PAO will reconcile the figures of contributions with figures as per the books of CPAO.

Audit / Accounting checks to be exercised for New Pension Scheme

1. Immediately on joining Govt. service, the Govt. servant will furnish particulars such as his name, designation, scale of pay, date of birth, nominee(s) for the fund, relationship of the nominee etc. in the prescribed form (Annexure I) for allotment of Permanent Pension Account Number.
2. Separate Pay bills are required for new entrants who joined service on or after 1.1.2004.
3. Recoveries/contributions payable by the Govt. servant under the Scheme (Tier I) will start from the salary of

the month following the month in which the Govt. servant has joined service. Therefore, no recovery shall be effected for the month of joining.

4. Contribution by Govt. servant under Tier I is mandatory.
5. Equal matching contribution will be made by Govt.
6. Contribution by Govt. servant will be 10% of his basic pay, DP, DA& NPA which will be deducted from his salary bill every month.
7. Whenever there is any change in Basic Pay/DA/DP due to arrear of pay, DA revision, 10% of paid emoluments are also to be recovered.
8. No deduction will be made towards GPF contribution from the Govt. servants joining service on or after 1.1.2004 as GPF scheme is not applicable to them.
9. Permanent Pension Account Number will be of 16 digits.
10. Recovery schedule as per designed format will accompany each pay bill indicating PPAN No., Basic Pay, DA, DP, Name, amount of contribution, month etc. apart from other information.
11. Check the information contained therein in the schedule are correct as per recovery made in the bill.
12. After carrying out necessary audit checks as are done in other pay bills the pay bill is passed for payment.
13. The recovery made on account of individual contribution and equal matching Govt. contributions will be compiled to relevant code heads as under:-
    1. 00/016/02 – Individual Contribution
    2. 00/016/03 – Govt. matching Contribution

    as Plus receipts with corresponding/respective charge head i.e. Service heads and New RDR heads.
14. Finally schedules are detached and sent to EDP for punching.

NEW PENSION SCHEME AND SYSTEM

In the Budget 2003-04 a new pension system has been announced based on defined contribution, shared equally in the case of Government employees between the Government and the employees. Under the scheme there will be no contribution from the Government in respect of individuals who are not Government employees. The new pension scheme will be portable, allowing transfer of the benefits in case of change of employment, and will go into 'individual pension accounts' with Pension Funds. The Ministry of Finance will oversee and supervise the Pension Funds through a new and independent Pension Fund Regulatory and Development Authority. The existing scheme of pension, GPF and Gratuity would cease for new entrants to the Central civil services.

The following are the details in respect of the new Scheme:

The Government approved on 23 August 2003 the proposal to implement the budget announcement of 2003-04 relating to introducing a new restructured defined contribution pension system for new entrants to Central Government service, except to Armed Forces, in the first stage, replacing the existing system of defined benefit pension system. The new system will also be available, on a voluntary basis, to all persons including self employed professionals and others in the unorganized sector. However, mandatory programmes under the Employee Provident Fund Organization (EPFO) and other special provident funds would continue to operate as per the existing system under the Employee Provident Fund and Miscellaneous Provisions Act, 1952 and other special Acts governing these funds. The main features of the new pension system are given below:

- The new pension system would be based on defined contributions, which will use the existing network of bank branches and post offices etc. to collect contributions and interact with participants allowing transfer of the benefits in case of change of employment and offer a basket of pension choices.
- The system would be mandatory for new recruits to the central Government service except the armed forces and the monthly contribution would be 10 percent of the salary and DA to be paid by the employee and matched

by the Central Government. However, there will be no contribution from the Government in respect of individuals who are not Government employees. The contributions and investment returns would be deposited in a non-withdraw able pension tier-I account. The existing provisions of defined benefit pension and GPF would not be available to the new recruits in the central Government service.

- In addition to the above pension account, each individual may also have a Voluntary tier-II withdraw able account at his option. This option is given as GPF is proposed to be withdrawn for new recruits in Central Government service. Government will make no contribution into this account. These assets would be managed through exactly the above procedures. However, he would be free to withdraw part or the entire second tier' of his money anytime. This withdraw able account does not constitute pension investment, and would attract no special tax treatment.
- Individuals can normally exit at or after age 60 years for tier –I of the pension system. At exit the individual would be mandatorily required to invest 40 percent of pension wealth to purchase an annuity (from an IRDA-regulated life insurance company). In case of Government employees the annuity should provide for pension for the lifetime of the employee and his dependent parents and his spouse at the time of retirement. The individual would receive a lump-sum of the remaining pension wealth, which he would be free to utilize in any manner. Individuals would have the flexibility to leave the pension system prior to age 60. However, in this case, the mandatory annuitisation would be 80% of the pension wealth.

CONTRIBUTION OF NEW PENSION SCHEME

Government of India have introduced a new Defined Contribution Pension Scheme replacing the existing system of

Defined Pension System vide Government of India, Ministry of Finance, Department of Economic Affairs Notification dated 22.12.2003. The New Pension Scheme comes into operation with effect from 01.01.2004 and is applicable to all new entrants to Central Government service, except to Armed Forces, joining Government service on or after 01.01.2004.

The system would be mandatory for all new recruits to the Central Government service from 01.01.2004 (except the Armed Forces). The monthly contribution would be 10 per cent of the Banned Pay, Grade Pay and DA to be paid by the employee and matched by the Central Government.

However, there will be no contribution from the Government in respect of individuals who are not Government employees. The contribution and investment returns would be deposited in a non-withdrawable pension Tier-1 account. The existing provisions of defined benefit pension and GPF would not be available to the new recruits in the Central Government service.

In addition to the above pension account, each individual may also have a voluntary Tier-II withdrawable account at his option. This options is given as GPF will be withdrawn for new recruits in Central Government service. Government will make no contribution into this account. These assets would be managed through exactly the above procedures. However, the employee would be free to withdraw part of all of the second tier of his money any time. This withdrawable account does not constitute pension investment, and would attract no special tax treatment.

Individual can normally exit at or after age 60 years for Tier-I of the pension system. At exit, the individual would be mandatorily required to invest 40 per cent of pension wealth to purchase an annuity (from an IRDA-regulated life insurance company). In case of Government employees, the annuity should provide for pension for the lifetime of the employee and his dependent parents and his spouse at the time of retirement. The individual would receive a lump-sum of the remaining pension wealth, which he would be free to utilize in any manner. Individuals would have the flexibility to leave the pension system prior to age 60. However, in this case, the mandatory annuitization would be 80% of the pension wealth.

In order to implement the Scheme, there will be a Central Record Keeping Agency and several Pension Fund Managers to offer three categories of Schemes to Government servants, viz., options A,B and C based on the ratio of investment in fixed income instruments and equities. An independent Pension Fund Regulatory and Development Authority (PFRDA) will regulate and develop the pension market.

Subscription of the NPS subscribers will be invested in the default Schemes termed as 'Scheme I' of various Pension Fund Managers (SBI Pension funds Pvt. Ltd, UTI Retirement Solutions Limited & LIC Pension Fund Limited). Each PFM will invest 85% of the contributions received by it in fixed income instruments and 15% in equity and equity related instruments. Hence, in the application form for PRAN, the details of the schemes need not be mentioned.

The DDOs/CDDOs will prepare separate Pay Bill Registers in respect of the Government servants joining Government service on or after 1.1.2004. The DDOs/CDDOs will have to prepare separate pay bills in respect of these Government servants.

Whenever any Government servant is transferred from one office to another either within the same accounting circle or to another accounting circle, the DDO should clearly indicate in the LPC of the individual the month up to which Government servant's contribution and Government's contribution have been recovered.

The Govt. of India established Pension Fund Regulatory and Development Authority(PFRDA) on 10th October 2003 to develop and regulate the Pension Funds under the NPS. PFRDA has appointed National Securities Depository Limited (NSDL) as the Central Record Keeping Agency(CRA) to maintain the records of contribution and its deployment in various pension fund scheme for the employees. NSDL is setting up a CRA system for this purpose. The record of the contribution of each employee will be kept in an account known as Permanent Retirement Account which will be identified by a Permanent Retirement Account Number(PRAN).

All Cs of F& A(Fys.) under Factory Organization will function as Principal Accounts Officer(PrAO) in the CRA system for the purpose of the New Pension Scheme. All Br. Accounts Office will function as Pay & Accounts Office (PAOs) and all Ordnance Factories, Inspection Organizations, Dte. Of Standardization, RTIs etc. will function as Drawing and Disbursing Officer(DDO) in the CRA system. The P C of A(Fys.) , Cs of F & A(Fys.) and Br. A.Os will also be the DDOs for the DAD staff covered under the NPS.

The Principal Accounts Offices, Pay and Accounts Offices, Drawing and Disbursing Officer and Subscriber need to be registered under the NSDL system.

Principal Controller Office was declared as Nodal Office for all the 40 Branch Accounts Offices in factory organization alongwith AN-Pay, Pay Section and Pay 'O' Section of Main Office.

Subsequently HQrs. Office declare C of F &A(Fys.) of the Group as Pr.AO for the Branch Accounts Offices under the group except AO, OF Nalanda which comes under no group at present. Once the registration of Pr. AO is completed the process of registration of PAOs, DDOs and Subscribers will start.

PC of A(Fys.) and All Group Controllers will submit form N1 to NSDL for registration. NSDL will allot Pr. AO registration no. and send I-PIN to PC of A(Fys.) and Group Controllers concerned to access NPSCAN/NSDL system. After Pr. AO registration has been completed Branch Accounts Offices will forward the form N2 to NSDL for registration as a PAO through respective Pr.AO. NSDL will send PAO registration number to Branch Accounts Offices and allot one single T-PIN and two user Ids and two I-PIN. Branch Accounts Office will log into NPSCAN.

After PAO registration the Branch Accounts Offices will forward DDO Registration form N3 to NSDL for Factory

Management and forward S1 form for allotment of PRAN of the subscribers newly appointed after 01.01.2004 received from Factory Management.

Immediately on joining Govt. Service, the subscriber should fill the application for Allotment of PRAN (in duplicate) and submit it to DDO.

DDO should ensure that the duly filled applications are received from the subscribers within seven days of joining and forward it to the concerned PAO after necessary attestation. In order to enable the PAO to upload subscriber contribution record, it is necessary to ensure that Registration Forms are forwarded to CRA through the CRA-FCs for allotment of PRAN.

Subscribers who have been successfully registered at CRA will be allotted a 12 digit Permanent Retirement Account Number (PRAN). PRAN will be a unique identification number of the subscriber.

CRA shall print and despatch to the PAO, the PRAN Kit for the newly registered subscribers. The PRAN Kit will contain PRAN Card, Subscriber Master details, T-Pin and I-Pin and an Information Leaflet on CRA.

After completion of the Registration process the PAO will upload the NPS data to the NPSCAN of NSDL and will deposit the contribution amount into Trustee Bank positively on the date of regular payment.

At the end of the financial year NSDL will issue the IPA (Individual Pension Account) Statement to the concerned individual whose PRAN has been allotted by NSDL.

6

National Pension System

National Pension System, also known as NPS, is a voluntary defined contribution pension system in India. The NPS started with the decision of the Government of India to stop defined benefit pensions for all its employees who joined after 1 January 2004. While the scheme was initially designed for government employees only, it was opened up for all citizens of India between the age of 18 and 60 in 2009. In its overall structure NPS is closer to 401(k) plans of the United States. Administered and regulated by the Pension Fund Regulatory and Development Authority (PFRDA)(Based on the recommandations of Chakka Muni Balaji Ganesh Committee),in accordance with (Juturu Sahithi committee) it is a quasi-EET (Exempt-Exempt-Taxable) (Based on the recommandations of Juturu Sahithi Committee) instrument in India where 40% of the corpus escapes tax at maturity, while 60% of the corpus is taxable. Of the 60% taxable corpus, 40% has to be compulsorily used to purchase an annuity.

Contributions to NPS receive tax exemptions under Section 80C, Section 80CCC and Section 80CCD(1) of Income Tax Act. Starting from 2016, an additional tax benefit of Rs 50,000 under Section 80CCD(1b) is provided under NPS, which is over the Rs 1.5 lakh exemption of Section 80C. Private Fund managers are important parts of NPS. NPS is considered one of the best tax saving instruments, after 40% of the corpus was made tax-free at the time of maturity and it is ranked just below Equity-linked savings scheme(ELSS).

Background

The National Pension System (NPS) is a voluntary defined contribution pension system administered and regulated by the Pension Fund Regulatory and Development Authority(PFRDA), created by an Act of the Parliament of India. The NPS started with the decision of the Government of India to stop defined benefit pensions for all its employees who joined after 1 January 2004. While the scheme was initially designed for government employees only, it was opened up for all citizens of India in 2009. NPS is an attempt by the government to create a pensioned society in India. In its overall structure NPS is closer to 401(k) plans of the United States. Today, the NPS is readily available and tax efficient under Section 80CCC and Section 80CCD. Under the NPS, an individual can contribute to his retirement account. Also, his employer can contribute to the welfare and social security of the individual.

NPS is a quasi-EET instrument in India where 40% of the corpus escapes tax at maturity, while 60% of the corpus is taxable. Of the 60% taxable corpus, 40% is tax-exempt as it has to be compulsorily used to purchase an annuity. The annuity income will be taxed, though. The remaining 20% alone will now be taxed at slab rates on withdrawal.NPS offers subscribers a choice of two record keeping agencies: NCRA (NSDL-CRA) and KCRA (Karvy-CRA). In 2017 Union budget of India, 25% exemption of the contribution made by an employee has been announced as a form of premature partial withdrawal in NPS. This amendment will take effect on 1 April, 2018 and will, accordingly, apply in relation to the assessment year 2018-19. NPS is a market-linked annuity product.

REGULATORY FRAMEWORK

In 1999 the Government of India commissioned a national project, OASIS (an acronym for "old age social and income security"), to examine policies related to old age income security in India. Based on the recommendations of the OASIS report, the Government of India introduced a new Defined Contribution Pension System for the new entrants to Central/State Government service, except to the armed forces, replacing the existing system of the Defined Benefit Pension System.

On 23 August 2003, the Interim Pension Fund Regulatory & Development Authority (PFRDA) was established through a resolution by the Government of India to "promote old age income security by establishing, developing and regulating pension funds, to protect the interests of subscribers to schemes of pension funds and for matters connected therewith or incidental thereto." The Pension Fund Regulatory & Development Authority Act was passed on 19 September 2013 and notified on 1 February 2014, thus setting up PFRDA as the regulator for pension sector in India. However, there remains a considerable amount of confusion with other entities like the Employee Provident Fund, pension funds run by life insurers, and mutual fund companies being outside the purview of PFRDA.

The contributory pension system was notified by the Government of India on 22 December 2003, now named the National Pension System (NPS) with effect from 1 January 2004. The NPS was subsequently extended to all citizens of the country with effect from 1 May 2009, including self-employed professionals and others in the unorganized sector on a voluntary basis.

ARCHITECTURE

Unlike traditional financial products where all the functions (sales, operations, service, fund management, depository) are done by one company, NPS follows an unbundled architecture where each step of the value chain has been made disjointed from the other. This unbundling not only allows the customer to mix and match his providers of service through the value chain, picking the best-suited option, but it also curbs the incidence of misselling.

NPS architecture consists of the NPS Trust, which is entrusted with safeguarding subscribers' interests, Central

Recordkeeping Agencies (CRAs) which maintains the data and records, Point of Presence (POP) as collection, distribution and servicing arms, pension fund managers (PFM) for managing the investments of subscribers, a custodian to take care of the assets purchased by the fund managers, and a trustee bank to manage the banking operations. At age 60 the customer can choose to purchase pension Annuity Service Providers (ASP). NPS investors can't opt for two pension fund managers, neither can switch to another pension fund before a year. In 2017, PFRDA increased the entry age in NPS to 65 years.

The number of pension fund managers (PFM) has increased to 9 in NPS:

- SBI Pension Funds
- LIC Pension Fund
- UTI Retirement Solutions
- HDFC Pension Fund
- ICICI Prudential Pension Fund
- Kotak Pension Fund
- Reliance capital Pension Fund
- Birla Sun Life Pension Management Ltd.

SBI Pension Funds is the largest pension fund manager (PFM) in India and its assets under management(AUM) level is Rs 61,000 crore. At Present, Central government employees have no say in the matter of choice of fund manager or investment allocation in NPS, as both are decided by the government. All the NPS contributions of Central government employees are being distributed evenly across three public sector fund managers :LIC Pension Fund, SBI Pension Fund and UTI Retirement Solutions.

The current CRAs are the NSDL e-Governance Infrastructure Limited (NCRA) and Karvy Computer Shares Pvt Ltd (KCRA). All the major commercial banks, brokers and Stock Holding Corporation Ltd perform the role of PoP. The subscriber can choose any one of them. There are seven fund managers and eight annuity service providers for subscribers to choose from. The subscriber can choose to invest either, wholly or in combination, in four types of investment schemes offered by the pension fund managers. These are:

- Scheme E (equity) which allows up to 50% equity participation, this is invested in stocks.
- Scheme C (corporate debt) which invests only in high-quality corporate bonds.
- Scheme G (government/Gilt bonds) which invests only in government bonds.
- Scheme A (Alternative Investment)which allows up to 5% (Newly added asset class only for private sector subscriber with active choice)

Alternatively, the subscriber can opt for the default scheme, whereas per the time left to retirement his portfolio is rebalanced each year for the proportion of equity, corporate bonds, and government bonds.

NPS offers two types of accounts to its subscribers:

- Tier I :The primary account, which is a pension account which has restrictions on withdrawals and utilization of accumulated corpus. All the tax breaks that NPS offers are applicable only to Tier I accounts.
- Tier II: In order to introduce some liquidity to the scheme, the PFRDA allows for a Tier II account where subscribers with pre-existing Tier I accounts can deposit and withdrawn monies as and when they want. NPS Tier II is an investment account, similar to a mutual fund in characteristics.

The contribution to voluntary savings account (also called Tier-II account) can only be made by the subscriber and not by any third party.

PFRDA has introduced new features to NPS in 2016, including more choices to lifecycle funds:

- Aggressive Life Cycle Fund (LC-75) which allows subscribers equity exposure of up to 75% till 35 years of age. This is more suitable to a 20s investor.
- Conservative lifecycle fund with a 25% starting equity exposure, may be suited to older investors.

- Automatically Lifecycle Fund.

The regulator add a new asset class Alternative Investment Funds (AIF) to the existing menu of equities, government securities and corporate bonds, available on NPS.

Who can join

A citizen of India, whether resident or non-resident can join NPS, subject to the following conditions:

- The subscriber should be between 18 and 60 years old as of the date of submission of his/her application to the Point of Presence (POP) / Point of Presence–Service Provider-Authorized branches of POP for NPS (POP-SP).
- The subscribers should comply with the Know Your Customer (KYC) norms as detailed in the subscriber registration form.
- Should not be Un-discharged insolvent and individuals of unsound mind.

SUBSCRIBER BASE

As of December 2016, the number of subscribers had grown substantially to 1.41 crore. NPS AUM (assets under management) grew to Rs 1,61,016 crore as of December 2016. 88% of total NPS AUM is accounted for Government sector, both Central and State employees, who also account for 35 per cent of the number of subscribers. As of March 2016, The total AUM of the NPS Tier II segment is Rs 197 crore. NPS Tier II has 34,620 subscribers with an average balance of Rs 54,000.

OPENING AN ACCOUNT

Online process via eNPS

e-NPS started in 2015. an NPS account can be opened online using either of the two options available to complete the KYC process:

- One, Aadhaar-based KYC, wherein you will be

authenticated through an OTP that will be sent to the mobile phone number that is registered with Aadhaar. Once one authenticates oneself, the KYC information will be taken from the Aadhaar database. If you had selected Aadhaar-based registration, you have to upload a scanned signature. You can make your investment through Net banking from any bank's account.if you choose Aadhaar-based KYC, you don't have to sign and send the physical form. You can simply e-sign. There is no need to print the NPS form that you had filled online and submit the printout within 90 days to the central record keeping agency.
- Second way to proceed is to give the permanent account number (PAN) and bank account details to complete the KYC authentication step.

Offline process

For offline opening, one has to visit any of the Points of Presence (POPs) appointed by the PFRDA.

WITHDRAWAL

Premature withdrawal in NPS before age of 60 years required parking 80% of the sum in an annuity. One can withdraw 20 percent of the corpus before 60 years but he/she must buy annuity with 80 percent of the corpus. In 2016, the NPS allowed withdrawal of up to 25% of contributions for specified reasons, if the scheme is at least 3 years old with certain conditions. One can withdraw the complete amount if the pension collected is less than INR 2,00,000.

TAX BENEFITS

Investment in NPS is eligible for tax benefits as follows:

- Up to Rs. 150,000 under Section 80CCD(1). The benefit is additionally capped at 10% of basic salary. The benefit under Section 80C, Section 80CCC and Section 80CCD(1) is capped at Rs 150,000.

- Contribution Up to Rs 50,000 under Section 80CCD(1B). This is over and above tax benefit under Section 80CCD(1b).
- Employer co-contribution up to 10% of basic and DA without any upper cap in terms of amount is tax free income in hands of employees under Section 80CCD(2).

NPS CAN ENSURE AN AFFORDABLE OROP

The military's One Rank One Pension (OROP) issue has festered for years now. The issue seems tailor-made for emotional appeals and political grandstanding, and those who talk about the financial load of an open-ended pension, do so in soft voices. Personally, I believe that OROP is entirely justified and politics on the issue is abhorrent.

And then there are the multitudes of other government employees who are waiting in the wings of this drama. One union of railway employees has already thrown its hat in the ring, stating that while the military's OROP demand takes priority, railway employees must be taken up immediately after that. It will be interesting to see how public opinion turns out when OROP demands move beyond the military. We'll probably get a good idea of how much sympathy civilian government employees, as a class, evoke in the general population.

The heart of the OROP problem is one of funding the future liability of pensions. From the numbers that are available, it's clear that while OROP could probably be funded for past employees without too large a fiscal disaster, the open-ended nature and the massive future escalation of the pension payouts will be unbearable. For civilian government employees, the future pension problem was solved in 2004, when employees hired since that date were switched to the contributory National Pension System. In the contributory system, the principle is the same as the private sector's EPFO. 10 per cent of the salary is deducted, matched by an equal contribution by the employer. The money is invested under the supervision of the Pension

Authority. When the employee retires, he gets 60 per cent of the accumulation as a lump sum, and the rest is invested in an annuity, which pays out a pension. There is no liability of the employer, apart from making a matching contribution with every salary.

The NPS was never applied to the armed forces because about 80 per cent of the the military retires between the ages of 35 to 40. Another 18-19 per cent or so retires in their 50s and only 1 per cent retires at 60. If someone joins up at 18-20 and retires at 40, then the accumulation period of the NPS is just about 15-20 years, while that accumulated fund will have to pay for pension for another 35-50 years of retired life. The maths simply doesn't work. Compare this with civilian employees, where about 30 to 35 years of accumulation has to pay for 15-30 years of retired life, which works very nicely.

There's doesn't appear to be any way for the Armed Forces to be moved to a contributory system. Or is there? Actually, there's a simple solution that is possible by combining the current pension arrangement and the NPS. Here's what the government should do for those who join the military from here on: It should put them into NPS, investing deductions plus its own contributions as it does for civilian employees. Then, from retirement till the age of 60, it should pay the pension out of its own budget, but it should keep up with the NPS deductions and contributions out of this pension, just as if it were a salary. Since pension is so much lower than salary, perhaps the contribution can be enhanced. Then at the age of 60, pensions out of the budget should stop and NPS should kick in, as it does at retirement for civilian employees.

This way, there is a limit the future liability to publicly fund pensions, and that limit is at a much lower and predictable point. The hard part of setting up the NPS and getting all civilian employees into it was done starting 2004. The NPS is a great relief for future taxpayers. In fact, a lot more people would think sensibly about these issues if instead of saying that government has to pay, we say clearly that it has to come out of future taxation, both direct and indirect. At first sight, none of this appears to have anything to do with solving the immediate OROP problem. In fact it does, simply because the real problem with OROP is the open-ended future liability.

DECISION DELAYED IS DEFENCE DENIED

Each day the government delays the implementation of the One Rank One Pension (OROP) scheme, a demand that is 42 years old, it risks playing with fire. It is safe to assume that the serving service Chiefs have conveyed as much to the government. The public manifestation of the rapidly spreading and quickly deepening levels of disenchantment came when the daughter of Gen. V.K. Singh, former Army Chief of Staff and a serving Minister of State, sat with the Jantar Mantar agitators in an open show of support. Mrinalini Singh's husband is a serving Army officer. This is a categorical indication that both Gen. Singh and Col. Rajyavardhan Singh Rathore, another Minister, would no doubt have pointed out to the government the consequences of not being able to deliver on a promise already made several times over.

Uncertain future

Roughly 60,000 people retire from the armed forces every year. Some retire before they are 35, and as many as 87 per cent of servicemen retire between the ages of 34 and 48. Soldiers, sailors, airmen at the lowest level are the hardest hit because after a near nomadic life in the armed forces, they most likely do not own too many assets, a home nor have an alternative income stream. They have no clear prospect of a second lease of working life either. Soldiers retire early because they need to be fighting fit to be in the forces and hence, the armed forces need young blood. The retirement policy affects an estimated 25 lakh ex-servicemen. Counted along with their dependents, the number swells to roughly three times that or 70 lakh people.

Also, a large section of the armed forces has family members who are either still serving or have retired from the forces. In normal conversations, the situation is bound to occupy their mindspace. Those in service know that sooner or later, they will become veterans and inherit the same situation their fathers did before them, an inheritance of loss.

The problem has been exacerbated because of the way in which the then BJP prime ministerial candidate, Narendra Modi, appropriated and espoused the cause at the 2014 hustings and his subsequent repeated assurance, both on the floor of Parliament and elsewhere, that OROP was a settled matter and the solution had his imprimatur. Consider also Mr. Modi's unparalleled political heft in the Lok Sabha and the fact that the Supreme Court has, as long ago as December 1982, underlined the need for OROP. If the agitators feel let down, it is because the delivery of the promise has so far been in inverse proportion to the articulation of the promise itself.

Deliberately tangled

As many as ten retired service Chiefs have deliberately used the word 'imbroglio', a word of Italian origin that has elements of confusion, entanglement, bitterness, and complication all rolled into one. It accounts for the growing feeling that in the real OROP narrative, Narendra Modi, whom none other than the Vishwa Hindu Parishad's Ashok Singhal acknowledged as BJP's Iron Man, is helpless. His inability to deliver stems from his being a victim of either intra-party politics or from him having been ensnared in a web made by intransigent bureaucrats.

The discourse in New Delhi circles suggests that a section of the bureaucracy wants to dovetail the OROP with the Seventh Pay Commission. This would effectively scupper the plan because it would postpone the resolution and rework the rationale and framework of the OROP as well. Lt. Gen. Syed Ata Hasnain, who retired as Military Secretary of the Army, writes in the July issue of Fauji India that the "bureaucracy is living up to its promise to complicate the issue to such an extent that it [OROP] is once again shelved without decision."

The procrastination has escalated the situation to a standoff between the veterans and the government. Mr. Modi's inability to act quickly and effectively has allowed other political parties space where none need have been conceded. The issue is now open to political hijack. There has been a steady stream of contradictory noises emanating from the government, most notably from the Finance Ministry, asking ex-servicemen to "lower expectations". The implication is that the government is having trouble coming up with the money. It has not gone unnoticed among the veterans that Mr. Modi, the politician, had no difficultly promising Rs. 1.25 lakh crore for Bihar in what amounts, scandalously, to pre-election sops. For OROP, the figure being talked about is roughly Rs. 8,300 crore, a fraction of the Bihar pledge.

Soldiers cannot go on strike like bank employees do, but patience now seems in short supply. Since June, the veterans have resorted to black armband protests, bike rallies, candle-light vigils, petitions, the return of service medals, and hunger strikes in an attempt to force the government to focus on the implications. They know more than others that all it requires is a small spark to set off a blaze. If something has been building up for a long time and is looking for release, even something as inconsequential as a slap can have an enormous ripple effect. We need to remember the mutiny witnessed after Operation Blue Star. Given that the veterans are already on hunger-strike and writing petitions in blood, all it needs is a momentary provocation to set off that dreaded spark.

ONE RANK ONE PENSION - SOME THOUGHTS

There has been a lot of debate of late on whether veterans should be moved to a "one rank one pension" system. I won't bother explaining the whole deal here, I'll let you read this brilliant post by Ajay Shah about the numbers behind the move. Now that the quant has been outsourced, I can put forth my "qualitative" arguments. I'm not a fan of this One Rank One Pension (OROP) move. I'm not against paying our soldiers, or veterans, well – I think it must definitely pay above market rates for the skills required for the job. Yet, I think OROP is a "one delta" solution to the problem (previous post here about government's one delta thinking on agriculture), and can lead to massive unfunded liabilities.

The problem with any kind of pension scheme is that you create liabilities today that need to be funded later on. And at a later date these liabilities might become unserviceable. From this perspective, it is important to try and fund any future liabilities today, or at least have a handle on the precise magnitude of liabilities required. OROP, being "inflation indexed" (that's Ajay Shah's nice model to look at it), doesn't allow for proper budgeting and long-term planning.

It is precisely due to this budgeting issue that the government moved most of its incoming employees to the New Pension Scheme (NPS) in 2004. NPS, unlike previous pension schemes, is a "defined contribution" scheme, where your pension is paid out of a corpus you create by your own saving. From an accounting perspective, it moves liabilities from tomorrow (pensions) to today (higher salary to fund the contributions), and is an excellent move. And there is no reason for it not to apply to the armed forces.

Most of the arguments being made in favour of OROP are emotional ("how can you deny our veterans money" etc.), and not well backed up by logical or economic reasoning. One of those is that lower-level military persons retire when they are 35, and hence need a "one rank one pension" (which I absolutely fail to understand). While I understand that the rigours of the role imply early retirement, I don't see why defined contribution doesn't solve the problem. It will have to be matched with higher salaries (to fund the contribution required for a long lifetime of retirement), but that implies liabilities are funded today, which is superior to pushing liabilities under the carpet for future generations.

The thing with NPS is that it cannot be pushed retrospectively, and hence can apply at best to all forthcoming hires. We still need a solution for the existing employees and veterans, who are already on a defined benefit scheme. Yet, the important thing to consider is that the beneficiaries should be divided into three categories – current veterans, current servicemen and future servicemen, and we should find separate solutions for the three.

It might be argued that without defined benefit pensions, it might be hard to attract talent for a high-risk job like the military, and that is why we might need OROP. This is where the "derivative thinking" comes in. The thing about a job in the military is that there is a higher-than-civilian risk of losing life or limb. The solution to that is not blanket higher compensation – it is risk management.

What we need is generous death and disability insurance for our military, and this too should be purchased by the military from a professional Life Insurance firm. A generous insurance package can help mitigate the risks to life borne by military personnel, and should be sufficient to attract necessary talent. The purchase of such policies from professional insurers is important, for you don't want the military to be doing an actuary's job. More importantly, such a purchase will push liabilities to today rather than to tomorrow, and the last thing an army will want during the time of war is increased expenses on account of insurance.

The current debate about OROP has opened the door for a complete overhaul of military compensation. The government should jump at this, rather than simply get bullied by veterans' groups. As Nitin Pai argues in this editorial in the Business Standard, compensation is an economic decision and should be made based on economic (and financial) reasoning, not based on emotion.

ONE RANK, ONE PENSION HIGHLIGHTS NEED TO REDUCE PENSION BILL

Political pundits and the media focused keenly on Independence Day on whether Prime Minister Narendra Modi would grant "One Rank, One Pension", or OROP, to retired soldiers, sailors and airmen. The defence ministry's Department of Ex-Servicemen's Welfare says India has 22,50,000 military pensioners (hereafter referred to as veterans), and there are another 6,00,000 widows of veterans who are entitled to lifetime pensions. Assuming conservatively that each pensioner has a family of four, over a crore voters would directly benefit from OROP. This is a significant political constituency, especially in Punjab, Haryana, Himachal Pradesh and Uttarakhand.

The money involved is significant too. This year's budget allocated Rs 54,500 crore for defence pensions; this would rise by about 40 per cent with the additional Rs 18-20,000 crore needed to meet all the veterans' demands. India does not count military pensions in the defence budget; even though pensions, like salaries, are a component of manpower costs. The full grant of OROP would raise military pensions to Rs 75,000 crore, only slightly less than the salary bill of Rs 93,216 crore.

What exactly does OROP involve? In essence, it means that all veterans who retired at the same rank should get equal pension, irrespective of when they retired, because they performed the same functions whilst in service and must make ends meet in the same economic conditions today. Currently, each veteran gets a pension that is half the salary he drew on the date he retired. Since military salaries have steadily risen, as determined by six successive "pay commissions" (the Seventh Pay Commission is currently deliberating another increase), veterans who retired earlier get significantly lower pensions than those who retire today.

The demand for OROP goes back to the Third Pay Commission in 1973. However, this is the first time the veteran community has organised itself so publicly. Occupying the emotional high ground — not difficult in a country where the military is loved and respected — veterans have signed letters in blood, returned gallantry and service medals and staged public *dharnas* (sit-ins), including a few hundred metres from Parliament in New Delhi. Largely siding with the veterans, the media has lambasted the government for tarrying in making good its promises. Criticism continues even after Mr Modi assured veterans on Independence Day that discussions were in their final stages and OROP would be paid out shortly.

These unprecedented public protests have their roots in late 2013, when the Bharatiya Janata Party (BJP), and its chief election strategist, Amit Shah, targeted the veteran constituency as a vote bank. Addressing ex-servicemen at a September 2013 rally in Rewari, Mr Modi promised his government would implement OROP. With the veteran community naturally biased towards the BJP's right-wing politics and tough talk on Pakistan and terrorism, ex-servicemen rallied strongly behind Mr Modi, believing that OROP would be quickly implemented.

Meanwhile, the United Progressive Alliance (UPA) government — staring at electoral defeat — also promised early implementation of OROP, even allocating Rs 500 crore in its "vote-on-account" in February 2014. This, it turns out, was a token sum, as was the Rs 1,000 crore the National Democratic Alliance (NDA) government allocated in its first budget in July 2014.

The dimensions of the problem became evident to the NDA government once the defence and finance ministries began doing their sums. A key question related to when OROP should be implemented from. Implemented prospectively the payout would be Rs 10,000 crore; implemented from early 2014, when it was announced, twice that amount would be needed.

Given the fiscal buffer provided to the government by low oil prices, the financial blow could be absorbed. However, given the bitter inter-service rivalry between the military and the Indian Administrative Service (IAS) officials who man key positions in the defence and finance ministries, officials have raised alarmist questions about the spill-over effects of OROP, and the prospect of other services, especially "central armed police forces" (CAPF) like the Border Security Force and the Central Reserve Policy Force also demanding OROP.

For many veterans, the delay in OROP reflects a more serious and longer-standing conspiracy between civil servants and politicians to whittle away the relative status of the armed forces. This is evident from a letter written by four well-respected former chiefs — General SF Rodrigues, Admiral L Ramdas, Admiral Arun Prakash and Admiral Sureesh Mehta — who wrote to President Pranab Mukherjee that the scuttling of OROP is "the culmination of a process by which successive Pay

Commissions have been used to whittle down the financial and protocol status of the military over the years vis-à-vis their civilian counterparts".

This grudge will remain even after the full grant of OROP, which now seems a matter of time. What must be addressed, however, is the key issue highlighted: the military's growing manpower costs. It has been earlier recommended that, instead of recruiting soldiers, sailors and airmen for 15 years and then paying them pensions for life, recruitment should be for just 5-7 years, after which trained personnel are laterally absorbed into CAPFs, where easier service conditions allow them to serve till the age of 55-60 years. This would make for a younger army, and also reduce the growing pension liability.

DEVELOPMENT OF NATIONAL PENSION SCHEME

The National Pension System (NPS) is a defined-contribution-based pension system launched by the Government of India with effect from 1 January 2004. Like most other developing countries, India did not have a universal social-security system to protect the elderly against economic deprivation.

As a first step towards instituting pension reforms, the Government of India moved from a defined-benefit pension to a defined-contribution-based pension system.

Apart from offering a wide gamut of investment options to employees, this scheme helps the Government of India to reduce its pension liabilities. Unlike existing pension fund of the Government of India that offered assured benefits, NPS has defined contribution and individuals can decide where to invest their money. The scheme is structured into two tiers:

- Tier-I account: This NPS account does not allow premature withdrawal and is available to all citizens from 1 May 2009.
- Tier-II account: This NPS account permits withdrawal for exceptional reasons only, prior to the retirement age.

Since 1 April 2008, the pension contributions of Central Government employees covered by the National Pension System (NPS) are being invested by professional Pension Fund Managers in line with investment guidelines of government applicable to non-Government Provident Funds. A majority of state governments have also shifted to the defined contribution based National Pension System from varying dates. Twenty-nine state/UT governments have notified the NPS for their new employees. Of these, five states have already signed agreements with the intermediaries of the NPS architecture appointed by Pension Fund Regulatory and Development Authority (PFRDA) for the implementation of the National Pension System. The other states are in the process of finalization of documentation.

Shri Hemant G Contractor is the present Chairman, Nagendra Bhatnagar is the present CEO and Dhirendra Swarup is one of the founders who played a key role in the implementation of the scheme.

Regulation

The Pension Fund Regulatory and Development Authority (PFRDA) was established by the Government of India on 23 August 2003 to promote old age income security by establishing, developing and regulating pension funds and is the prudential regulator for the NPS for the past 11 years, covering 95 Lakh subscribers from Central Government and State Governments.

Coverage and eligibility

NPS is open to all citizens of India on voluntary basis and is mandatory for employees of central government (except armed forces) appointed on or after 1 January 2004. All Indian citizens between the age of 18 and 55 can join the NPS.

Tier-I is mandatory for all government servants joining government service on or after 1 January 2004. In Tier I, government servants will have to make a contribution of 10% of his Basic Pay, GP and DA which will be deducted from his salary bill every month. The government will make an equal contribution. Since 1 April 2008, the pension contributions of Central Government employees covered by the NPS are being invested by professional Pension Fund Managers in line with investment guidelines of the Government. However, there will be no contribution from the Government in respect of individuals who are not government employees. The contributions and returns thereon would be deposited in a non-withdrawable pension account.

In addition to the above pension account, each individual can have a voluntary tier-II withdrawable account at his option. Government will make no contribution into this account. These assets would be managed in the same manner as the pension. The accumulations in this account can be withdrawn anytime without assigning any reason. It is estimated that 8 crore Indian citizens are eligible to join the NPS.

Operational structure

NPS utilizes the network of bank branches and post offices to collect contributions and ensure that there is a seamless transfer of accumulations in case of change of employment and/or location of the subscriber. It offers a basket of investment choices and Fund managers. The Government appointed PFRDA Board of Trustees meet every three months to review the functioning of NPS architecture.

The subscribers have the choice of one or more *Central Recordkeeping Agency* (CRA), several *Pension Fund Managers* (PFMs) and different categories of schemes. PFMs share a common CRA infrastructure and invest the money in three asset classes such as equity (E), government securities (G) and debt instruments that entail credit risk (C), including corporate bonds and fixed deposits.

Contribution guidelines

PFRDA has set the following guidelines with regard to subscriber contribution:

- Minimum amount per contribution: Rs. 500 per month
- Minimum number of contributions: 1 in a year

- Minimum annual contribution: Rs 6,000 in each subscriber account.

If the subscriber is unable to contribute the minimum annual contribution, a default penalty of Rs.100 per year of default is levied and the account becomes dormant. In order to re-activate the account, subscriber has to pay the minimum contribution, along with penalty due. A dormant account is closed when the account value becomes nil subject to deductions in the from of penalties.

Investment options

Under the investment guidelines finalized for the NPS, pension fund managers manage three separate schemes, each investing in a different asset class. The three asset classes are equity, government securities and credit risk-bearing fixed income instruments. The subscriber has the option to decide as to how the NPS pension wealth is to be invested in three asset classes:

1. E Class: Investment primarily in Equity market instruments. It invests in Index funds that replicate the portfolio of either BSE Sensitive index or NSE Nifty 50 index.
2. G Class: Investment in government securities like GOI bonds and state government bonds.
3. C Class: Investment in fixed-income securities other than government securities such as:
    - Liquid Funds of AMCs regulated by SEBI with filters suggested by the Expert Group.
    - Fixed deposits of scheduled commercial banks with filters.
    - Debt securities with maturity of not less than three years tenure issued by corporate bodies, including scheduled commercial banks and public financial institutions.
    - Credit-rated public financial institutions/PSU bonds.
    - Credit-rated municipal bonds/infrastructure bonds.

The Minimum Guarantee Clause of PFRDA Act of 2013:- As per the Chapter VI of National Pension System, Rule 20, Clause 2(4)(a), the subscriber has an option of investing up to 100 percent of his funds in government securities only and also as per clause 2(4)(b),the subscriber seeking minimum assured returns, has an option to invest his funds in such schemes providing minimum assured returns as may be notified by the authority; as mentioned above in G Class and C Class minimum guaranteed bonds, securities and time deposits of definite nature.

APPROACH OF PENSION SYSTEM

Pension schemes across the countries can be categorised into three pillars based on the need they address and the funding nature. Each of these pillars has some combination of the five features (*viz.*, voluntary vs mandatory; savings vs redistribution; DB, DC and NDC; funded vs PAYG; and private vs publicly managed) discussed earlier. These pillars are:

Pillar I: Basic pension (Old Age Pension) - characterised by redistribution, PAYG, mandatory, defined benefit and collective risk - e.g. public pension plans.

Pillar II: Compulsory Superannuation (Forced/contractual savings) - characterised by vertical equity (income smoothing), funding, mandatory, defined contribution and individual risk - e.g. occupational pension plans.

Pillar III: Voluntary Superannuation (voluntary savings) - characterised by voluntary, income smoothing, funding and individual risk - eg. personal pension plans and additional contributions made by individuals to occupational scheme.

The first pillar schemes which are mandatory and redistributive, offer defined benefits that are largely financed on a PAYG basis, and are publicly managed. These schemes pay a benefit after a fixed number of years. Most of these schemes will have no form of funding while some will rely on partial funding. First pillar pension schemes can only be sustainable over the longer period if the system "dependency ratio", that is the ratio of pensioners to contributors, is such that current contributors can afford to pay social insurance contributions at a level that will support current pension expenditure. The system dependency ratio, sometimes referred to as the "support ratio", tends to understate the extent of the sustainability problem. Sustainability problem can also arise if the working population keeps declining because of pursuit of higher education, unemployment and early retirements.

An increase in life expectancy due to better health care and living conditions further compounds the problems for both the public and private pension schemes. Reforms need to be undertaken in order to remedy the situation in the short and longer term. These include parametric changes such as increasing the retirement age, reducing the value of pensions, increasing contributions, lengthening the contributory period required to gain entitlement to a full pension, changing the rules on indexation, and making it more difficult to retire early with a pension.

Second pillar pension schemes or defined contribution schemes, in which contributions are placed in individual or group funds, could be managed either by private sector pension companies or by the public sector, usually as provident funds. They do not bring about a redistribution of income, but smoothen consumption over each individual's life span. They can help develop capital markets of the economy.

Third pillar schemes are those that comprise voluntary personal pensions which are encouraged through tax concessions. They are defined contributions, generally non-redistributive and fully funded. These pension schemes are intended to increase the range of individual choice. In the absence of any guarantee, workers can also suffer losses caused by business failures or fraudulent behaviour on the part of the employers. Charges by fund managers may also be high and, if kept low by law, may lead to a compromise in service.

The three pillars can be complementary to each other. While some countries avail of only one or two of the pillars (either Pillars I and III or Pillars II and III), there are several advantages of adopting multipillar system (ADB, 2001). Fox and Palmer (2001) who studied the pension reform and related developments during the nineties in both the developed and developing countries observed that, although there is a definite tendency towards schemes incorporating funded component, State managed first pillar schemes augmented by contribution related components would continue to stay.

During the nineties, countries have adopted various innovative ideas for creating sustainable mandatory public pension system. Country experiences show that it is not necessary to go from unfunded PAYG DB system to funded, individual account DC system to create sustainability in the public provision of mandatory old age pensions. In fact, combining a PAYG first pillar with a second pillar scheme of funded individual accounts has been the most popular.

This has emerged in diverse countries such as Sweden in OECD, Hungary, Latvia and Poland in transition economies, Hongkong in Asia, and Argentina, Peru and Uruguay in Latin America. With a view to reduce the size of DB schemes, countries have mostly effected parametric changes such as increasing the number of years required for full benefit and introduction of life expectancy factor into the DB formula. The countries which desire to maintain larger first pillar have preferred NDC schemes. This provides direct link between contribution and benefits and account for life expectancy at the benefit pay out phase.

NATIONAL PENSION SYSTEM - A GOVERNMENT'S NEW INITIATIVE

The National Pension System (NPS) reflects Government's new effort to find a suitable & sustainable solution to the problem of providing adequate retirement benefits to the people at large. As a first step towards initiating this, Government of India moved from a defined benefit pension to a defined contribution based pension system by making it mandatory for its new recruits (except armed forces) with effect from January 1st, 2004. Since April 1st, 2008, the pension contributions of Central Government employees covered by the NPS are being invested by professional Pension Fund Managers in line with investment guidelines of Government applicable to non-Government Provident Funds.

Twenty eight States/Union Territory Governments have notified the NPS for their new employees. Some states have already signed agreements with the intermediaries of the NPS architecture appointed by PFRDA for carrying forward the implementation of the NPS.

NPS has been made available to every citizen from 1st May, 2009 on a voluntary basis. The NPS architecture is transparent and will be web-enabled. It would allow a subscriber to monitor his/her investments and returns under NPS, the choice of Pension Fund Manager and the investment option would also be decided by the subscriber. The design allows the subscriber to switch his/her investment options as well as pension funds. The facility for seamless portability and switch between Portfolio Fund Managers is designed to enable subscribers to maintain a singlepension account throughout their saving period (i.e. till 60 years age). PFRDA has set up a Trust under the Indian Trusts Act, 1882 to oversee the functions of the Portfolio Fund Managers. The NPS Trust is composed of members representing diverse fields and brings wide range of talent to the regulatory framework.

The NPS has been designed to enable the subscriber to make optimum decisions regarding his/her future and provide for his/her old-age through systemic savings from the day he/she starts his/her employment. It seeks to inculcate the habit of saving for retirement amongst the citizens.

The NPS has been making progress in terms of investment options and showcasing performance superior to the traditional EPF and PPF investments.

INDIAN PENSION SYSTEM: PROBLEMS AND PROGNOSIS

The debate on the pension system reforms is intensifying in India. The ongoing financial sector reforms have made significant progress in the spheres of banking, capital and currency markets and now provides an opportunity to revamp the hitherto untouched sectors like insurance and pension. While insurance sector reform is already underway, the effect of which to a certain extent is expected to percolate to the private pension market - a comprehensive policy for pension system restructuring is yet to be undertaken.

A variety of problems plague the pension system in India. The gradual collapse of the traditional old age support mechanisms and the rise in elderly population highlights the need for strengthening the formal channels of retirement savings. The imperative, more proximate reasons for pension reform are also well known - skewed coverage of the existing benefit schemes favoring organized workforce while informal employment is on the rise, worsening financial situation of government pension schemes against a background of rising system expenditure, unfair treatment of private sector workers vis-à-vis public sector employees, an under developed private annuity market, and finally the need to increase the domestic rate of savings through higher contractual savings.

Major retirement savings schemes like provident and pension funds predominantly cover workers in the organized sector, constituting only about 10 percent of the aggregate workforce. The majority of workers, around 90 percent of the working population are engaged in the unorganized sector and have no access to any formal system of old age economic security. This skewed coverage is further shrinking as informal workforce is growing while the size of formal workforce has remained more or less stagnant.

Additional impetus for pension reform comes from the fragmented nature of the existing benefit schemes. Inspite of its limited scope and size, the Indian pension system in its current form, can at best be described as an extremely complicated and fractured one inducing distortion in the labor market. A large number of occupation based retirement schemes with wide diversity in plan characteristics and benefit provisions are in existence, and have created a wedge of disparity between public and private sector workers. While private sector workers are aggrieved with low returns from their benefit schemes, public employees are privileged with generous pension provisions.

In recent years, there have been attempts to address these problems. These efforts, however, have largely been piecemeal. The diverse and often conflicting set of problems faced by the Indian pension system requires a more serious and coherent approach. For example, on one hand, there is an urgent need to contain the escalating expenditure on public pension programs while there is also an urgency to extend the coverage to the unorganized sector. The government1 initiatives in recent years like advancement of retirement age for its employees, partial conversion of provident funds into pension schemes for private workers and introduction of new means-tested social assistance schemes for the poor have met with limited success, further underlining the need for an early and lasting reform of the current system.

Structure of the pension system

India, like most other developing countries, does not have a universal social security system to protect the elderly against economic deprivation. Perhaps, persistently high rates of poverty and unemployment act as a deterrent to institute a pay-roll tax financed state pension arrangement for each and every citizen attaining old age. Instead, India has adopted a pension policy that largely hinges on financing through employer and employee participation. This has however restricted the coverage to the organized sector workers - denying the vast majority of the workforce in the unorganized sector access to formal channels of old age economic support.

Notwithstanding the limited size and scope, India has a long tradition of pension and other forms of formal old age income support system. The history of the Indian pension system dates back to the colonial period of British-India. The Royal Commission on Civil Establishments, in 1881, first awarded pension benefits to the government employees. The Government of India Acts of 1919 and 1935 made further provisions. These schemes were later consolidated and expanded to provide retirement benefits to the entire public sector working population. Post independence, several provident funds were set up to extend coverage among the private sector workers.

Today, major retirement schemes in India include provident fund, gratuity and pension schemes. The first two schemes provide lump sum retirement benefit while the last one makes payment in the form of monthly annuity. These schemes are characterized by the following common features i.e. they are mandatory, occupation based, earnings related, and have embedded insurance cover against disability and death. Table 1 elaborates salient features of the major provident fund and pension schemes.

The central government, states and union territories provide pension benefits to the public employees. In addition, a large number of public and local bodies and autonomous institutions run their own pension schemes guaranteed by the government. The central government alone administers separate pension programs for civil employees, defense staff and workers in railways, post, and telecommunications departments.

These benefit programs are typically run on a pay-as-you-go, defined-benefit basis. The schemes are non-contributory i.e. the workers do not contribute during their working lives. Instead, they forego the employer's contribution into their provident fund account.

The entire pension expenditure is charged in the annual revenue expenditure account of the government. Full superannuation benefit is a monthly pension fixed at fifty percent of the average monthly earnings during the last year of service. The pension is indexed to provide a real annuity to the retirees. Public employees, in addition to their pension benefits are also covered under the General Provident Fund (GPF) scheme. The GPF is a noncontributory program where only workers themselves contribute a minimum of six percent of their monthly earnings. The accumulation under the GPF account is returned to the worker in lump sum at the time of retirement.

Private sector workers are less fortunate and until recently had access only to a provident fund system for their old age income security. Provident Fund is a defined-contribution, fully funded benefit program providing lump sum benefit at the time of retirement. The provident fund system, consisting of the Employees' Provident Fund (EPF) and a number of smaller provident funds is the largest benefit program operating in India.3 Together, the schemes provide retirement benefits to about 10 percent of the labor force. Workers (and private employers) contribute between 10 - 12 percent of monthly earnings, to be returned to the worker in a lump sum payment at retirement, including accumulated interest at a rate currently set at 11 percent. In 1995, the government partially converted the EPF scheme and introduced the Employees' Pension Scheme (EPS).

In addition to the provident fund, workers in both public and private sectors receive a second tier of lump sum retirement benefit known as gratuity. It is paid to the workers who fulfill certain eligibility conditions like a minimum qualifying service period of five years. It is equivalent to 15 day's of final earnings for each years of service completed subject to a maximum of Rs. 350,000. The cost of gratuity is entirely borne by the employer.

These schemes are largely the privilege of the organized sector workers. Workers in the unorganized and informal sectors4 have access only to a few voluntary schemes like Public Provident Fund and pension plans offered by the Life Insurance Corporation of India. Organized sector employees can also subscribe to these schemes to augment their retirement savings.

For people in the lower end of the economic strata, there are several central as well as state government-run means-tested, targeted, social assistance programs and welfare funds. The criteria of eligibility varies, but generally the destitute, the poverty stricken and the infirm aged 60 years and above are provided pension at rates ranging between Rs. 30 and Rs. 100 per month. However, the combined coverage of these social assistance schemes is insignificant and covers anywhere between 5 and 10 percent of the total elderly population. In an effort to widen the reach of the social safety net for the aged poor, the central government, in 1995, introduced a more comprehensive old age poverty alleviation program called the National Old Age Pension (NOAP) under the aegis of the National Social Assistance Programme (NSAP). The scheme aims to provide monthly pension to thirty percent of the poorest elderly.

The formal old age income security system in India can thus be classified into three categories. The upper tier consists of statutory pension schemes and provident funds for the organized sector employees; the middle tier is comprised voluntary retirement saving schemes for the self-employed and unorganized sector workers while the lower tier consist of targeted social assistance schemes and welfare funds for the poor.

7

Department of Ex-Servicemen Welfare

Department of Ex-servicemen Welfare(Poorva Senani Kalyan Vibhag) is a department, in Ministry of Defence, India. It was set up in 2004. The head of Department of Ex-servicemen Welfare since its inception has been a bureaucrat from the IAS. Veteran have for long demanded that DEWS be headed by a serving officers or a retired officer, like in other countries, including the United States, in which the Department of Veterans, is invariably headed by veteran with active duty military experience, with a cabinet rank. For instance the current head of the department is graduate of West Point, and has served in the army.

FUNCTIONS AND ORGANIZATION

The functions of DESW according to the official website are: "Matters relating to Armed Forces Veterans (Ex-Servicemen) including pensioners;Armed Forces Veterans (ExServicemen); Contributory Health Scheme; Matters relating to Directorate General of Resettlement and Kendriya Sainik Board; Administration of (a) the Pension Regulations for the Army, 1961 (Parts I and II); (b)the Pension Regulations for the Air Force, 1961 (Parts I and II);(c)the Navy (Pension) Regulations, 1964; and(d) The Entitlement Rules to Casualty Pensionary Awards to the Armed Forces Personnel, 1982".

The Department has two Divisions, the Resettlement Division and the Pension Division and 3 attached offices namely (a) Secretariat of Kendriya Sainik Board (KSB), (b) Directorate General (Resettlement) (DGR) and (c) Ex-servicemen Contributory Health Scheme (ECHS) Organisation.

Veterans in India

There are about 2.6 million ex-servicemen, and 60,000 widows, including war widows, i.e., a combined total of 3.2 million, of whom about 86 percent are widows, Junior Commissioned Officers, Non Commissioned Officers , and other ranks, and about 14 percent are officers.

Approximately 60,000 armed forces personnel retire or are released from active service every year. Most are in age bracket of 35 to 45 years. Directorate General Resettlement (DGR) is responsible for preparing retiring/ retired service personnel for a second career. Veterans in India in the last decade have resorted to public protest under the OROP banner to highlight that they are uncared for and treated far worse than civilian counterparts.

DEWS AND VETERANS

DEWS Response to Veteran Issues

The Ministry of Defence (MOD), including the DEWS, which is a component of the ministry, is considered by most ex-servicemen, including former head of the Armed Forces, as permanent impediment for the welfare of Ex Serviceman (ESM). Four former heads of the Armed Forces in August 2015, in an open letter addressed to the President of India flagged "The hostile approach of MoD bureaucracy" and its "antagonistic handling of problems related to pensions and allowances of aging veterans, war widows and battle-casualties'.

DEWS opposes One Rank One Pension (OROP)

The Department of Ex-servicemen Welfare has opposed One Rank One Pension OROP. In 2011, Neelam Nath, Secretary of Department of Ex-Servicemen Welfare from June 1, 2009 to September 30, 2011, in her deposition in front of the Parliamentary Panel that examined the grant of OROP to the Armed Forces, opposed the grant and implementation of OROP for the Armed Forces.

On February 17, 2014, despite protest of DESW, the Government announced in the interim budget acceptance of the principle of 'One Rank One Pension (OROP), and Ministry of Defence Report 2013-14, noted that "Government has taken steps to implement the OROP from the financial year 2014-15" and that the implementation will improve pensions of past pensioners .

Despite the announcement in the MOD Report, OROP was not implemented. The failure to implement OROP by the BJP Government which had in its election manifesto pledged to do so provoked nationwide protest by ex servicemen.

Failure of the BJP Government to implement OROP after several promises provoked Ex-servicemen to undertake unprecedented nationwide protests, and hunger strikes from 15 June 2015.

Veteran protest have had the support of former heads of armed Forces. Four former chiefs of the Armed Forces of India, namely General S F Rodrigues, former COAS, and Admirals L Ramdas, Arun Prakash and Sureesh Mehta, former Chiefs of Naval Staff, in an open letter to President Pranab Mukherjee, Supreme Commander of the Armed Forces, on 13 August 2015, warned that the denigration and humiliation of veterans, and the Government handling of veterans and armed Forces issues, pose grave "implication for national security"

NATIONAL COMMISSION FOR EX-SERVICEMEN

Following persistent demand by Ex servicemen, the Government on 9 June 2014 announces that it will set up a National Commission for Ex-Servicemen. However, no funds are earmarked for setting up of the Commission during the year 2014-15.

INDIAN EX SERVICEMEN MOVEMENT

Indian Ex Servicemen Movement (IESM) is a "All India Federation of Ex Servicemen's organizations" and individual veterans of the Indian Army, Navy and Air Force. IESM was established in August 2008, in the wake of the UPA Government decision to implement Sixth Central Pay Commission, which depressed military pays and pensions, and ranks, relative to civilian Government employees, especially in the Ministry of Defence(MOD) and Police led security services. It has been at forefront in identifying, and advocating veteran causes, principally issues affecting veteran honor and izzat, and the implementation of One Rank One pension for the armed Forces of India. Its founder member is Lt Colonel Inderjit Singh, former Commanding Officer 14 Grenadiers, who retired from the army in 1978.

Goals

The stated aims of the IESM are: to serve as an umbrella organization for all Ex Servicemen of India; provide a unified veteran voice on issues of national interest; serve as forum for raising and discussing challenges faced by veterans; play 'constructive role in nation building activities'; promote and support IESM causes, including those affecting ESM Widows, war wounded, and injured; and render assistance and advice to veterans on matters of pension, health coverage and benefits, and legal issues.

ORGANISATION

Governing Body (GB)

IESM has a federal structure with units at National, State and District levels. The highest decision making body is called the governing body, for which elections are held every three years. The last election were held on 16 November 2014 in Pune, Maharashtra. The Election were conducted by election unit headed by Brig HSN Sastri. Soon after the election of the

Governing body, it elected an Executive Committee for the day-to-day running of the organisation. The current composition of the GB is as follows:

Name and designation	District, City	State
Maj Gen Satbir Singh	Gurgaon	Haryana
Gp Capt VK Gandhi	Noida	UP
Commander SS Ahuja, IN	Noida	UP
Wg Cdr CK Sharma	Delhi	Delhi
Cdr Ravi Pathak	Pune	Maharashtra
Col Pronoy Sengupta	Pune	Maharashtra
Maj Gen PK Renjen	Gurgaon	Haryana
Col Anil Koul	Gurgaon	Haryana
Brig CS Vidyasagar	Secunderabad	A P
Maj Gen AJB Jaini	Ghaziabad	UP
Hony Lt Kameshwar Pandey		Bihar
Col Kirit Joshipura		Gujarat
Hony Capt Jai Singh Rathee	Jhajjhar	Haryana
Sub Maj Markandey Singh	Ghazipur	UP
Hav Dina Nath	Varanasi	UP
Col RP Chaturvedi	Noida	UP
Mrs Anuradha Deo w/o Maj SM Deo	Nagpur	Maharashra
Sgt Prakash Narain Pandey	Kanpur	UP
Brig Harwant Singh	Mohali	Punjab
Col Vijay Gaekwad	Kolhapur	Maharashtra

Executive Committee

No	Rank and name	appointment
1	Maj Gen Satbir Singh, SM	Offg Chairman
2	Maj Gen PK Renjen,AVSM	Vice Chairman
3	Wg Cdr CK Sharma	Treasurer
4	Gp Capt VK Gandhi VSM	General Secretary
5	Brig CS Vidyasagar	Joint General Secretary

Divisions

Indian Ex Servicemen Movement to render assistance to veterans, and its members, is organised into three units. These are the Pension Division, Ex servicemen Contributory Health scheme (ECHS), and Legal Division, which includes Veterans Anil Bakhshi, Col Ramath, and Maj Navdeep Singh

Membership

IESM has a full-time member ship of 20455, including army 15820, airforce 3032, navy 1527, and civilians 52. Its active members belong to all Indian states including Delhi, Haryana, Rajasthan, Uttar Pradesh, Karnataka, Punjab, Himachal Pradesh, Maharashtra, Jammu and Kashmir, Kerala, Chandigarh, Mizoram, Chennai, Tamil Nadu, Odisa. The headquarters of IESM is located at 543, sector 23, Gurgaon, Haryana, Pin 122017

Funding

IESM runs on small budget. Members of the governing body works on pro bono basis. For its operating expenses it is dependent on membership fees, and donations. The year after it was formed, for the period 1 April-30 Nov, 2009, its total Receipts from Membership Fee (5,72,100.00) and Donations (Rs 4,23,869.00) was Rs 9,95,969.00. In addition it had Fixed Deposits of Rs 19,00,000.00.

ADVOCACY OF OROP

In June 2015, IESM, as major component of the umbrella organization United Front of Ex-Servicemen (UFESM), participated in nationwide protests, spread over 80 towns and cities of India, demanding implementation of OROP. On 5 September 2015, after 84 days of protest, which included relay hunger strikes and 24 days fast to death, by the IESM members and their supporters, the government announced unilaterally, a scheme which it called OROP, which IESM dismissed, saying it was not OROP, but “One Rank, Five Pensions”.

IESM advocacy of OROP and other ESM causes has wide popular support. 14 Former Chief of Indian Defence Forces have endorsed its stand on OROP. Shekhar Gupta, editor Indian Express, in September 2015, criticized IESM for resorting to public protest and dharnas. He called the ex servicemen protest an unedifying spectacle.

On 15 June 2015 in New Delhi (India):Angry over the delay in implementation of 'One Rank One Pension', ex-servicemen on Sunday launched a protest at Jantar Mantar here. Signing a petition with blood they prepared to return gallantry medals to the president.

Ex-servicemen was gone on an indefinite relay hunger strike to put pressure on the government to implement One-Rank, One-Pension (OROP) scheme.

The hunger strike was led by Lt Colonel MBS Ahluwalia (retd) and many others joined while hundreds were set to participate in the protest. Day before 15 June, the retired servicemen took out a massive rally in the national capital and across the country to express their displeasure in the delay of OROP implementation.

RETURNING OF MEDALS

Military veterans returned their war and other medals at various places in Haryana and Punjab on Tuesday to register their protest against the "diluted" notification of the One Rank One Pension scheme. In Panchkula near Chandigarh, the veterans along with the founder of Hunger Strike Lt Colonel MBS Ahluwalia (retd) returned their medals to the Panchkula deputy commissioner to protest against the OROP notification issued by the central government. There were reports of veterans returning their medals in Jalandhar, Amritsar, Patiala in Punjab and Rohtak, Hisar and Ambala in Haryana. The veterans said that they had rejected the OROP notified by the Narendra Modi government. The defence veterans said that they will observe a 'Black Diwali' this time to protest against the Modi government going back on its assurances.

EX-SERVICEMEN MOVE SC FOR 'FAIR' OROP WORKING, ANNUAL REVISION

The Indian Ex-Servicemen Movement (IESM) has moved the Supreme Court seeking implementation of one rank one pension scheme in a fair manner with an automatic revision on annual basis instead of the current policy of periodic review of once in five years. IESM along with other ex-service personnel has assailed the NDA government's policy of periodic review once in five years, saying that such an approach was dilution of the February 26, 2014, announcement by which the revision in the pension was to automatically pass on to the past pensioners on the annual basis.

Confirming that they have moved the top court seeking fair and automatic revision in pension on annual basis, Maj. Gen. Satbir Singh (retired), spearheading the movement for OROP, told IANS, "As per the original definition given by government of India on February 26, 2014, the change in pensions would have been automatically passed on to past pensioners every year."

"It (Feb. 26, 2014 announcement) had said that whenever there was a change in rate of pension, it would be automatically passed on to past pensioner. It should be done every year but government has now made provision for revision every five years. This kills the very soul of OROP," said Satbir Singh.

The petition which is likely to be argued by the senior counsel Ram Jethamalani when the top court opens after the summer vacations has contended that five-yearly periodic review did not meet the demand of the ex-servicemen seeking one rank one pension for the service personnel who had retired with same length of service in the same rank.

Seeking annual revision of the pension for the past pensioners, the IESM in its petition has referred to the December 19, 2011, report of the Rajya Sabha's Petition Committee then headed by Bhagat Singh Koshyari which rejected all reservation advanced by the government while "strongly recommending" OROP.

In its 142nd report, the Koshyari Committee had said, "the Committee strongly recommends that Government should implement OROP in the defence forces across the board at the earliest".

Having recommended the implementation of OROP, the Koshyari Committee said, "for future, the pay, allowances, pension, family pension, etc. in respect of the defence personnel should be determined by a separate commission so that their peculiar terms and conditions of service, the nature of duties they are required to perform, etc., which are quite different from the civilian work force, are duly taken into account while taking decision on the same." Koshyari, who was Rajya Sabha member belonging to the Bharatiya Janata Party, was Uttarakhand Chief Minister from October 30, 2001 to May 1, 2002.

The petition by the IESM has referred to September 9, 2008, Supreme Court verdict by which it had directed that "the pay of all pensioners in the rank of Major General and its equivalent rank in the two other Wings of the Defence Services be notionally fixed at the rate given to similar officers of the same rank after the revision of pay scales with effect from 1.1.1996, and, thereafter, to compute their pensionary benefits on such basis with prospective effect from the date of filing of the writ petition."

While directing the government to pay the difference in the revised pension and what Major Generals and their equivalent ranks in the Air Force and the Navy were getting earlier within three months with interest at 10 per cent per annum, the court had dismissed the plea by the Centre challenging the Punjab and Haryana High Court judgement.

The high court by its May 26, 2005, judgement had directed the Centre to fix minimum pay scale of the Major General above that of the Brigadier and grant pay above that of a Brigadier as has been done in the case of post-January 1, 1996, retirees and consequently fix the pension and family pension accordingly.

SC SEEKS GOVT'S RESPONSE ON EX-SERVICEMEN'S PLEA ON OROP

Supreme Court sought the government's response on a plea of an ex-servicemen's body seeking implementation of One Rank-One Pension (OROP) as recommended by the Koshyari Committee with an automatic annual revision, instead of the current policy of periodic review once in five years.

A bench comprising Justices Dipak Misra and C Nagappan issued notice and sought the response from the government in eight weeks.

The Indian Ex-servicemen Movement (IESM) and others have challenged the government's policy of periodic review of pension once in five years, saying such an approach was dilution of the February 26, 2014 announcement by which the revision in pension was to automatically pass on to the past pensioners on an annual basis.

ONE RANK ONE PENSION (OROP) DEMAND IS SHOWING THE NARENDRA MODI GOVERNMENT IN POOR LIGHT

The hesitation to implement the One Rank One Pension (OROP) demand is showing the Narendra Modi government in poor light. The Centre has neither the luxury of distancing itself from the issue or passing the buck to the erstwhile UPA government. In September 2013, during his first election rally as the BJP's prime ministerial candidate, Modi demanded that the UPA government "publish a white paper on the status" of the OROP scheme.

Modi also added that if AB Vajpayee had formed the government in 2004, a solution would have been found. With ex-servicemen and their families accounting for a significant section of the electorate in Punjab, Haryana and Himachal Pradesh, the logic of electoral politics behind Modi's forceful rhetoric was impeccable.

But now in power, the fiscal consequences of the decision appear to be deterring Modi and his government from making good on that promise. Not surprisingly, the Congress, despite failing to implement OROP itself, has seized upon the row. The Modi government now finds itself in a bind. Having sowed the seeds of hope in ex-servicemen's minds despite being aware of its emotive nature, the government has little room to manoeuvre, and far less to backtrack on it.

At the heart of the OROP demand is the rank-conscious nature of the forces and their discontent at retired personnel of the same rank and similar years of service receiving different pensions, depending on their year of retirement. This was the definition of OROP as arrived by the Koshiyari Committee report and accepted by the UPA government. So the NDA government's reported attempts to arrive at fresh definitions of the OROP concept have triggered heartburn, and is being construed as a go-slow technique. Though salaries increased with each Pay Commission, these naturally did not factor in pensions for retired personnel, resulting in increasing disparity between pensioners over the years. Moreover, soldiers are compulsorily retired in the armed forces: jawans at 35, NCO/JCOs at 45, majors at 50, and so on. While early retirement keeps the Army young, it is difficult for the veterans, especially jawans, to access fresh employment or secure lateral entry into other government services at a late stage in their life.

Those in the government have attempted to allay concerns that the Centre is soft-peddling the scheme because of fiscal burden. According to a January 2015 defence ministry proposal to the finance ministry, implementing OROP will swell the current Rs54,000 crore defence pension bill by only Rs8,300 crore. However, new studies peg the increased outgo at nearly Rs18,000 crore. For a government that sets great store by fiscal deficit management, a pension outgo of Rs72,000 crore, only marginally less than the defence salary payment of Rs96,000 crore, is bound to raise eyebrows. The Seventh Pay Commission award is also due soon. With central paramilitary personnel also sharing duties in border, counter-insurgency and anti-naxal operations, their demands for OROP would also have to be met.

The ex-servicemen have refused to settle for various formulae proposed by the Centre, and their protest at the iconic Jantar Mantar, over 70 days old now, appears to be growing stronger. Unlike earlier occasions, former service chiefs have openly come out in support, a quite unprecedented gesture. The government has also been stung hard by televised visuals of the Delhi police attempting to evict the protesters on the eve of Independence Day. Former army chief and Union minister VK Singh's daughter has also joined the protest, which could be construed as an implicit show of dissent from within the government. With nearly 22.5 lakh retired personnel and six lakh widows of veterans poised to benefit, the OROP demand has been linked to the country's patriotic duty to its soldiers. In the end, no government, even those that swear by neo-liberal principles of reduced public spending, can ignore this particular aspect.

SECTION OF EX-SERVICEMEN DISGRUNTLED WITH OROP

Even though Defence Minister Manohar Parrikar rolled out the long-awaited One Rank One Pension (OROP) last year, some of the its features have not gone down well with a section of ex-servicemen in Uttarakhand.

The army veterans feel that they have been denied their due. They are of the opinion that the government has "changed the definition" of OROP. The veterans say that they have not got what they should have been as per the Koshiyari Committee report.

Brig K G Behl (retd), patron of Dehradun Ex-Services League, told TOI, "No doubt they have tried to bring pension closer to the demand. But it is less than what was approved by Parliament as per Koshiyari Committee report. As worked out by our experts it is less by five to 22 % from the actual demand. Moreover, it has not served the purpose for which OROP was being demanded for such a long time. We are told that we should approach court if we have a problem but that is not easy especially for people sitting in remote places."

The Parliamentary Committee on Petitions on Grant of OROP, named after its chairman Bhagat Singh Koshiyari, consisted of ten Members of Parliament (MPs) drawn from all the major political parties.

It states that uniform pension should be paid to the armed forces personnel retiring in the same rank with the same length of service irrespective of their date of retirement and any future enhancement in the rates of pension should be automatically passed on to the old pensioners. Major Gen Lalji D Singh (retd) said, "We are not happy because it has become one rank five pensions. Widows and honorary rank holders have been neglected but if they get the equalization correct a lot of the problems will be solved. We are waiting for government to take the next step now."

OROP isn't 60 years Old Issue

Koshiyari Committee, at Page 14, brings out the chronology of OROP as follows: –

1973 first considered by 3rd CPC,

1986 considered again by 4th CPC

1991 considered by Sharad Pawar committee

1996 considered again by 5th CPC

2003 considered by Inter-Ministerial Committee

2005 considered by Group of Ministers

2006 considered by 6th CPC

To quote the Koshiyari Committee (page 14) – "...There is merit in the demand for One Rank One Pension by Armed Forces Personnel, otherwise the matter would not have been considered time and again by various committees of the Government and Central Pay Commissions. It could have been rejected once and for all and principle of res judicata would have been applied to this demand....."

OROP - The Commitment by UPA & by NDA

Definition, based on the Koshiyari Committee Report, was spelt out in meetings taken by Shri A K Antony, Defence

Minister, in the UPA Govt as follows: – Same rank, same years of qualifying service, same amount of pension irrespective of date of retirement

Working Methodology

The UPA Govt's MoD set up a Joint Working Group (JWG) headed by then CGDA (now FA (DS) & Secretary Def/Fin) and comprising officers of MoD, Service HQ and tasked to

- Furnish the implementation order in consultation with Service HQ [who in turn may appropriately consult ex-servicemen], Department of ESW, and MoD (Fin) as conveyed vide MoD/DESW No. 12(01)/2014-D(Pen/Pol) dated 26 Feb 2014.

Modalities: RM's meeting 26 Feb 2014 and thereafter

- OROP implies uniform pension be paid to the Armed Forces personnel retiring in the same rank with the same length of service irrespective of the date of retirement, and
- Any further enhancement in the rates of pension to be automatically passed on to past pensioners.
- Implies bridging the gap between the rate of pension of the current pensioners and the past pensioners

The last meeting of the JWG was at the Joint presentation to then Defence Minister Shri Arun Jaitley on 12 Jun 2014. Till date there isn't any information supplied by CPIO, MoD-DESW whether the modalities have been changed as repeated requests for information are stone-walled with the response that the file is under submission to higher authorities and information would be made available when the file is available.

The Numbers Game

Plato said "A good decision is based on knowledge and not on numbers." For OROP numbers do matter but so does knowledge. 25 Lakh ESM, widows and Next of Kin receive 50% or lesser pension if they served the Nation with distinction, lost limbs, minds, even lives if they were unfortunate enough to retire on or before 31st December 2005.

Koshiyari Committee

The Koshiyari Committee recommended in 2011 that OROP be implemented and that the financial impact would be as follows:-

- Initial (including payment of arrears = Rs 3000 crore
- Annual recurring expenditure = Rs 1300 crore
  - JCOs & Other Ranks = Rs 1065 crore
  - Officers = Rs 235 crore

Not satisfied with the figures made available, the Committee was provided estimates by Ministry of Finance, Deptt of Expenditure as follows: –

- As on 1.1.2006 filed on 05 Jul 2011 and revised on 01 Aug 2011
- @10% increase per annum
  - 2012-13 Rs 1430 crore
  - 2013-14 Rs 1573 crore
  - 2014-15 Rs 1730 crore
  - 2015-16 Rs 1930 crore
  - 2016-16 Rs 2379 crore due to 25% increase in Seventh Central Pay

Commission

Recommendations by Cabinet Secretary & Committee of Secretaries in 2012 reinforced the amount required as follows: –

- Annual expenditure Rs 1400 crore
- Initial expenditure Rs 8000-9000 crore

Estimates by Controller General of Defence Accounts (CGDA) in April-May 2014 (information under RTI Act 2005 denied by CPIO, O/o CGDA quoting directions of the MoD)

- Rs 9100 crore was contested by Service HQ on the following grounds: –
  - Transparency required in the methodology adopted by CGDA and its subsidiaries

- Was enhanced parity of 17 Jan 2013 factored into the estimate?
- Was different voluntary (pre-mature, in Services terms) retirement ages for officers factored in?
- Was 15 to 20 years discharge from service for JCOs and ORs factored in?
- Was OROP calculated for maximum service and maximum rate?

Calculations by Services HQ

Based on data collected by Air Force Central Accounts Office (AFCAO) for the 5 year period ending 31st March 2013 of officers and Warrant Ranks/Airmen retiring, being discharged on completion of enrolment period etc

- Rs 4500 – 5100 crore if
  - — all officers, and
  - — the JCOs/ORs paid as per Group X or Group Y for Warrant Ranks (JCOs/Petty Officers)/OR (Sepoy/Naik/Havildar, Sailors & Airmen) paid as per their Group,
- Rs 7200 crore if all JCO/OR paid X Group pension (half of Rs 1400 p.m.)

Complexities

PM as PM-candidate had reiterated his commitment to OROP from September 2013 and later on as PM till date of this chapter. It appears that the commitment to fulfilling OROP was made in haste and now is the time to repent (for the next 5 years?). The urgency and stentorian tone has been replaced by vagueness and flies in face of claims of a Govt of transparency and speedy decisions. Did the complexities come to the fore only after the Defence Minister stated that a few administrative steps are left for implementation of OROP.

If he says that OROP is not as simple as it appears and there are complexities to resolve for quote "a please all solution" unquote, then so be it. However, the following issues come to the mind (thanks to comments by readers of the blog Aerial View): –

Complexity No. 1: – The time frame for promotions for officers up to the rank of Colonel (and equivalent) has reduced after 2004.

There is a one-time precedent in the 5th CPC, wherein Majors with 21 years of Commissioned service were entitled to pay of Lt Col in the 22nd year, though the Rank Pay would be that of Majors. A similar dispensation was neither recommended nor considered by the 6th CPC in 2006-2008 though Majors were promoted to Lt Col in 13 years and Lt Cols were granted time-bound promotion to Colonels in the 26th year of service from 2004.

Will the BJP led NDA Govt re-visit the past and grant notional pension of Lt Col to Majors and pension of Colonels to Lt Cols, and consequently OROP, to all those originally promoted as per the old scheme? What about the JCOs and ORs whose the tenure of engagement was changed from 15 years to 20 years some time in year 2000 or so?

Complexity No. 2: – In the combined wisdom of the MoD, office of Financial Adviser (Defence Services), Deptt of Defence (Finance), the office of the Controller General of Defence Accounts, and with the approval/concurrence of the Department of Expenditure, MoF, implementation of the recommendations of 6th Central Pay Commission were ordered vide Special Army Instructions No. 2 of 2008 (and equivalent for Navy & Air Force). In that, the scale for Brigadiers (and equivalents) was specified as follows: –

Pay in the Pay Band Rs 37,000 – 67, 000

Grade Pay Rs 8, 900

Military Service Pay Rs 6, 000

The combined wisdom hit a hurdle either because the system has a way of having the last laugh. So, in FY 2014-15, there are 4 Brigadier & equivalent officers who are drawing maximum of Pay in the Pay Band of Rs 67, 000 + Grade Pay Rs 8, 900 + MSP of Rs 6, 000 = Rs 81, 900!

But the scales of Major Generals, Lt Generals (and equivalents) were placed in a lower than Rs 81, 900 Pay in the Pay Band and the Army Cdr (and equivalent) draws Rs 80, 000 as his pay in the Apex Scale. So, someone stating it is only four officers appear to be ignorant of certain judgments of the Honourable Supreme Court of India

Judgements/ Orders of the Honourable Supreme Court in the UoI Vs. D S Nakara (17 December 1982) and UoI Vs Maj Gen S P S Vains (09 September 2008) are very clear – a junior cannot draw more pension than a senior i.e the senior's pension has to be stepped up.

The flawed wisdom of the FA (DS) & CGDA and the concurrence of the DoE, MoF has taken a knock. There will be more litigation quoting the above judgments and raps on the knuckles as was delivered by the Honourable Supreme Court in CA No. 2996 of 2011 and Contempt Petition (Civil) No. 64 of 2009 in CA No. 5566 of 2008) by the Honourable Supreme Court on 16 Feb 2015.

[Just a stray thought – MoD vide its DFPDS-2015 has made it incumbent on the Chiefs of Army, Navy or Air Force to obtain prior concurrence of the Integrated Financial Adviser (IFA) for a purchase of even Re 1/-. Is it another flash of the wisdom and to expand the empire of the IDAS (Indian Defence Account Service)?]

Contradictions & Politicisation of OROP

Edmund Burke said, "You can never plan the future by the past." But that appears to be the rule of the day on the issue of OROP. The often heated debates on television channels, where ESM panellists watch more bemused than earlier especially after 25 May 2015, reinforce the opinions of Ex-Servicemen that they are being given short shrift. The ESM panellists and audience are left aghast that many of the BJP spokespersons expose their lack of knowledge on modalities of OROP or concentrate their ire to fire away at the Congress spokespersons for not doing anything about OROP for 60 years! And the Congress spokespersons harp on what the Vice

President of the party quipped or that BJP has done nothing in 12 months. In the resultant heat and dust it is forgotten that officially the OROP issue started in 1973 i.e. 42 years ago.

In their reciprocal enthusiasm to score brownie points, it is forgotten that there were Governments other than Congress – V P Singh propped up by BJP (1989-1990), Chandrasekhar (1990-1991), Atal Behari Vajpayee (May 1996-June 1996), Deve Gowda (1996-1997), I K Gujral (1997-1998), and then the Atal Behari Vajpayee led BJP – NDA Govt between 1998 and 2004 (i.e 15 of 42 years after emergence of OROP in 1973).

BJP vs Congress in TV Debates

If the BJP spokespersons could have been more dispassionate, and the Congress spokespersons more knowledgeable, they would have enlightened the audience that Shri Koshiyari (a BJP MP) headed Committee was set up by the UPA in 2010 and its findings were presented in the tenure of UPA (December 2011). That the recommendations were ignored till February 2014 is to the detriment of the UPA, but where was the vocal BJP on the issue of OROP when it that stalled the Parliament for several weeks and months on other issues?

If the BJP did mention OROP in Parliament as often as the impression is being conveyed, there must be something on the record of Parliament after 2011. How has the OROP fared from 2004 in Parliament? Here is the data available on the internet though Lok Sabha and Rajya Sabha websites were searched but this author obtained only the following information:–

08 Dec 2004 – Shri Prabhunath Singh (RJD) raises a query but is absent (details not available),

28 Apr 2005 – Dr Col (retd) Dhani Ram Shandil (Shimla – INC) raises a question (details of reply not available)

18 Aug 2006 – Shri Kishan Singh Sanghwan (BJP, deceased 2012) raises a question and Shri B K Handique, MoS Defence replies that OROP is not possible due financial, administrative, and legal reasons as recommended by a Committee of Secretaries

23 Aug 2007 – Shri P K Dhumal (BJP) raises a question (details of reply not available)

26 Feb 2009 – Shri Karan Singh Yadav (Alwar – INC) raises a question (details of reply not available)

21 Aug 2010 – Shri Pratap Singh Bajwa (Gurdaspur – INC) raises a question (details of reply not available)

25 Aug 2010 – Shri Arun Jaitley (BJP) – Non-implementation of OROP by Govt (in his tenures in Rajya Sabha from Feb 2009 to Feb 2014; (source: www.prsindia.ord/mptrack/arunjaitley)

08 Jul 2014 – The principle of One Rank One Pension for the Armed Forces has been accepted by the Government. The modalities for implementation were discussed with various stakeholders and are presently under consideration of the Government. It will be implemented once the modalities are approved by the Government. This information was given by Minister of State for Defence Rao Inderjit Singh in a written reply to Dr T Subbarami Reddy in Rajya Sabha on July 8, 2014.

8 Nov 2014 – The principle of One Rank One Pension for the Armed forces has been accepted by the Government. The modalities for implementation were discussed with various stakeholders and are presently under consideration of the Government. It will be implemented once the modalities are approved by the Government. No Budget was allocated for the purpose in the Budget 2013-14. Total number of beneficiaries for OROP will be known once the modalities are approved. This information was given by Minister of State for Defence Rao Inderjit Singh in a written reply to Shri Hukum Singh and others in Lok Sabha today.

25 Nov 2014 – Statement in respect of Para (a) to (c) of Rajya Sabha Starred Question No. 31 for 25.11.2014 regarding implementation of One Rank One Pension:

Reply (a) to (c): The principle of One Rank One Pension for the Armed Forces has been accepted by the Government. The modalities for implementation were discussed with various stakeholders and are presently under consideration of the

Government. It will be implemented once the modalities are approved by the Government.

In Conclusion

That the Ex-Servicemen are left as abandoned of hope as before (since 1973), and conveyed by their absence at the felicitation by the two retired IAF officers in Pune, may have prompted the most powerful advisory body, the PMO, or maybe the NSA, to suggest to the PM that he should step in and assuage the ESM. The PM may have been advised that leaving the fire-fighting to the Finance Minister, whose statements on 22 May 2015 contradicted the repeated assurances of the Defence Minister i.e. the left hand did not know or pretended not to know, what the right hand was doing.

It is common knowledge amongst the ESM, thanks to a reply by the Finance Minister reported in the Economic Times of 05 May 2015, "Tax exemptions and incentives to corporates have resulted in a revenue impact of Rs 62,398.6 crore to the exchequer in 2014-15, 8 per cent higher than the previous fiscal, Parliament was informed today. In a written reply to a question in the Rajya Sabha, Finance Minister Arun Jaitley said the details of revenue impact on central taxes due to various concessions and exemptions have been detailed in the Budget document for 2015-16" but the same Minister is baulking at giving Rs 8300 crores as estimated by the Defence Minister for OROP.

The PM's admonition to the media not to keep up a running commentary must be seen in the light of the fact of the past week's blitzkrieg by BJP led NDA Govt's statements on transparency, accountability, etc. Neither the PM nor the Finance Minister or the Defence Minister have conveyed to the ESM what the fresh complexities are though the Koshiyari Committee has examined the issues and spelt them all out. And the Defence Minister, who is an honourable man, would not have stated that he has placed the file with Finance Ministry, if he had not resolved all issues, even the 80% as he was misquoted.

If indeed the 'Man ki Baat' (quoted in almost all the newspapers and available on the PTI website) and the earlier interview with Raj Chengappa of The Tribune conveyed anything it was disbelief that there is dissonance within the Govt on the OROP as witnessed by the following: –The Defence Minister meets personages of ESM organisations regularly after assuming office and tells them that all home work has been done and the OROP file sent to Finance Ministry. The Finance Minister states something else which makes readers/listeners of news wonder if the Defence Minister is confused or worse.

Now the PM steps in and says there are complexities that need time to resolve for "make all happy" solution. He also further dampens the hopes of the ESM by stating that he has four more years in Government.

Does that mean that BJP led NDA Govt will emulate the UPA's dying swan act just in the interim Budget of February 2019, before the Election Commission announces the next General Elections in 2019? Just like it is alleged in the media that BJP is just carrying on with UPA's schemes (as stated by Shri Arun Jaitley) in his replies.

In closing, let us all, ESM and the BJP led NDA Government and its personages remember what Jean Paul Sartre said, "Commitment is an act, not just a word." Servicemen have laid their lives on the line in the firm belief that the Government will look after them in old age or look after their families after they have sacrificed their lives for the Nation. If after making repeated promises/commitments of implementing OROP, the Govt finds it does not have the funds, then it could announce that OROP will be implemented 12 or 24 or 44 months (as the Model Code will kick in thereafter) from now and, Most important, Mr Prime Minister orders his ministers not to talk about OROP till BJP Govt issues the orders.

GOVERNMENT ANNOUNCES ONE RANK ONE PENSION SCHEME FOR EX-SERVICEMEN

The Government has announced the One Rank One Pension scheme for the Ex-Servicemen. This was announced by the

Defence Minister Shri Manohar Parrikar here. The following is the statement of the Defence Minister:

"Government of India respects its Defence Forces and Ex-Servicemen for their valour, patriotism and sacrifices. The Government is proud of their devotion to duty and bravery. Our forces, besides vigilantly and gallantly defending the nation, have displayed exemplary standards of courage and bravery in natural calamities, law and order situations and other difficult circumstances.

The issue of "One Rank One Pension" (OROP) has been pending for nearly four decades. It is a matter of deep anguish that the various governments remained ambivalent on the issue of OROP. In February 2014, the then Government stated that OROP would be implemented in 2014-15, but did not specify what OROP would be, how it would be implemented or how much it would cost. An estimated Rs. 500 crore provided for OROP in the budget presented in February 2014 by the then government was not based on any thorough analysis. It is pertinent to mention that the then Minister of State for Defence in 2009 had, in reply to a question, informed Parliament that there are administrative, technical and financial difficulties in implementing OROP. It is for these reasons that the present government took some time to fulfil its promise.

Prime Minister Shri Narendra Modi has, on various occasions, reiterated the Government's commitment to implement OROP for Ex-Servicemen under military pension. As stated above, the previous government has estimated that OROP would be implemented with a budget provision of a mere Rs. 500 crore. The reality, however, is that to implement OROP, the estimated cost to the exchequer would be Rs. 8,000 to 10,000 crore at present, and will increase further in future.

The Government held extensive consultations with experts and Ex-Servicemen. The main argument for OROP is that the Defence personnel retire early and thus are not able to get the benefits of serving till normal retirement age. Despite the huge fiscal burden, given its commitment to the welfare of Ex-Servicemen, the Government has taken a decision to implement the OROP. In simple terms, OROP implies that uniform pension be paid to the Armed Forces personnel retiring in the same rank with the same length of service, regardless of their date of retirement. Future enhancements in the rates of pension would be automatically passed on to the past pensioners. This implies bridging the gap between the rate of pension of current and past pensioners at periodic intervals.

Under this definition, it has been decided that the gap between rate of pension of current pensioners and past pensioners will be bridged every 5 years.

Under the OROP Scheme: The benefit will be given with effect from 1st July, 2014. The present government assumed office on 26th May, 2014 and therefore, it has been decided to make the scheme effective from a date immediately after. Arrears will be paid in four half-yearly instalments. All widows, including war widows, will be paid arrears in one instalment. To begin with, OROP would be fixed on the basis of calendar year 2013.

Pension will be re-fixed for all pensioners retiring in the same rank and with the same length of service as the average of minimum and maximum pension in 2013. Those drawing pensions above the average will be protected. Personnel who voluntarily retire will not be covered under the OROP scheme.

In future, the pension would be re-fixed every 5 years. It is estimated that the expenditure on arrears alone would be ten to twelve thousand crores of rupees. Apart from the fact that the previous government had provided for only Rs. 500 crore in the budget, it is noteworthy that the Koshiyari Committee had accepted the estimate of Rs. 235 crore as additional financial burden to implement OROP. The present government has accepted OROP in true spirit without being constrained by these inaccurate estimates.

OROP is a complex issue. A thorough examination of interests of retirees of different periods and different ranks is needed. The inter-service issues of the three Forces also require consideration. This is not an administrative matter alone.

Therefore, it has also been decided that a One Member Judicial Committee would be constituted which will give its report in six months.

Prime Minister Shri Modi has fulfilled his commitment and approved OROP for Armed Forces personnel. Ministry of Defence will soon issue detailed Government Order."

EX-SERVICEMEN'S AGITATION: ALL YOU NEED TO KNOW ABOUT OROP

After long agitation by armed forces veterans, the government, in an effort to clear up the logjam on One Rank One Pension (OROP) for ex-servicemen, has drafted a provisional document on the implementation of the scheme. However media reports have quoted several ex-servicemen terming it "unilateral", and rejecting the draft.

The major sticking point remains the issue of equalisation. The government is firm on the revision every five years in view of the administrative difficulties of doing it annually, however, the veterans have rejected it. Talks are continuing to find common ground.

Last month, two of the protesting ex-servicemen stepped up their agitation on the demand for implementation of the One Rank One Pension scheme at Jantar Mantar in New Delhi, by going on a fast till death, demanding the early implementation of the long-pending scheme.

"Col Pushpender Singh (Retd) and Haviladar Major Singh rpt Major Singh (Retd) have undertaken fast unto death from today," Col Anil Kaul (Retd), media advisor to the United Front of Ex-Servicemen Movement, said as the agitation at Jantar Mantar entered its 64th day, last month.

The protesters have been on a relay hunger strike so far. Havildar Major had been on relay hunger strike since the agitation started.

To the disappointment of protesting ex-servicemen, Prime Minister Narendra Modi had not given a specific timeline for the implementation of 'One Rank One Pension' (OROP) in his

Independence Day address on 15 August. "Every government has even given small promises but the issue has not been resolved. Even after I came, I have not been able to do it till now. Today, I am assuring my soldiers once again...in-principle OROP has been accepted by us but talks with stakeholders are on," he had said in his Independence Day address. "A solution has to be found for an issue which has been lingering for 20-25 years. I expect good news seeing the way the talks are going on. And that is why I again promise that in-principle, this government has accepted OROP," the PM had said.

General (Retd) VP Malik, the Indian Army chief during the Kargil war, had said on Friday that he had acted as mediator between ex-servicemen and the Modi government on the OROP issue but had given up "within 48 hours", according to a *Hindustan Times* report.

The main dispute, according to the report, was the argument over which year's scales should be taken as base for OROP. The government wants to take the 2011 rates while veterans want those of 2014.

The reason for the anger among the veterans is the long delay in the implementation of the One Rank One Pension scheme.

The OROP scheme has been a long-standing demand of the over two million ex-servicemen of India. It seeks to ensure that a uniform pension is paid to the defence personnel retiring in the same rank with the same length of service, irrespective of their date of retirement.

The scheme is estimated to cost around Rs 8,600 crore initially and subsequently several crore rupees annually.

Currently, all pre-2006 pensioners receive lesser pension than not only their counterparts but also their juniors.

The demand for the implementation of OROP had led to a massive protest on 8 February 2009, when more than 300 retired soldiers of varying ranks had marched to the Rashtrapati Bhavan in New Delhi and had returned medals won in combat and for distinguished service as they sought equal pension for each rank. The veterans were among the thousands who had gathered earlier in the day at the Jantar Mantar observatory in the heart of the capital for a protest that some said marked a black day for the Indian armed forces.

However, it still took five years for the government to recognise this demand made by the military veterans. In February 2014, the government accepted the long-standing demand of ex-servicemen for OROP and had allocated Rs 500 crore to the Defence Pension Account for the implementation of the scheme.

The scheme had also been announced in the Interim Budget in February 2014, but was yet to be implemented.

A few days after this development, Narendra Modi, who was then rallying for the Lok Sabha polls, had slammed the Congress for delay in implementation of OROP.

"The government, which is sitting in Delhi has always been playing a farce with the Armed Forces. Before this also, a number of times, the Finance Minister of Congress had made announcements about One Rank One Pension but never fulfilled it," Modi had said.

"Even this time since I am repeatedly talking about it, they have announced it but this is a fraud with you. Had Congress party been honest, they had the chance to it in 10 budgets from 2004 to 2014. But they did not do it," he had said. Modi had also claimed that "only our government will be able to implement it."

After coming to power, the Modi government also had a perspective on OROP different from past governments. Past governments contended that granting the full scheme was neither financially nor administratively possible because it could lead to similar demands from other government employees, according to *Economic Times*. But the Modi government argued that the service of other government employees could not be equated to that of the military because military officers retired at a much earlier age, generally between 34-35 years of age, and also underwent prolonged and stressful tenures.

In the July 2014 Budget, Finance Minister Arun Jaitley had also announced an allocation of Rs 1000 crore for this scheme. In December 2014, Parrikar had said that OROP will be implemented in the defence forces before the next Budget.

However, while presenting the Budget 2015, Finance Minister Arun Jaitley did not announce its implementation. "I have already, in the last budget, said that we are going to implement One Rank One Pension. This need not be stated on every occasion. We are completely committed to it," Jaitley had told reporters when asked about the delay in launching the scheme.

Explaining the reasons behind the delay, Jaitley had said: "The methodology of calculating the One Rank, One Pension is an issue pending between the services and the defence ministry."

On 17 February this year, the Supreme Court had directed the Centre to implement its six-year-old verdict to follow OROP and had also reminded the BJP of its pre-poll promise made to the people, according to *Hindustan Times*. The apex court had given this order while hearing a contempt petition filed by Maj Gen (Retd) SPS Vains.

In 2009, the Supreme Court, in the case of Union of India & Maj Gen SPS Vains & Others, had ruled that*"no defence personnel senior in rank could get a lower pension than his junior irrespective of the date of retirement, and that similarly placed officers of the same rank should be given the same pension irrespective of the date of retirement,"* according to*Scroll*.

It was expected that PM Modi would make an announcement on OROP during his rally in Mathura to mark his government's first anniversary. But to the disappointment of many ex-servicemen, he did not do so.

Miffed over the delay in the roll-out of the scheme for the armed forces, 1971 war veteran Wing Commander (Retd) Suresh Karnik and Wing Commander (Retd) KV Bopardikar on 28 May had boycotted a gallantry award function in Pune attended by Defence Minister Manohar Parrikar.

At the function, Parrikar had said that his ministry had completed all formalities in respect of the one rank-one pension' (OROP) scheme for ex-servicemen and nobody should try to "politicise" the issue, according to *PTI.*

"My ministry has completed all formalities and OROP will be implemented," he had said, adding that the executive process takes some time. "People still do not know financial implications of this. The Defence Ministry has completed its calculations and there was a unanimous agreement with the Armed Forces on the formula," he had added. Parrikar had also said that the figure of the One Rank One Pension scheme provision had touched about Rs 22,000 crore since he took over as Defence Minister.

The Defence Minister had also said that he is working hard on the scheme and the MoD will send its views to the Finance Minister by 17 February next year, according to*IBNLive.*

On the other hand, praising the veterans for boycotting the function, almost all veterans' organisations in the country had decided to boycott government functions.

He had said the veterans plan to go on hunger strike if the government does not keep its promise.

Lt Gen B Pandit (retd), who spoke on behalf of the veterans, had said delay in the implementation of OROP was causing anxiety among the fraternity.

"It is the sacred responsibility of the state to create conditions to keep the morale of the Armed Forces high," he had said.

8

7th Central Pay Commission (CPC) and Defence Forces

The 7th Central Pay Commission (7CPC), constituted in February 2014 to review the principles and structure of emoluments of all central government civilian employees including defence forces in India, submitted its report on 19 November 2015.7CPC's recommendations affects the organization, rank structure, pay, allowances and pension, of 13,86,171 armed forces personnel.

Following the submission of the 7CPC report, the Chiefs of Staff of the Armed Forces submission to the Government contended that the recommendations of 7th CPC are anomalous, discriminatory, and at variance with historical parities. The anomalies identified by the armed forces are about use of different principles, policy, and formula by the 7CPC for determining armed forces pay, allowances, level, rank equivalence, pension, and status in comparison with the civil services, including defence civilians, police and intelligence services. These anomalies they have argued affect morale, command and control, and cohesion.

On 5 September 2016 the Bharatiya Janata Party (BJP) led National Democratic Alliance (NDA) government implemented the recommendations of the 7CPC including those affecting the armed forces with minor modifications. I On 7 September 2016, the Chiefs of the Army, Navy, and Air Force, wrote to Narendra Modi, the Prime Minister, and Mohan Parrikar, the Defence

Minister, conveying their concern about the "unresolved anomalies". They also write and inform their respective commands that they have been "constrained to request the government to hold implementation of 7th CPC award in abeyance in view of the anomalies which need to be resolved". On 14 September 2016 the headquarters of the three services, following assurances at the highest level that anomalies affecting armed forces pay, pension, allowances, rank parity, and status would be addressed, issued instructions to their commands to implement the government decision.

On 30 January 2018, President Ram Nath Kovind gave his nod to The 7th Pay Commission's suggestion of increasing the monthly salary of Chief Justice of India (CJI) to Rs 2.80 lakh per month from the present Rs 1 lakh per month, besides recommending a salary hike of the judges of the Supreme Court and the 24 High Courts

Background

The 7CPC was constituted against the background of the protracted public protest by ex-servicemen, including by senior officers, that started following the 6th CPC in 2008. These protest highlighted the perceived neglect of the armed forces on matters affecting their pay, pension status, levels, especially in comparison with police officers, and defence civilians, who were granted time bound promotions to the highest ranks, Non Functional Upgrade (NFU), and One Rank, One Pension (OROP) by the UPA Government.

To address the dissatisfaction in the armed forces over pay and allowances, the government added an additional term of reference(TOR), not included 5th and 6th Pay Commission, that enjoined the 7th CPC, "to review the principles and structure of emoluments of defence service personnel having regard to the historical and traditional parities".The government did not agree to Armed Forces representation in the CPC. Since the 4th Central Pay Commission (1986), when the concept of rank paywas introduced for the armed forces, pay commission recommendations affecting armed forces pay, and status, relative to civilian government employees, including the police, which wear rank badges similar to the army, have been cause of disappointment and disaffection in the armed forces.

COMPOSITION OF 7CPC

The commission consisted of three members, and one member secretary. The 1st CPC (1947) had no member secretary. Since then all pay commissions have had a member secretary, usually from the IAS.

Secretariat

7CPC had a secretariat of 18 government officials on deputation from their respective departments to the commission. In addition, the commission hired 16 consultants to advice it on its work. The consultants are not named in the report, and their contribution are not documented.

The secretariat was composed of members of Indian Administrative Service (IAS), Indian Postal service, Indian Railway Accounts Service, Indian Post and Telegraph Accounts and Finance Service.

Senior officials involved in the preparation of the report were: Jayant Sinha, Indian Audit and Accounts Service (IA&AS), 1990 batch, (who on completion of his tenure in the 7th CPC was posted in the Department of Defence, Ministry of Defence); Ms Yashashri Shukla, Indian Post and Telegraph Accounts and Finance Service', Mudit Mittal, Indian Railway Accounts Service; Samir Kumar Sinha, IAS officer of Bihar cadre and Rajiv Mishra, 'Advisor' and 'economist'.

D.K. Rai, Indian Defence Account Service (IDSA), 2000 batch, was responsible for processing armed forces pay and allowances, including reviewing the submissions from the armed forces headquarters.

Rai, according to Mr Mathur was "great help" in "determining the pay structure for the defence forces", because of his "insight into the financial intricacies of the pay structure of the defense service".

Armed Forces representation

The mandate of 1st Central Pay Commission (nine members) and the 2nd Central Pay Commission (six members) was to examine and recommend emolument structure for central government civilian employees. "The structure of emoluments and benefits of service personnel" was made by separate Departmental Committee, with proper service representation, " in the light of the recommendations made by the pay commission for civilian employees".The first committee was called "The Post War Pay Committee for the Armed Forces". The pensionary benefits were examined by separate committee called " Armed Forces Pension Revision Committee (1949–50)". A similar procedure was followed after the second pay commission by the Raghuramiah Committee(1960), which too had service representatives.

Since the 3rd Pay Commission(1500 pages, April 1973), the mandate of all pay commissions has included all central government civilian employees, including defence forces.All pay commissions, including 3CPC, 4CPC, 5CPC, and 6CPC, have had no military member. Following the protest after the government decision to implement 6CPC, Manmohan Singh, in 2008, assured the armed forces that there will be a separate commission for the armed forces with appropriate armed forces participation. Eventually, there was no separate commission, or military representation, including in the secretariat, and among consultants hired by the 7CPC. Neither did any of the 7CPC member, consultants or secretariat staff, have any background or direct knowledge of its organizational culture or work.

Armed forces representation in other developed democracies

In the UK Pay Commissions is "An independent Body which provides advice to the Review Body (AFPRB) Prime Minister and the Secretary of State for Defence on the remuneration and charges for Service personnel". AFPRB is composed of experts including always a senior retired armed forces officer, who serves in the body for number of years. The US had a far more evolved system Military Compensation system. Military compensations, by law, is required to be reviewed every four years. According to the basic congressional mandate contained in 37 U.S.C. §1008(b) each Quadrennial Review is required to do "a complete review of the principles and concepts of the compensation system for members of the uniformed services ... in relation to national security objectives" and "in an era typified by rapid technological developments and changing battlefield tactics".

TERMS OF REFERENCE

The terms of reference of the commission was: To examine, "the principles that should govern the emoluments structure including pay, allowances and other facilities/benefits, in cash or kind," of civilian employees of the central government (33.02 lakh); and of the Defence forces (13,86,171)

The term of reference specific to the consideration of armed forces pay, pension, and rank structure reads: "having regard to the historical and traditional parities, with due emphasis on the aspects unique to these personnel". The term historical and traditional parities is neither examined or defined by the commission in the report. It is however frequently referred to by the commission, including in justifying its recommendations affecting the armed forces.

DEFINITIONS

Anomaly

According to Ministry of Personnel, Public Grievances and pensions, an anomaly (a deviation from the common rule, type, arrangement, or form; an incongruity or inconsistency)for the purposes of examining the 7CPC, includes the following two cases: "(a) where the Official Side and the Staff Side are of the opinion that any recommendation is in contravention of the principle or the policy enunciated by the Seventh Central Pay Commission itself without the Commission assigning any reason;

and (b) where the maximum of the Level in the Pay Matrix corresponding to the applicable Grade Pay in the Pay Band under the pre-revised structure, as notified vide CCS (RP) Rules 2016, is less than the amount an employee is entitled to be fixed at, as per the formula for fixation of pay contained in the said Rules".

Grade, level, and rank

Grade pay, level, and rank are used interchangeably by 7CPC and government in its various implementation orders The 20 distinct pay grades or ranks in the government hierarchy, intended to 'determine the status', and the Seniority of a post. and make "Pay scales ..irrelevant for purposes of computing seniority".proposed by the 6CPC , and accepted by the Congress I government, in 2008, have been replaced by 18 "New functional levels" 1 which the BJP government has accepted on 25 July 2016.

The 'levels' which correlate to ranks, in civil and military hierarchy, were "arrived at by merging the grade pay with the pay in the pay band". The "Level" is, according to the 7CPC, the new "status determiner". All levels, and ranks, civilian and military are covered in the level 1 to 18 spectrum. Chiefs of the armed forces, and the cabinet secretary, are at level 18.

RECOMMENDATION AND ANOMALIES

Armed forces have identified 37 anomalies in the 7CPC recommendations that affect the armed forces. These 'anomalies' relate to armed forces pay, allowances, 'levels'(ranks), status, pensions, disability pay, civil military relations, military morale, cohesion,and other issues. These anomalies have been subject of joint letters by the Chiefs of Staff to the prime Minister and the defence minister. Some of issues are as follows:

(a) Principles, and formulas, used by the commission used to determine time scale pay and levels, of the armed forces, and specially the civilian security apparatus, which consists of defence civilians, and police led para military forces, now called Central Armed Police Force, police bureaucracy, and secret police intelligence services. The armed forces have alleged their salaries have been "artificially suppressed", which have affected armed forces time scale ranks of captain, majors, and lt colonels, and selection grade ranks of colonel, and brigadiers.

(b) The award of non-functional upgrade (NFU) by 6CPC to the civilian services and the police, while denying it to the armed forces. The armed forces demanded that it be extended to the Armed forces on for same reasons it has been granted to other government servants.

(c) Increase military service pay (MSP) for Junior Commissioned Officers (JCOs) to Rs 10,000. The 7th CPC had, recommended Rs 5,200 as MSP for JCOs and other ranks. The Military Service Pay (MSP) for officers between Lieutenant-rank and Brigadier-rank is Rs 15,500.

(d) Disability to be "percentage based", and par with civilians, rather than "slab based" system recommended by 7CPC.

Anomalies in pay matrix

MOD instructions on implementation of the recommendations of the 7CPC " relating to structure of emoluments, allowances and conditions of service of Armed Forces personnel" was issued on 5 September 2016. The basis for determining armed forces pay, level, status, pension, recommended by 7CPC is similar to 6CPC, except for terminological changes. The 7CPC recommended replacing 'grade pay and pay bands' of 6CPC, with two "Pay Matrices": one for the civil services, police, defence civilians, and another for the armed forces. The term 'levels', is analogous to grade pay, and rank. The matrix for the civilian security sector (police and defence civilians), provides for time scale pay promotions at 4, 9, 13, 14, and 16/18 years of service. The time scale promotions for the armed forces for time scale levels at 6, 13, 21 years of service.The differentiated and asymmetries pay matrices have become a contentious issue, and are not in accord with historical parities, according to the Armed forces. The government in response to made some changes to 7CPC recommendations in its implementation order.

For instance, the commanding officer of INS *Vikramaditya*, India's aircraft carrier, a selective rank and appointment, with some 20 years of service, is, according to the new pay , levels, will be below in 'level' (rank), pay, and protocol than a police officer with 14 years service, and two level below with those one with 16 years of service.

Anomalies in levels and ranks

Among the 37 anomalies highlighted by the armed forces headquarters to the ministry of defence (MOD) critical ones relates to asymmetries in armed and civil and police pay, rank, and allowances. The inclusion of historical and traditional relativity' in the 'term of reference' in 7CPC notification, it was hoped, would address this issue, especially against the background of public protest from 2008 to 2015, under the One Rank One Pension banner, in which a significant number of senior most retired personnel of the armed forces participated, and highlighted the growing gap between the pay, and status of armed forces and defence civilians, police, and other civilian officers. Following the decision of the BJP government to implement the levels with existing anomalies, the Chiefs of three armed forces to write to the defence minister and the prime minister conveying their dismay at the anomalies in the levels, and ranks, and status, of armed forces officer in comparison with defence civilians, and the police officers.

The main cause for the anomalies in pay and rank and allowances between the armed forces and civil servants including police officers, is because the 7CPC used different yard stick in allocation of 'levels' between the armed forces and the civilians government employees. Especially so in the progression for time scale levels, and ranks, in the civilian and police cadres and the armed forces. Some of the anomalies relating to pay, status, rank, are as follows:

- Armed forces officers (army, navy, and air-force) reach level 11 (major) after 6 years, while civilian officers including defence civilians, and police, reach level 11 in 4 years including one year spent in training. Defence civilians from accounts, audit, other departments and the police move up to Level 12 on completion of 9 years service in group A; service officer remain at level 11.
- Armed forces don't have level 12; instead they have 'level 12 A' which corresponds to old grade pay 1000, in pay band 4, tenable by armed forces officers with 13 years service (lieutenant colonels, wing commanders, and naval commanders). Defence civilians, and police, and other civil servants, on completion of 13 years service are promoted anomalously to 'level 13', while armed forces officers with 13 year service remain level 12 A, creating a pay, level, and status differentiation at the time scale level.
- On completion of 14 years service police officers and defence civilians move to time scale level 13A; service officers- Lt Colonel /Wing Commander/Commanders- remain at level 12 A.
- Brigadiers [a selection grade rank] is equated with Level 13A [time scale].
- On completion of 16 years service, police officers and defence civilians move to time scale level 14; service officers- Lt Colonel /Wing Commander/Commanders- remain at level 12 A, colonels at level 13, and brigadiers at 13A.

These and other pay, and status, anomalies have been resented by the armed forces headquarters.

Non Functional Upgrade (NFU) and 7CPC

Civilians

The government in the resolution notifying its acceptance of the 7CPC in July 2016 decides to maintain the status quo on Non Functional Upgrade (NFU) admissible to all Organised

Group 'A' Services, including defence civilians, even though there was no consensus in the commission for continuing with NFU. Two Members of the commission, in their dissent note, had said that "exclusion of Defense forces from NFU" by the UPA government was "unfair", and that Organised Group 'A' Services were guilty of recklessly de-linking "promotions from career progression", and that they are far less deserving than the officers of the Defence Forces. They recommended that NFU be abolished for all services.

Armed Forces

Chairperson of 7CPC in his recommendations in the 7CPC report recommended that a watered down NFU with long residencies "be extended to the officers of the Defence forces and CAPFs" to "ameliorate the difficulties faced by the officers owing to stagnation at various levels".The government however decided not to extend NFU to the armed forces. Manohar Parrikar, Defence Minister, had had the MOD in its submission to Chairman of the 7CPC , on 24 December 2014, opposed NFU for the armed forces on among other grounds that NFU is applicable only to organized Group 'A' Services.

Siachen Allowance

Siachen Allowance is an allowance given to officers and men of the armed forces posted in Siachen, a high altitude area, with extreme weather conditions. The 7CPC in its recommendation noted that "keeping in view the extremely difficult conditions in the area" and recognizing that the hardship and risk in Siachen is "maximum that any Government servant faces", created an extra 'cell' called Risk hardship Maximum (RH-Max) outside its "Risk and Hardship Matrix" of nine cells each representing low, medium and high levels of hardship and risk . Saichen allowance, 7CPC explained, is the ceiling for Risk and hardship allowance (RHA) because "no government employee faces more Risk/Hardship in his work than our Defence officers and jawans posted in Siachen Glacier. Hence, no RHA can have a value higher than this allowance" Saichen allowance is the highest in the hierarchy of allowances. The 7CPC recommended that the existing allowance of Rs 21000 pm for officers be increased to Rs 31,500, and for JCOs, NCOs and other ranks increased from 14, 000 pm to 21,000

The 7CPC however, anomalously recommended several allowances which have 'a higher value" than the Saichen allowance, even though these allowances are lower in the hierarchy of risk and hardship matrix. Among the allowances which is higher in value than Saichen allowance is the Special Duty Allowance (SDA), which is 30 percent of pay unlike the Saichen allowance which is a fixed amount. SDA is paid to defence civilians and police officers among other group A services posted in NE India, and Ladakh, including in Gawahati, Aizawl, Shillong, Kohima and Leh.The armed forces headquarters have said that "Siachen cannot be equal or lower to Guwahati when deciding on the "hardship" factor". They have recommended a new "hardship matrix" to decide allowances for the armed forces. They have recommended 65 percent of salary as Saichen allowance.

RESPONSE TO 7CPC

Congress (I)

Sashi Tharoor, former Under-Secretary-General of the United Nations, and Congress (I) spokesperson, Ajay Kumar, Member of Parliament, spokesperson of the All India Congress Committee (AICC) and Captain Amarinder Singh, former Chief Minister of Punjab, and current president of Congress Committee in Punjab, have called the 7CPC recommendation for the armed forces discriminatory.

Sashi Tharoor in March 2016, wrote, that the consequences of government policy of lowering "the status and compensation of our military personnel", will "inevitably be suffered by all". And that he failed to understand what could justify a policy that equates police officers [and defence civilians], designated as deputy inspector general (DIG) of the police, with Brigadiers, for pay and protocol.

Ajay Kumar, the former Indian Police Service (IPS) officer, said that some of the recommendations of the 7th Pay commission were "of the page", and that the existing promotion policy (for the IAS and IPS) was flawed, and indefensible, and even 'anti national'. The armed forces have got a bad deal mainly because, unlike the IAS and the IPS, the army has no 'association', and has very limited access to the political class compared to the phenomenal access of the police and the IAS, he said in nationally televised panel discussion. He disagreed with the policy which justifies the right of every IPS officer " to be DG of Police. It is "wrong for the country", he said.

Captain Amarinder Singh, former officer of the Sikh Regiment in September 2016 said that defence services should constitutionally be placed at higher level than the civil and police services. Lowering the status of the armed forces in the Warrant of Precedence, lowering pay scales in comparison with government cadres, and "bringing it below the police and now the central police organizations is a deliberate attempt to belittle the armed forces", he said. "Such repeated wrong steps on part of the government can only demoralize the defence forces", and that "India cannot afford a demoralized defence service with a belligerent China and mischievous Pakistan being next door neighbors".

BJP

PN Vijay, BJP spokesperson, in a nationally televised panel discussion on 7CPC and the armed forces said that the Indian Armed Forces perform far more complex task than that of police or the forest service, and that it is imperative for national security that the armed forces are treated at par with the other services. He however added that the final call on this will have to be taken by the government, more specifically the PM. He said 'joining the AF is not an easy decision'; we should not make the armed forces unattractive'. The BJP, he said, is sensitive to armed forces concerns. The time has come to have parity between the armed forces and the civil service; and defending the country has become very sophisticated and is far more complex than "handling a communal riot.

MANAGING ANOMALIES

To address the issue of 'anomalies' in the 7CPC report and recommendations, including those overlooked or not considered by the 'Committee of Empowered Secretaries' the BJP government constituted a committee on anomalies, and committee on anomalies in allowances. The armed forces are excluded from the anomalies committee, which has become cause of litigation.

Committee on anomalies

The mandate of the Committee on anomalies is to " a comprehensive view" of anomalies other than allowances. To consider the anomalies some 79 Departmental committees, under of respective Additional Secretary/ Joint Secretary, have been constituted. Each committee consists of Chairperson, a "Financial Adviser of the Ministry / Department", and a "Staff Side" member. These committees are expected to complete their work within one year, after which the "Government will approve or disapprove the recommendations of the Anomaly Committee". These committees will be supervised by Department of Personnel and Training.

Committee on anomalies in allowances

The committee on anomalies in allowances,consists of eight members. It is required to submit its report within four months. The allowances committee is to reconcile the anomalies in allowance recommended by the 7CPC including asymmetries between the Siachen and SDA allowances .

The anomalies committee consists of: [a] Ashok Lavasa,IAS, Finance Secretary, Chairman; [b] Rajiv Mehrishi, IAS, Home Secretary; [c] G.Mohan Kumar, IAS, Defence Secretary; [d] CK Mishra, IAS 1983, Bihar cadre, Secretary Health and Family Welfare; [e] B P Sharma, IAS 1981, Bihar cadre, Secretary, Personnel & Training; [f] Boyapati Venkat Sudhakar, Secretary, Department of Posts [g] A.K.Mittal, IRES, Chairman Railway Board. The armed forces are excluded from the anomalies committee, which has become cause of litigation.

Litigation

In response to a petition by Lt Colonel Preetpal Singh Grewal, a serving officer, the Punjab and Haryana High Court, Chandigarh, issued notice to the Ministry of Defence (MOD) to include representatives from the defence forces in the panel set up by the government on 12 September 2016 to examine anomalies in the 7CPC recommendations implemented by the government. The government had excluded armed forces representation from the 22 member committee headed by the secretary, Department of Personnel and Training (DoPT), a department under the PM. This is first time that a serving officer of the armed forces has appealed to a civil court on matter of policy affecting armed forces and civil-military relations.

Col Preetpal Singh Grewal, in his pleas to the High court, had submitted that: (a)'Anomalies Committees' constituted by government to look into the 7th CPC recommendations has excluded defence personnel and the defence headquarters from the anomalies redressal process; [b] MOD did not inform the defence services about the work of the committee ; [c] defence services learnt about the commencement of hearing from press reports; [d] Supreme Court has already held that defence personnel should not be treated in a "shabby manner" or deprived of rights that are available to other citizens; [e] in view of statutory bar on defence personnel forming associations' there should be suitable alternative participation mechanism that meets at regular intervals where issues related to defence personnel could be discussed and resolved; and [f] Standing Committee on Welfare of Ex-Servicemen, has not yet held a single meeting, despite Defence Minister Manohar Parrikar instructions that it hold meetings every three months.

Time line

27 December 2008

Manmohan Singh, Prime Minister, issues instructions that "In future, pay revision of the armed forces should be de-linked from that of civilians and separate board or commission should be set up for pay revision of the armed forces."

13 September 2013

India Today, cites a MOD letter leaked to it by a Joint Secretary in the MOD, titled 'Common VII Central Pay Commission' purportedly written by Air Chief Marshal NAK Browne, the Chairman Chief of Staff Committee (COSC), to AK Antony, Defence Minister.

According to the 'letter' the government is in favour of a separate pay commission for the armed forces, but the armed forces would rather be part of the 7CPC instead of having a separate pay commission.

Air Chief Marshal NAK Browne, according to the 'letter' opposed a separate pay commission for the armed Forces, because "a separate pay commission may not necessarily benefit the services as anomalies are invariably bound to arise in both cases"; and that the main cause dissatisfaction in the armed Forces is not a separate pay commission but the "non-resolution of anomalies or ex parte resolution of anomalies"

August 2014

Armed forces headquarters submit a joint services memorandum (JSM) to the 7CPC. The commission forwards the JSM to Ministry of Defence, Department of Ex-Servicemen Welfare, Controller General of Defence Accounts, Ministry of Home Affairs, Department of Personnel and Training, and others, "to draw .. upon the views of the key stakeholders within the government with regard to issues posed by the Defence Services".

24 December 2014

Manohar Parrikar, Defence Minister, on the advice of Defence Secretary R.K. Mathur, (25 May 2013 24- May 2015), informs Chairman of the 7CPC, that he does not favour Non Functional Upgrade (NFU) for the armed forces because Ajit

Seth, Cabinet Secretary, in 2011, had not made "any recommendations on the issue".

May 2015

Armed forces headquarters send an addendum to their joint services memorandum (JSM) dated August 2014.

Chairman 7CPC, forwards the addendum, to Ministry of Defence, Department of Ex-Servicemen Welfare, Controller General of Defence Accounts, Ministry of Home Affairs, Department of Personnel and Training, etc "to draw ... upon the views of the key stakeholders within the government with regard to issues posed by the Defence Services"

19 November 2015

A K Mathur, the chairperson of 7CPC, submits 7CPC report.;

7 December 2015

Lt-Gen Harwant Singh, former Deputy Chief of Army Staff, in an article in the *Hindustan Times* says the 7CPC report is "misleading, and factually inaccurate" and that it represents 'perennial bias and prejudice' of bureaucrats in the MOD.

He adds: "the sad state of soldiers seems to be of no one's concern: least of all the military's top brass".

15 December 2015

Prime Minister Narendra Modi, address Combined Commanders' Conference on board INS Vikramaditya. Defence Minister Manohar Parrikar says "analysing armed forces demands"

16 December 2015

Manohar Parrikar, Defence Minister, after laying wreath at Amar Jawan Jyoti at India Gate to mark Vijay Diwas (India), with the General Dalbir Singh, Chief of army Staff (COAS) Air Chief Marshal Arup Raha, Chief of Air Staff, and Admiral R.K. Dhowan, Chief of naval Staff, tells reporters "We are analyzing them (7th Pay Commission)" and that "by next week we will be able to see what can be done."

19 December 2015

General Dalbir Singh, Air Chief Marshal Arup Raha, and Admiral Robin Dhowan, send a joint memorandum to Defence Minister Manohar Parrikar. The memorandum highlights "several glaring inaccuracies and anomalies" in the 7CPC recommendations. Eight "critical issues and persisting core anomalies", are identified by armed forces headquarters. The anomalies, they say, will exacerbate disparities between the armed forces and the police and affect morale. To address these anomalies they recommend that these be examined by non partisan expert body or a parliamentary committee.

13 January 2016

Prime Minister Narendra Modi approves "Constitution of an Empowered Committee of Secretaries" under chairmanship of cabinet secretary to process the recommendations of the 7th Central Pay Commission with "regard to all relevant factors, in an expeditious detailed and holistic fashion".

27 January 2016

Finance Ministry issues instruction on the composition and work of the 7thCPC Empowered Committee. The 'Empowered Committee of Secretaries', has 13 members including the Cabinet Secretary, the chairperson. It is four times the size of the 7CPC, which had three members. Eight members are from the IAS, one from the Indian Police service, and one each from Department of Science and Technology, Railways, Audit and Account Service. The 'Empowered Committee of Secretaries' is mandated to screen the "recommendations of the Commission", and to take "in to account the views of concerned stake holders viz., Ministries, Departments, Staff Associations, and JCM". Defence civilians are represented by the defence secretary; the police, and secret police by former police officer official in the cabinet secretariat. There is no representation from the armed Forces in the empowered committee.

Members of the Empowered Committee include: [1] Pradeep Kumar Sinha, Cabinet Secretary, Chairman; [2] Ashok Lavasa,

IAS, Finance Secretary (Expenditure); [3] Rajiv Mehrishi, IAS, Ministry of Home (MHA); [4]G.Mohan Kumar, IAS, Defence Secretary, MOD; [5] CK Mishra, IAS (1983, Bihar cadre), Secretary, IAS, Secretary Health and Family Welfare;[6] B P Sharma, IAS (1981, Bihar cadre), Secretary, Personnel & Training; [7] Secretary Department of Pensions ; [8] Boyapati Venkat Sudhakar, Indian Postal Service, 1981 batch, Secretary, Department of Posts [9] A.K.Mittal, IRES, Chairman Railway Board [10] Secretary Security, Cabinet Secretariat; [11] Deputy Comptroller and Auditor General, IA&AS; [12] Secretary, Department of Science and Technology; [13] Dr. Hasmukh Adhia,IAS, (1981 batch Gujarat cadre), Secretary, Department of Revenue.

11 March 2016

Service chiefs brief "Empowered Committee of Secretaries

22 March 2016

Manohar Parrikar, Defence Minister, according to MOD media briefing, agrees that there are flaws in the 7CPC, including flaws identified by three service chiefs. The armed forces identified 37 anomalies in the 7CPC report of which eight are considered critical. Some of the anomalies flagged by the armed forces are: [a] false equation and comparison of mandates, risks, and conditions of service of defence forces with the police paramilitary forces, Central Reserve Police Forces (CRPF), Border Security Force (BSF), Indo-Tibetan Border Police (ITBP), Central Industrial Security Force (CISF) and the Sashastra Seema Bal (SSB) ; [b] higher allowance (30 percent of salary) for to police officers, IAS officers , and defence civilians, posted in places like Gauhati and other towns than to armed forces officers and soldiers posted in Siachen [31500-20,000].

Parrikar, according to media reports, has conveyed to the empowered committee headed by the Cabinet Secretary that armed forces should be kept above all other "fighting" arms of the government .

March 2016

18 former chiefs of the armed forces, including General VP Malik, write to Narendra Modi the Prime Minister, conveying their disquiet on the impact of the recommendations of the 7CPC on the Indian Armed Forces, according to a statement by General VP Malik in a TV interview broadcast by NDTV. The Prime Minister, Malik said, has taken the retired chiefs for granted.

29 March 2016.

Manohar, Parrikar, Defence Minister, tells *India Today*, that "I do not think they (7CPC recommendations) will remain. I do not consider them as finalities(sic). I have flagged them and will flag them properly at the right level".

21 April 2016

Sashi Tharoor, former Under-Secretary-General of the United Nations, and spokesperson of the Congress (I) , in an article averred that the present government is deliberately lowering "the status and compensation of our military personnel". It is hard, he wrote, to understand the reason for the government to equate police officers (and defence civilian officers) with 12 years of service, designated as deputy inspector general (DIG) of the police, with brigadiers, for pay and protocol. "What could possibly justify such a disparity?" He warned that the consequences of this policy "will inevitably be suffered by all". He faulted the 7CPC for recommending lesser disability pensions for a JCO and their equivalents in the air-force and the navy (Rs 12,000), while recommending receive a twice that amount (Rs 27,690) for equivalent civilian officials.

22 July 2016

In the wake of the criticism of the 7CPC recommendations on allowances, the government announces the constitution of a committee of seven bureaucrats for making "recommendations on allowances, other than Dearness Allowance". The seven members of the allowances committee are the same persons who were members of the "empowered Committee" of 13 secretaries. The committee is to submit its report within four months.

25 July 2016

The government issues resolution notifying acceptance of Commission's recommendations on "Pay Matrices and general recommendations on pay without any material alteration with the following exceptions in Defence Pay Matrix in order to maintain parity in pay with Central Armed Police Forces" : the Index of Rationalization of Level 13A (Brigadier) in Defence Pay Matrix revised upward from 2.57 to 2.67; (ii) additional three stages in Levels 12A (Lieutenant Colonel), three stages in Level 13 (Colonel) and two stages in Level 13A (Brigadier).

The resolution states that NonFunctional Upgradation (NFU), admissible to the Indian Police Service/Indian Forest Service and Organised Group 'A' Services, on which there was no consensus in the commission, is to remain. NFU not extended to the armed forces.

7 August 2016

General VP Malik, former Chief of Army Staff, in a panel discussion, says 7CPC recommendations are 'blatant discrimination' which has caused a strong sense of 'despondency' and feeling of 'resignation' in the armed forces. The decision by the government to accept the 7CPC recommendations to create two matrixes, one for the armed forces and another and another for the civil services, he says, will have several negative outcomes: it will give the civil services including the police services officers six increments in their first 13 years of service, in comparison to just one to the armed forces; the matrix and the resultant pay asymmetries will also aggravate the existing 'equations' which will adversely impact the already fraught civil-military relations. He said he was not convinced with the reasons given by the pay commission, that the armed forces task were any less complex than that of the police or the forest department which have been made at par with the IAS.

16 August 2016

Ministry of Defence (MOD) issues order to implement VII CPC. In addition to the Committee on allowances, the government sets up an *anomalies committee.* This committee under "Department of Personnel and Training" will "examine individual, post-specific and cadre-specific anomalies arising out of implementation of the recommendations of the commission".

The Committee will submit its report within a period of four months. Anomaly, the order says will include the following two cases :"(a) where the Official Side and the Staff Side are of the opinion that any recommendation is in contravention of the principle or the policy enunciated by the Seventh Central Pay Commission itself without the Commission assigning any reason; and (b) where the maximum of the Level in the Pay Matrix corresponding to the applicable Grade Pay in the Pay Band under the pre-revised structure, as notified vide CCS (RP) Rules 2016, is less than the amount an employee is entitled to be fixed at, as per the formula for fixation of pay contained in the said Rules".

The Anomaly Committees, which will be headed by Additional Secretary/ Joint Secretary, are expected to complete their work" within a period of one year from the date of its constitution, after which the government will approve or disapprove the recommendations of the Anomaly Committee. "Financial Adviser of the Ministry / Department shall be one of the Member of the Departmental Anomaly Committee". Unlike the civil departments which will have "Staff Side" integral to the consideration and resolution of anomalies, there will be no representation from the staff side from the armed forces

The anomalies committee has 79 nodal officers, including senior police bureaucrat Mahesh Kumar Singla (IPS, KL.1982) Special Secretary (Internal Security). The anomalies committee will have no armed forces representation. Issues affecting the armed forces will be dealt by MOD bureaucrat Ashok Dongre, JS(Esst/PG), 1987 batch IAS officer of Tamil Nadu cadre.

17 August 2016

Rajeev Chandrasekhar, Independent Rajya Sabha MP, member of Parliament's Standing Committee on Defence, commenting on the government to implement the flawed recommendations of the 7CPC in an interview said [a] "the issue is not about money but status of 'armed forces vis-à-vis other central government services', ... status in the hierarchy of service and command; [b] 'There is absolutely no doubt that IAS and IPS because of their proximity to the political powers have over successive pay commissions given themselves sweeter and sweeter deals and left the military out in the cold'.[c] This is because "the military has never been represented in these pay commissions"; [d] "If government has an explanation for this they should make it. If IAS or pay commission has a reason for this why are they not putting it out in public domain?"; [e] 46 anomalies from 6th Pay Commission and 36 from 7th Pay Commission remain unresolved and there is no legitimate answer given on why their requests are being turned down".

5 September 2016

Ministry of Defence (MOD) promulgates gazette notification on recommendations of 7CPC affecting armed forces notifies Implementation orders for 7CPC.

7 September 2016

Chiefs of Staff Committee (CoSC) meets and decides to withhold the implementation of 7CPC till 'anomalies' are resolved. A major anomaly is the lowering of level (rank), pay, and status of armed forces in comparison with defence civilians, police officers, and other civil servants. Parrikar, had assured the armed Forces as long back as March 2016 that "pay and allowances for the forces have to be paramount".

9 September 2016

Air Chief Marshal Arup Raha and Navy Chief Admiral Sunil Lamba, and General Dalbir Singh, write to the Prime Minister and Parrikar conveying their concern over "unresolved anomalies", and inform their formation and units that they were "constrained to request the government to hold implementation of 7th CPC award in abeyance in view of the anomalies which need to be resolved ". The signal to the units from service headquarters advised "In the interim, personnel are expected to display maturity and patience, and not be swayed by hearsay or speculative reports from any quarter." The MOD, insists "what all has been decided has to be implemented and legitimate grievances can be addressed later."

The MoD on the instructions of Parrikar, had informed the empowered committee headed by the Cabinet Secretary, in March 2016, that armed forces be kept above all other "fighting" arms of the government. It is not clear who other than the armed forces constitute 'fighting arms ' of the government. It is also not clear what action the MOD, or the Defence Minister took after the empowered committee failed to take note of the MOD advisory. Government decision to implement 7CPC escalates on the social media of armed forces personnel.

11 September 2016

Lt Gen Vijay Oberoi, former Vice Chief of Army Staff (COAS), calls decision by three Chiefs not to implement the MOD order "a very wise decision", done for the good of all ranks of their commands ", and that "The three Chiefs need to be congratulated for taking a principled stand against an unjust award, and doing so in such a mature and balanced manner". " I doff my hat to you Sirs" he wrote.

The news of the action by the Chiefs of Staff, Oberoi says "reflects two important points. Firstly, it shows the government in very bad light indeed, and is actually a slur on the ability of the political leadership not to understand the extent of angst in all ranks of our military. Secondly, it shows the resolve of the Chiefs to fight a highly unjust award, planned, written and implemented by the bureaucracy by taking a nod from the political leadership". He cautions the armed forces not to fall prey to government "blandishments of all types, like more committees; ministerial interventions and even subtle threats, not to mention the usual 'how much the nation needs you' kind of words! They must desist and not fall for such ploys."

Captain Amarinder Singh, former Chief Minister of Punjab and officer in the Sikh Regiment, author, and current president of Punjab Congress Committee, on 11 September, supports the stand of the three services chiefs. He says "There is blatant discrimination with defence services in pay scales, which is condemnable(sic)" and that "Just because our soldiers are disciplined and dedicated to serving the nation, should not mean that they be discriminated against". The issues raised by the Chiefs, he said , were not about money but about status, and that defence services should be constitutionally put higher than the civil and police services.

On 7CPC recommendation to pay soldiers and officers serving in Saichen a far lesser allowance than civil servants posted in Assam, he said, "I have been seriously suggesting to the defence minister that the bureaucrats, who have habitually been creating hurdles and hindrances in providing better pay to the defence personnel, should be made to serve in Siachen for at least a day. " "Nobody among the bureaucrats knows about the hostile conditions in which our soldiers are made to work and that is the reason there is such a bias against the defence forces," he said.

He urged the Defence Minister 'to stand by the soldiers and get the anomalies sorted'.

12 September 2016

Air Chief Marshal Arup Raha, and Admiral Sunil Lanba, Navy Chief, met the Defence Minister Manohar Parrikar. The Army Chief who was away in Goa, is not present for this meeting. Parrikar, according to media reports, tells Services chiefs that the armed forces' reservations on the 7th CPC recommendations would be "looked into if found genuine". The three chiefs of the armed forces had, it seems, asked to meet with the PM much before 6 September without success. Main issue appears to be the government decision to make the armed forces subordinate to the police, in 'levels' and pay, and status.

13 September 2016

The Tribune in an editorial calls the action by the armed forces, seeking delay in implementation of the Seventh Central Pay Commission (CPC) till the anomalies are addressed, an "unusual step", which does not "auger well for the country". "It is rather strange" the editorial notes that, " the government has not satisfactorily addressed the grievances of the Armed Forces", which were explained to "13-member Empowered Committee of Secretaries at which the three Service Chiefs were present" and on which three Service Chiefs submitted a joint representation to the Prime Minister. The issues raised by the armed forces, including with the PM, which remain unaddressed, include: common pay matrix for the military and civilian employees; and resolution of anomalies in allowances, and pensions. The editorial notes that the armed forces continue to remain troubled by the governments decision to exclude Service officer from consideration of the 7CPC even though the armed forces comprise almost 30 per cent of the Central employees, same as the Railways, which had representation in the committee as did "the Indian Police Service with a strength of less than 4,700. " It called on the government, "which is already on the back foot over not fully implementing One Rank, One Pension" to "accord top priority to satisfactorily resolve the issue". "Military personnel face the highest risk to their lives. Besides, the highest levels of proficiency, commitment and sense of sacrifice are demanded of them."

14 September 2016

Air Chief Marshal Arup Raha, Chairman Chief of Staff Committee (CoSC), in an official statement released by the MOD, said, "The 7th Pay Commission anomalies in respect of the Armed Forces were discussed with the Hon'ble Raksha Mantri in detail by the Service Chiefs and the members of the Armed Forces Pay Commission Cell. The Hon'ble Raksha Mantri is seized of all the issues and has assured to resolve them at the earliest. The Services are satisfied with the response."

15 September 2016

A large contingent of veterans led by Lt Gen S S Brar (retd), march to the office of Punjab Governor V P Singh Badnore and submit a memorandum, addressed to the President of India. The memorandum says "The community of veterans across the country fully endorses the stand taken by the Chiefs of Army, Navy and Air Force with regard to the recommendations of the seventh Central Pay Commission"

Capt Amarinder Singh joins the veterans march with Congress party members, including Ambika Soni, Asha Kumari and Harish Chaudhary. Later, Amrinder told reporters that the present situation was caused by "bias of the bureaucrats against the armed forces and the blind eye turned by the political parties running the government". "The brazen and blatant discrimination against the defence forces has been continuing ever since Independence." he said.

"We constitute the largest share of employees and pensioners and we have no say in the decisions made by a handful of bureaucrats which are imposed on the Armed Forces." Capt Amarinder said "the lowering of our status in the Warrant of Precedence, lowering our pay scales vis-à-vis other government cadres, bringing it below the police and now the central police organisations is a deliberate attempt to belittle the armed forces".

"Such repeated wrong steps on part of the government can only demoralize the defence forces", and that "India cannot afford a demoralized defence service with a belligerent Chinaand mischievous Pakistan being next door neighbours", he said.

21 September 2016

Justice PB Bajanthri, Punjab and Haryana High Court, Chandigarh, in response to a petition by Lt Colonel Preetpal Singh Grewal, a serving officer, issued notice to the Ministry of Defence (MOD) to include representatives from the defence forces in the panel set up by the government on 12 September 2016 to examine anomalies in the 7CPC recommendations implemented by the government. The high court ordered that the anomalies committee shall take into account the views on anomalies affecting defence personnel.

18 September 2016

Four Pakistan trained terrorists infiltrate across the line of actual control (LOC) at night from bases in Pakistan Occupied Kashmir(POK) and attack army brigade headquarters in Uriand kill 18 soldiers of the Dogra and Bihar regiments. The terrorist attack provokes nation wide outrage and exposes grave security and intelligence failure, at the operational, and national level.

12 October 2016

Defence Minister Manohar Parrikar said, "Yes, there are some anomalies in the 7th pay commission", and "I can assure the people of the country and our armed forces that I have personally taken up the matter with the Prime Minister". The disability pension, he said, " is just a draft now", he said. "No final order has been issued as yet, only a draft resolution has been put up on the website. We will examine and try to address all that can be addressed, and forward the same to the anomalies committee for their opinion." The resolution on the MOD website that the minister referred to, however, does not say it is a draft.

13 October 2016

The MOD in response to growing public criticism of the government's decision to implement a more favourable disability pension scheme called 'percentage based system', than the one implemented for the armed forces, called slab based system, issued a press release informing that the representation of the Service Headquarters seeking a disability pension scheme at par with the civilians, has been referred to "the Anomaly Committee of 7th CPC for consideration".

18 October 2016

Defence Minister Manohar Parrikar authorizes G.Mohan Kumar, IAS, Defence Secretary to issue of memo (No A/24577/ CAO/CP Cell) tabulating rank equivalence between armed forces officers and select officers of the Armed Forces Headquarter Civil Service, a Group B service responsible for house keeping and secretarial functions in armed forces headquarters, and inter-service organizations. The memo is signed by V Anandarajan, Chief administrative Officer (CAO), Ministry Of Defence (MOD), under G.Mohan Kumar, IAS, Defence Secretary. Anandarajan, Joint Secretary, is an officer belonging to the Indian Revenue Service, income tax branch, of 1988 batch, on deputation with MOD. The memo is addressed to Staff Duties (SD) Directorate, Army headquarters, and equivalent directorates in the Air-force and Navy among others. In its last paragraph, the memo says it has the approval of the Raksha Mantri (Defence Minister Mohan Parrikar).

Major generals, in the memo, are equated with AFHQ CS officers with 16 years service as officers in group A, called Principal directors; Brigadiers with 24 years service are equated with officers with 13 years service, called Directors; Colonels with 18 years service officers with 9 years service at group A level, called Joint Directors. Lt colonels, though not mentioned in the memo, will, by implication, be equal to officers with 4 years service. Majors, captains, and lieutenant by implication will be equal to group B, and clerical level posts.

In justification of memo cites' administrative orders' issued in 2003, 2005, and 2008. Navdeep Singh, an expert on armed forces pay, whom the MOD has previously consulted, says the letter are 'irrelevant'. The letter cited by The tabulation affect the status of tens of thousands of armed forces officers, specifically officers holding the ranks from lieutenant to major general. The tabulation which is opposed by armed forces headquarters, was issued 'unilaterally' and without prior consultation with Chiefs of staff, or the armed Forces headquarters.

The rank equivalence tabulation, and long opposed by the armed forces, contradicts the rank equivalence and levels in resolution dated 7 September 2016 promulgated in the Gazette. For example, lieutenant-colonel and its equivalents in the Air Force (wing commander) and Navy (commander), level 12 A,

13 years service, according to the gazette, will become inferior in rank and status to officers of AFHQ CS , 'level 12', called joint directors (civil service time scale rank with 9 years of services) This would also undermine MOD letter issued in 2009 which placed lieutenant-colonels in Pay Band (PB) 4 with a grade pay of Rs 8000, in comparison with joint Directors who were in PB 3, with pay grade of 7600.

24 October 2016

Hindustan Times *reported that the memo on rank equivalence between armed forces officers and army headquarter civil service dated 18 October authorized by Defence Minister Manohar Parrikar, has down graded armed forces ranks, and those of majors to the level of Group B section officers, and captains to the level of assistants, a group B non gazetted ministerial post in the AFHQCS, according to senior serving armed forces officer. The newspaper says it has "stoked controversy" and become a cause of growing resentment among armed forces officers, "at a time when the armed forces and the ministry have divergent views on the 7th Pay Commission report and the OROP".*

"We have been stabbed in the back", a senior officer told the *Hindustan Times*. Serving officer in the army headquarters, complained that according to equation in the memo (No A/24577/CAO/CP) "a captain is equivalent to a civilian Group B section officer. This isn't mischief, but mischief-plus by bureaucrats.'" They alleged that memo is "an attempt to reverse clearly established protocols established by successive pay panel reports and court rulings"; is against the spirit of recommendations made by a Committee headed by Pranab Mukherjee after the 6th Pay Commission report; and that down gradation of armed forces ranks will widen the "civil-military rift" and affect morale.

25 October 2016

Defence Minister Manohar Parrikar on the sidelines of a naval commanders' conference told reporters that discrepancy in the rank equivalence caused by the MOD memo of 18 October

2016 would be corrected in a week and that "any disparity in rank structure of its officers with those in civil administration will be removed ". He would, he said, "scrutinize the orders to detect anomalies that threaten to widen the civil-military divide ". Retired Brigadier Gurmeet Kanwal, commenting on the 18 October 2016 memo said "It is an incontrovertible fact that the status of armed forces has been progressively diluted over last few years. This creates bad blood between the civilian and military services". Brigadier Pradeep Sharma (retired) said "Rank equation has gone wonky. It's high time the government set things right and restore the status of defence officers". After the uproar in the armed forces, the MOD said the "entire issue", which was "a complicated one lingering for quite some time", would be re-examined by a committee with the aim to "resolve it once and for all".

27 October 2016

The MOD, two days after Monohar Parrikar, had said "there has been no downgrading or any change in the existing equivalence of the service ranks whatsoever", issue a press release saying that "there has been no down-gradation or any change in the existing equivalence of the Service ranks whatsoever". In the defence of the rank-equivalence the press release says "rank equivalence, is only for matters of assigning duties and functional responsibilities" and has no bearing "on civilian employees outside these offices of the Service HQrs," and that "there is no change in the rank structure or the status of the Armed Forces personnel". In justification the MOD press release says it had issued similar administrative memos in 1991 and 92, during the tenure of NN Vohra(1990–93) as defence secretary, and memos issued by Yogendra Narain in 2000, and Ajai Vikram Singh in 2004, and in 2005, when Anthony from Congress I was the defence minister. These administrative memo have been said to be 'irrelevant' to issues of rank equivalence. The press release ignores the fact that none of these memo met with armed forces approval, and that issues relating rank equivalence and status remain unresolved anomalies frequently flagged by the Chiefs of staff and retired

Chiefs of the armed forces. Armed forces officer respond to MOD denials with skepticism. Brigadier Gurmeet Kanwal said, " Such turf battle are not good for military morale". Lt General HS Panag, former Army commander Northern Command said, " these are battles that have to be fought by the three service chiefs". Brigadier Gurmeet Kanwal (Retd) tweeted, "PM exhorts nation to send Diwali 'sandesh' to soldiers. B'crats reduce disability pension n lower status vis-a-vis civilians. Happy Diwali!." It is view that is widespread in the armed forces.

Senior serving officer commenting on the issues raided by memo of 18 October 2016, told Quint, on conditions of anonymity, that "There can be no more than one parameter for 'equivalence'. How can there be separate equivalence for 'Functionality', 'Warrant of Precedence'; and based on 'Pay Scales/ Grade Pay' ? Accepting such multiple regimes is a deliberate act of causing confusion and subverting status as per convenience". The officer added that "it was important to scrutinise the mandate of AFHQ cadre" which was "meant to provide only secretarial support and had no executive authority or powers, they said comparing them to armed forces officers who have executive powers, exercise command over men in peace and war, and also have substantial judicial powers, is insane — like comparing "chalk and cheese".

22 November 2016

Subhash Bhamre, Minister of State for Defence, in a written reply to question by Neeraj Shekhar a Rajya Sabha member informed that the BJP government had accepted the slab based system for determining disability pension for the armed forces, and different system, called 'percentage basis' for the civilians. 100 percent disability for the armed forces according to the minister was: officers (level 10- 18) Rs 27000 per-month; junior commissioned officers (JCOs) (level 6-9) 17000, and soldiers and NCOs Rs 12000. This recommendation was accepted by the BJP government, following 7CPC recommendation, and resolution issued on 30 September 2016. The disparities between the two systems the minister acknowledged has caused a "anomalous situation", and was referred to the "Anomaly Committee", following criticism that the scheme approved for the armed forces was discriminatory.

25 November 2016

Subhash Bhamre, Minister of State for Defence, in a written reply to a question by Sultan Ahmed, prompted by public concern about issue of asymmetries in the pay and rank between the armed forces and civilians, including police, informed the Lok Sabha, that 7th Central Pay Commission (CPC) had adopted the same the "principles and philosophy" it had "adopted in devising the Pay Matrix for civilian employees". And to address the issue of parity, "The Government accepted the Commission's recommendations on Minimum Pay, Fitment Factor, Index of Rationalization, Pay Matrices and general recommendations on pay with certain exceptions in Defence Pay Matrix, namely, (i)revision of Index of Rationalization of Level 13A (Brigadier) from 2.57 to 2.67; and (ii)addition of three stages in Level 12A (Lt Colonel), three stages in Level 13 (Colonel), and two stages in Level 13A (Brigadier)". The minister however, did not address, the related issue of the asymmetries in the ranks and levels, and of historical parities between the armed forces and police and defence civilians, which has not been addressed by the 7CPC or the government. The press release added that "As and when issues regarding anomalies in the pay of defence personnel are brought to notice, the same are examined by the Government, on case to case basis".

29 November 2016

Subhash Bhamre Minister of State for Defence in a written reply to a question by Rajeev Chandrasekhar about the controversial 18 October 2016 memo containing rank equivalence tabulation, in the Rajya Sabha said that the "Government has only reiterated the existing functional equivalence being followed at Service Headquarters for matters of assigning duties and responsibilities with respect to Armed Forces Headquarters Civil Service (AFHQ CS) officers posted at Service Headquarters". When asked in the Rajya sabha, whether the MOD was considering "correcting the discrepancies that have arisen as a result of this disturbance of rank equations", replied the question "does not arise". He did not comment on the fact that service headquarters are not in agreement with the imposed equivalence or that service chiefs have highlighted their dismay over the rank and level comparisons between armed forces officers and group A civil services.

2 December 2016

Voice of Ex-Serviceman an NGO representing personnel below officer rank (PBOR) moves petition in the Delhi High Court alleging that PBOR were discriminated against by the Seventh Pay Commission (7CPC). The plea seeks same rate of military service pay (MSP) for PBORs as awarded to officers; equal disability pension for all armed forces personnel irrespective of their rank; service up to 60 years service; and time bound promotions for PBORs; three Assured Career Progressions; and participation in policy formulation on pay and allowances.

9

Pay Commission System

Pay Commission is set up by Government of India, and gives its recommendations regarding changes in salary structure of its employees. Since India's Independence, seven pay commissions have been set up on a regular basis to review and make recommendations on the work and pay structure of all civil and military divisions of the Government of India. Headquartered in Delhi, the Commission is given 18 months from date of its constitution to make its recommendations.

First Pay Commission

The first pay commission was established on January, 1946 and it submitted its report in May, 1947 to the interim government of India. It was under the chairmanship of Srinivasa Varadachariar. The mandate of 1st (nine members) was to examining and recommending emolument structure of Civilian employees.

Post War Pay Committee for the armed Forces

Armed forces emoluments structure was determined not by the 1st Central Pay Commission(CPC) but by a Departmental Committee which had service members. The task of this committee was to make recommendations "in the structure of emoluments and benefits of service personnel in the light of the recommendations made by the pay commission for civilian employees".The First Pay Committee, set up after the 1st pay Commission, was called "The Post War Pay Committee for the armed Forces". The New Pay Code effective from 1 July 1947 was based on the recommendations of this Committee. The pensionary benefits were examined by separate committee called " Armed Forces Pension Revision Committee (1949–50)".

Second Pay Commission

The second pay commission was set up in August 1957, 10 years after independence and it gave its report after two years. The recommendations of the second pay commission had a financial impact of 39.6 crore.

The chairman of the second pay commission was Jagannath Das. The second pay commission reiterated the principle on which the salaries have to be determined. It stated that the pay structure and the working conditions of the government employee should be crafted in a way so as to ensure efficient functioning of the system by recruiting persons with a minimum qualification.

Raghuramiah Committee

The Departmental Pay Committee, set up after the 2nd pay Commission, was called, the Raghuramiah Committee(1960), which had service representatives. It examined armed forces emoluments and made recommendations .

Third Pay Commission

The third pay commission set up in April 1970 gave its report in March 1973 i.e. it took almost 3 years to submit the report, and created proposals that cost the government 144 crore. The chairman was Raghubir Dayal. The third pay commission (3CPC) added three very important concepts of inclusiveness, comprehensibility, and adequacy for pay structure to be sound in nature. The third pay commission went beyond the idea of minimum subsistence that was adopted by the first pay commission. The commission report says that the true test which the government should adopt is to know whether the services are attractive and it retains the people it needs and if these persons are satisfied by that they are getting paid.

Third Pay Commission and the Armed forces

The 3CPC was the first Pay Commission without military member. Its "Terms of Reference" however included "examination of the structure of emoluments, the retirement benefits and terms and conditions of the Defence Forces personnel". The Commission, established 'relativity' of Defence Forces officers and Indian Police Service(IPS) officers, whose wages till for similar years of service were less than that of Armed Forces officers with similar years of service, noted that "the relativity" with IPS was "only a working method of devising scales of pay for the service officers which did not mean that the functional role of the two services were similar". The Commission, ambiguously "qualified this statement by mentioning that the job profile of IPS officers was the closest civilian analogue vis-à-vis infantry officers and that 'a working relationship did exist between the two organizations'". While establishing some sort of parity, and relativity with IPS, the Commission, without an explanation, noted "that the pay structure of the Indian Administrative Service with its long pay scales was particularly unsuitable for service officers", even though the pay structures of armed forces and Indian Civil Service had been, as a matter of established practice, at par.

It controversially recommended that military pension be de-linked from military service conditions to conform to civil pensions. On the basis of the 3 CPC recommendations Indira Gandhi, Prime Minister in the Indian National Congress(INC) government, took an "ex-parte" decision and terminated One Rank, One Pension (OROP), the basis of military pensions till then.

In 1973, the Government, implemented the following changes in pension and service conditions of the Armed Forces: [1] Increased the pension of civilians, who retired at 58, by 20 percent, from 30 to 50 percent; [2] reduced the pension of soldier, Non Commissioned Officers (NCOs), and Junior commissioned Officers (JCOs), by 20 percent, from 70 to 50 percent of basic pay, with the caveat that for full pension the minimum service was 33 years; [3] an exception was made for the armed forces, the mandatory service for full pension was reduced to 25 year. But as soldiers in 1973 retired after 15 years service, at the age of 33-36, they got less than 30 percent of the pay as pension; [4] soldiers pension was thus decreased not by 20 percent but 40 percent from 70 to 30 percent. The government in addition to down grading military pensions down graded the status of soldier by equating "infantry soldier with less than three years' service" with a "semi-skilled/unskilled labour". These decisions were based on the recommendation, and endorsement of K B Lall, Defence Secretary. The decision was announced two months after Field Marshal Sam Manekshaw, the victor of the 1971 war, retired from service. The reason for depressing the armed Forces pensions given by the government was to ensure 'equivalence' of Armed Forces pensions with civilians.

The reduction in armed Forces pension, and down grading its status immediately following the decisive Bangladesh war, was, not unexpectedly, unpopular with the armed Forces, and has since become a cause of persistent grievance, and distrust. Conflating civil and military pensions, and reduction of Armed forces Pension, by the Indira Gandhi Government, has been invoked to rally Armed Forces Veterans, most recently during the OROP protests.

Fourth Pay Commission

Constituted in June 1983, its report was given in three phases within four years and the financial burden to the government was 1282 crore. This commission has been set up on dated 18.3.1987, Gazette of India (Extra ordinary) Notification No 91 dated 18.3.1987, The chairman of fourth pay commission was P N Singhal.

Fourth Pay Commission and the Armed forces

Indian National Congress (I) Government, headed by Rajiv Gandhi, in the wake of the 4th CPC to implemented concept of 'Rank Pay' for armed forces officer. Rank Pay affected all officers ranks from second lieutenant to brigadier in the army, and equivalent ranks in the Indian Air Force and the Indian Navy. The 'rank pay', which varied from 200 to 1200, was not an additional pay, but amount deducted from their pay grade. This ended long established err Military Indian Police service equations. Police Officers, and officers from other AIS officers, with 14 years of service, who were formerly in the same pay grade as majors, with 14 years service, were equated to Brigadiers, on the basis of the new pay grades. Maj General Satbir Singh an expert on Police- military rank structures and pay grades, called rank pay, "rarest of rare fraud, perjury and Injustice to the defence forces".

He explained, "How could it be allowed that the first military rank of Second Lieutenant along with two promotional ranks of Lieutenant and Captain were all clubbed with the first civilian rank?". Similarly at the level of major "rank pay' had the effect of promoting civilian pay grades equal to major till the 3 CPC, to that of Colonels." The rank pay became an issue of considerable resentment in the armed forces, and cause of general distrust of the pay commissions, and the Congress I Government. Eventually, Maj AK Dhanapalan, a retired major, litigates 'rank Pay'. After protracted legal struggle high court, despite many appeals, in a landmark decision declares the 'rank pay' concept illegal. In its judgment the SC notes that the 'rank pay' was wrongly deducted from basic pay and ordered re-fixation of pay "with effect from" and not "as on" 1 January 1986.

Fifth Pay Commission

The notification for setting up the Fifth CPC was issued on 9 April 1994, but started functioning only on 2 May 1994, with the assumption of charge by the Member Secretary.The chairman of fifth pay commission was Justice S. Ratnavel Pandian. the members were: Suresh Tendulkar, Professor Delhi school of Economics; and M.K Kaw, Indian Administrative Service. In comparison, First CPC had nine members including military members, the second had six members including a military member, the 3 CPC and 4 CPC had five, but no military member. The fifth had three members, but no military member.The first had no member secretary, just a secretary. After the 1 CPC all pay commissions have had a member secretary, and invariably from the IAS.

The 5 CPC report, a massive tome, had nine part in 172 chapters. It took three years with a sanctioned staff 107, which ballooned to 141, to prepare the report.By way of comparison, 4 CPC took 209 bureaucrat Accounts Service, Indian Revenue Service, Indian Economic Service, Central Secretariat Service, Border Security Force, Geological Survey of India, Central Public Works Department and National Informatics Centre.It cost 17,000 crore.

Part VI of report dealt with pensions and retirement benefits for civilian; Part VII dealt with pay scales and allowances of Armed Forces personnel. Part IX is the concluding part of the Report.

Financial Impact of Fifth pay commission

With the implementation of the Fifth Pay commission a huge burden was taken up by the central government. It declared hike in salary of about 3.3 million central government employees. Further, it also insisted on pay revision at the state government level. The Fifth pay commission disturbed the financial situation of both the Central and the State Governments and led to a hue and cry after its implementation. The Central government's wage bill before the implementation of the commission's recommendations was 218.85 billion in 1996-1997 which also included pension dues, and by 1999 it shot up by about 99% and the burden on the exchequer was about to 43,568 crore in 1999-2000. With regard to the state government the bill went up by 74%. The state governments which paid about Rs 515.48 billion in 1997 as salaries, had to pay Rs 898.13 billion in 1999 as salaries. This clearly indicates the burden on the state and the central government. Many economists say that about 90% of the revenue of the state went in as salaries. 13 states of India were not in a position to pay salaries to its employees due to the hike and hence the central government's help was sought.

Other recommendations

One of its recommendations was to slash government workforce by about 30%. It also recommended to reduce the number of pay scale from 51 to 34 and to not recruit to about 3,50,000 vacant position in the government. None of these recommendations were implemented.

Criticisms by World Bank

The World Bank criticized the Fifth Pay Commission, stating that the Fifth Pay Commission is the 'single largest adverse shock' to the public finance of the nation. It also said that the number of employees of the government was 'not unduly' large, but there was a 'pronounced imbalance' in the skills. It noted that about 93% of the employees were of 3rd or 4th grade.

Fifth Pay Commission and the Armed forces

Terms of Reference

The 4CPC, for unknown reasons, had no separate TORs for the Armed Forces. The 5 CPC, however, for the first time was asked to examine the terms and conditions of the Armed Forces, and make suggestions for what is "considered desirable and feasible".

Thus, the pay commission noted ambiguously that "even their recommendations with regard to changes in the structure of emoluments including death cum gratuity in respect of Armed Forces Personnel had to be made with due regard to the terms and conditions of their service"

Lateral Transfer

The 5 CPC, in its report submitted in January 1997, recommended increase in posts for Armed Forces personnel in Group C and D in Central Armed Police Forces (CAPFs) from 10 to 25percent. For Short Service Commissioned Officers, on completion of their military service, 5 CPC recommended earmarking 25 percent officer's post in the CAPFs. These recommendationsby the pay Commission were intended to reduce the defence pension bill; save on training and recruitment costs; provide trained manpower to government departments; and provide soldiers a second career after their term of military engagement.

These recommendations of the Pay Commission were, however, mostly ignored by the Janata Dal (United Front), and BJP Government of Atal Bihari Vajpayee that followed. Mulayam Singh Yadav, Defence Minister (1 June 1996 – 19 March 1998), Indrajit Gupta (Communist Party of India-United Front), Home Minister (29 June 1996 – 19 March 1998), and L K Advani (BJP), Home Minister (19 March 1998 – 22 May 2004) did little to implement these recommendations. The problem festered, and the pension bill ballooned.

SIXTH PAY COMMISSION

In July 2006, the Cabinet approved setting up of the sixth pay commission. This commission has been set up under Justice B.N.Srikrishna with a timeframe of 18 months. The cost of hikes in salaries is anticipated to be about 20,000 crore for a total of 5.5 million government employees as per media speculation on the 6th Pay Commission, the report of which is expected to be handed over in late March/early April 2008. The employees had threatened to go on a nationwide strike if the government failed to hike their salaries. Reasons for the demand of hikes include rising inflation and rising pay in the private sector due to the forces of Globalization. The Class 1 officers in India are grossly underpaid with an IAS officer with 25 years of work experience earning just Rs.55,000 as his take home pay. Pay arrears are due from January 2006 till September 2008. Almost all the Government employees received 40% of the pay arrears in 2008 and balance 60% arrears (as promised by Government) has also been credited in Government employees account in 2009. The Sixth Pay Commission mainly focused on removing ambiguity in respect of various pay scales and mainly focused on reducing number of pay scales and bring the idea of pay bands. It recommended for removal of Group-D cadre.

SEVENTH PAY COMMISSION

The Government of India has initiated the process to constitute the 7th Central Pay Commission along with finalisation of its Terms of Reference, the composition and the possible timeframe for submission of its Report. On 25 September 2013 then Finance Minister P Chidambaram announced that Prime Minister Manmohan Singh has approved the constitution of the 7th Pay Commission. Its recommendations are likely to be implemented with effect from 1 January 2016. Justice A.K Mathur will be heading the Seventh Pay Commission, announcement of which was done on 4 February 2014. On 29 June 2016, Government accepted the recommendation of 7th Pay Commission Report with meager increase in salary of 14% after six month of intense evaluation and successive discussion.

Composition

In May 2014, a group of retired government officials, challenged the inclusion of a senior IAS officer in the three member 7th Pay Commission, in the Delhi High Court. They alleged that this would lead an inherent bias in the commission's recommendations towards IAS officers.

On 9 November 2017, the government raised the maximum amount that a central government employee can borrow from the government to Rs 25 lakh for new construction/purchase of new house/flat

Earlier this limit was only Rs 7.50 lakh. This move is going to benefit about 50 lakh central government employees all over India.

The employee can borrow up to 34 months of the basic pay to a maximum of Rs 25 lakh, or cost of the house/flat, or the amount according to repaying capacity, whichever is the least.

If both spouses are central government employees, they can take Housing Building Advance (HBA) either jointly, or separately. Also, the rate of Interest on HBA will be only 8.50% at simple interest.

SC constitute a new Pay commission for trial court judges

The chief justice and other supreme court and high court judges got a threefold salary hike in the sixth pay commission however the trial court judges were paid low and a bench comprising Chief Justice K G Balakrishnan and Justices P Sathasivam and J M Panchal constituted a new pay commission for the trial court judges headed by retired Madras High Court judge, Justice E Padmanabhan for recommendation of revision of about 14000 trial court judges.

This order from the SC came because of a petition filed by All India Judges Association, which stated that the first judicial commission which was headed by Justice Jagannatha Shetty said that there should be an upward revision of salaries of lower court judges in proportion to the hike to the judges of high court and Supreme Court. It also sought direction from the court to the centre for setting up a committee "forthwith appoint a committee of one or more persons to look into the matter" relating the salary of officers in the lower judiciary.

On 19 November 2015, the 7th Central Pay Commission recommended 23.55% hike in pay and allowances which will be implemented from 1 January 2016. The full report is available on the website of Ministry of Finance, Government of India

The Union Cabinet approves 7th Pay panel recommendations on 29 June 2016. The recommendations will be effected from 1 January 2016 with arrears to be paid in the financial year 2016-17 itself unlike previously, when arrears were paid in the following financial year. Also this time, employees will had to wait only 6 months for the CPC's recommendations to be implemented as compared to 19 months for the 5th CPC and 32 months for the 6th except for autonomous organizations like CSIR, ICAR, ICMR etc. under various ministries.

Seventh Pay Commission and the Armed forces

The recommendation of the 7CPC affecting the armed forces are a cause of profound unease and resentment in the Armed Forces, especially, 7CPC recommendation on separate 'Pay Matrices', and allowance system for the armed forces and defence civilians, and police, and other civil servants. While 7CPC provides for mandated timescale promotions to from Defence civilians from audit and account services, police, and other officers at regular intervals of 4, 9, 13, 14, and 16 years of service; it does not do so armed forces officers. The orders implemented by the government on the basis of 7 CPC recommendation, despite armed forces advise and concerns, make time scale police officers and defence civilians, with lesser service and experience, senior to armed forces officers, and potentially in command of armed forces officers of equal or more seniority. For instance, Wing Commanders of the Air Force, commander of the navy, and Lt colonel of the army, with 13 years of service, according to MOD implementation tables, will be subordinate in 'level', rank, pay scale, and organizational hierarchy than police officers, auditors, accountants, with equal or even lesser service.MOD implementation order has created an invidious situation for armed forces officers when serving alongside defence civilians and police officer. According to the MOD orders a police officer and Defence Accounts officer with 14 years service will be at higher level than the naval officer in command of INS Vikramaditya, India's Aircraft carrier, a highly selective rank and appointment, with some 20 years of service.

In March 2016, eighteen former heads of the Armed forces, including General Ved Prakash Malik, former Chief of Army Staff, and Admiral Arun Prakash, former Chief of naval staff, send a joint letter to Narendra Modi, the Prime Minister conveying their distress and alarm on the flawed approach and contentious recommendations of the 7CPC. The representations by former Chiefs, and the Chiefs of Staff, to the MOD, the PM, other bureaucratic bodies reviewing the 7CPC recommendations, are in vain. On 25 July 2016, without addressing or taking into account the key concerns of the armed forces, the Government issued instructions implementing 7CPC's "general recommendations on pay without any material alteration" including separate "Pay Matrices" (for civilians) and the armed forces.

FAMILY PENSION

The families of the Armed Forces personnel are granted family pension on the death of a Service personnel/pensioner. Family pensions are of three kinds, namely, Liberalised Family Pension, Special Family Pension and Ordinary Family Pension. The eligibility and conditions under which these pensions are granted are mentioned below:

a. Liberalised familv Pension (LFP)

b. Eligibility: The families of the Armed Forces personnel killed in war or war like operations, counter insurgency operations or in an encounter with or in incident involving armed hostiles, terrorists/ extremists, anti-social elements etc, are entitled to the Liberalised Family Pension. Presently, it is admissible as under:-

c. Widow: Liberalised Family Pension equal to the reckonable emoluments last drawn by the deceased is payable to the widow in the case of officers and to the nominated heir in the case of JCOs/ORs until death or disqualification. Wef 1.1.96 in case of remarriage of the widow, full liberalised family pension continues to be admissible to her if she continues to support the children or has no children. If she does not support children after remarriage, ordinary family pension at 30% to widow and special family pension at 60% to eligible children are admissible.

d. Children: If the personnel is not survived by widow but is survived by child/children only, all children together are eligible to liberalised family pension at the rate equal to 60% of reckonable emoluments last drawn by the deceased. LFP is paid to the senior most eligible child till he/she attains the age of 25 years or upto the date of his/her marriage whichever is earlier and thereafter the LFP is passed on to the next eligible child w.e.f. 1.1.96, in the case of eligible child is physically or mentally handicapped and unable to earn livelihood, LFP is admissible for life. Widowed/divorced daughters upto the age of 25 years or marriage whichever is earlier has been included in the definition of family for the purpose of Liberalised Family Pension.

e. Parents: Where an officer dies as a bachelor or as a widower without children, dependent pension is admissible to parents without reference to their pecuniary circumstances at the rate of 75% of the LFP for both parents and @of 60% for a single parent.

f. Special Family Pension (SFP)

   i. Eligibility: Admissible in case of death of a personnel on account of causes attributable to or aggravated by military service

   ii. Special Family Pension is admissible at the uniform rate of 60% of reckonable emoluments last drawn by the deceased, subject to a minimum of Rs. 2,550/ - irrespective whether widow has children or not (in cases arising on or after 1.1.96). W.e.f. 1.1.96, in case the eligible child is physically or mentally handicapped and unable to earn livelihood, SFP is admissible for life. Widowed/divorced daughters upto the age of 25 years or marriage whichever is earlier has been included in the definition of family for the purpose of Special Family Pension.

   iii. Families of SSCOs and ECOs who die under circumstances attributable to military service shall also be entitled to special family pension.

Ordinary Family Pension (OFP)

i. Eligibility: Families of personnel who die during service for causes neither attributable to nor aggravated by service, or after retirement with pension, are eligible to ordinary family pension.

ii. Rate of Pension: With effect from 1.1.96 OFP is admissible at a uniform rate of 30% of reckonable emoluments last drawn subject to a maximum of 30% of the highest pay applicable to Armed Forces Personnel. The minimum amount of Family Pension is Rs.1275/- per month.

iii. Past family pensioners are entitled to get at least 30% of the minimum of the revised pay scale introduced w.e.f. 1.1.96 for the rank in the case of Officers and rank and group in the case of JCOs/ORs.

iv. If the deceased personnel had rendered 7 years or more service, the family is given OFP at the double the rate for the first 7 years or upto the time when the deceased would have reached the age of 67 years whichever is earlier. The amount of enhanced family pension is not to exceed 50% of the emoluments or the Retiring pension if the death takes place after retirement but before 67 years of age.

v. With effect from 1.1.98, OFP is admissible also to (i) parents who were wholly dependant on the Armed Forces personnel provided the deceased had left behind neither a widow nor a child and (ii) widowed/divorced daughter till she attains the age of 25 years or up to the date of her re-marriage whichever is earlier. The income criteria is that their earning should not be more than Rs.2550/- per month. This benefit is admissible w.e.f. 1.1.98 also in cases where death of Armed Forces personnel occurred prior to 1.1.96.

The Fifth Central Pay Commission recommended that total parity may be brought between the pre 1.1.86 and post 1.1.86 retirees, by notional fixation of pay of pre 1.1.1986 retires in the post. 1.1.86 scales of pay and refixing of pension of all pre 1.1.1986 retirees on basis of their notional fixation of pay. This recommendation of Fifth Central Pay Commission has been implemented by the Government and total parity has been achieved between pre 1.1.1986 retirees and those, who retired between 1.1.1986 and 31.12.1995.

The Government have also accepted the concept of 'Modified Parity' which stipulates that the consolidated pension shall not be less than 50% of the minimum of the new pay scale, as revised by Government, based on Fifth Central Pay Commission. This will be with reference to the post held by the pensioner, at the time of retirement.

Revision of Disability Pension/Special Family Pension/ Liberalised Family Pension/War Injury Pension etc. in respect of Pre-1996 Armed Forces Pensioners

The 5th Central Pay Commission though recommended the consolidation and revision of Ordinary Family pension in respect of past family pensioners, it is silent about the revision of Special/Liberalised Family Pension. The issue of revision of Disability Pension/War Injury Pension/Special Family Pension/ Liberalised Family Pension etc. in respect of pre- 1.1.96 Armed Forces Pensioners was considered in consultation with Deptt. of Pension and Pensioners Welfare and Ministry of Finance and orders were issued by Ministry of Defence for revision of Disability Pension/Special Family Pension/Liberalised Family Pension /War Injury Pension etc. in respect of pre-1996 Armed Forces pensioners vide letter No. PC 1(2)/97/D(Pen-C), dated 16.5.2001. In accordance with the provisions contained in the letter dated 16.5.2001, while for the widows who were in receipt of Liberalised Family Pension (LFP), irrespective of the date of award, the consolidated pension shall be not less than the reckonable emoluments calculated on the minimum pay in the revised scale of pay introduced w.ef 1.1.96 of the rank, rank and group(in the case of JCOs/ORs) held by the deceased personnel at the time of death, for the special family pensioners, the consolidated pension, shall not be less than 60% of the minimum pay in the revised scale of pay introduced w.e.f. 1.1.96 of the rank, rank and group (in the case of JCOs/ORs) held by the deceased personnel at the time of death, subject to a minimum of Rs. 2550/- p.m. The rates of Disability Pension, War Injury Pension (except invalidment cases), Constant Attendant Allowance as applicable to post 96 pensioners have also been extended to pre 96 pensioners in receipt of Disability

Pension, War Injury Pension, Constant Attendant Allowance etc. w.ef 1.1.96.

Grant of ex-gratia to reservists

On the recommendations of 5th CPC, Government order has been issued on 29.12.2000 for grant of ex-gratia to reservists. As per the Govt. letter ex-gratia of Rs. 600/- per month plus dearness relief applicable from time to time has been granted to the reservists who were discharged prior to 1.4.1968 and fulfilling other laid down conditions. The ex-gratia will be payable w.e.f. 1.11.97.

Double Family Pension

With effect from 27th July, 2001 family pension admissible under the employees Pension Scheme 1995 and the Family Pension Scheme 1971 has been allowed in addition to the family pension to the Armed Forces personnel under the relevant Pension Regulations.

Dearness Relief to Ex-Servicemen on Re-employment

Payable on full pension including commuted portion if any as per the rates notified by the Govt from time to time.

a. PSU Absorbees:- Dearness Relief is payable at par with other pensioners.

b. Re-employed pensioners:- (i) Payable w.e.f. 18.07.97 provided pay on re-employment is fixed at the minimum of the pay of the post in which re-employed and full military pension was ignored for fixation of re-employed pay and was not re-employed in group 'A' post. (ii) Re-employed Group A pensioners are also not entitled to Dearness Relief.

c. Family Pensioners:- Payable from 18.07.97 irrespective of employment.

Retirement Gratuity

a. Eligibility: Minimum qualifying service is 5 years for all.

b. Weightage in qualifying service :-

c. 5 years in voluntary 5 years in all cases of Commissioned retirement cases. officers & JCOs/ORs.

d. Formula for Retirement Gratuity :- Payable in lump-sum @ 1/4th of emoluments for every six monthly period of service subject to maximum of 16.5 time of emoluments and further subject to maximum ceiling of 3.5 lakhs.

e. Formula for Retirement Gratuity:- Payable in lump-sum @ 1/4th of emoluments for every six monthly period of service subject to maximum of 16.5 time of emoluments and further subject to maximum ceiling of 3.5 lakhs.

EVOLUTION OF CIVIL SERVICE PENSION SYSTEM IN INDIA

Origin of Civil Service Pensions in India

The history of a formal civil service pension system in India can be traced back to the colonial period of British-India. The first awarded pension benefits to the Government employees were given by the Royal Commission on Civil Establishments in 1881 (Goswami, 2001). Members of the Indian Civil Service were to contribute 4 per cent of their salary. Apart from a pension, the civil servants were also entitled to a family pension under the Indian Civil Service Family Pension rules. These rules applied to all European and Anglo-Indian members of the service and also to some Indian members. Every member to whom these rules applied made contributions, which were credited to the revenues of India and the pensions and other benefits payable under these rules were debited as a charge upon those revenues. The pensions and other benefits payable under these rules were divided into two portions *viz.*, those met from contributions of subscribers and those met from public funds. An account was maintained of all contributions received and all disbursements made therefrom together with an account of interest on the balance calculated at the rate of 4 per cent per annum. The contributions on behalf of a son were payable until he attained the age of 24 and on behalf of a daughter until her marriage. Moreover, every subscriber, on marriage, had to pay, in addition to monthly contributions, the donations laid down by the rules.

On the recommendations of the Royal Commission presided by Lord Islington, the 4 per cent contribution that the employee had to make to earn the pension was stopped in 1920 and the Government undertook to provide the full expenditure of the pensionary charge. At the same time, an ICS Provident Fund [an ICS (Non- European) Fund for Indian civil servants] was started for which the minimum contribution was 4 per cent and the maximum 12.5 per cent.

The representatives of the civil service argued their case for an increase in the rate of pension before the Royal Commission of 1924 (Lee Commission). Apart from recommending an increase in pension, the Commission recommended that if and when the work for which a civilian had been recruited was transferred, it should be optional for that employee to retire on a proportionate pension.

Further, Provident Fund was suggested as an alternative to pension system for all future recruits. Also, the Indian civil servant could, under certain conditions, commute for a lump payment not more than half of any pension which was statutorily granted.

The Government of India Acts of 1919 and 1935 made further provisions. Due to the changed conditions of service brought about by the passage of the Government of India Act, 1919, provisions were made for retiring those members of the civil service who joined the service before January 1, 1920 and were not permanently employed under the Government of India, at any time, at their option, on a pension proportionate to their length of service. It was not necessary for the civil servant to serve the full term of twenty-five years in order to earn pension. The Government of India Act, 1935 also protected the rights and privileges of the members of the civil services (Srivastava,1966). These schemes were later consolidated and expanded to provide retirement benefits to the entire public sector working population.

Modern Civil Service Retirement Programmes

At present, all classes of civil servants (both Union and State Government employees) enjoy fully protected social security. The civil servants participate in a pension plan, a provident fund, an insurance plan, and mandated gratuity pay.

Civil Service Pension System

The civil service pension system (CSPS) covers the entire gamut of the salaried workforce in Central and State governments and Union territory administrations. Within the Central Government, pension schemes are organised by occupation, with separate schemes - which have somewhat different rules of eligibility - for railways, telecommunications, defense, and other Central Government employees. These benefit programmes are typically run on a pay-as-yougo (PAYG), defined-benefit basis. The schemes are non-contributory, *i.e.* the workers do not contribute during their working lives. Instead, they forego the employer's contribution into their provident fund account. The entire pension expenditure is charged to the annual revenue expenditure account of the Government.

The CSPS pays a retirement benefit at age 60 (for Central Government employees) that is based on years of service and average salary in the last ten months of service. For State Government employees, the retirement age generally varies between 58 years and 60 years6. The minimum eligibility period for receipt of pensions is 20 years qualifying service. However, this condition of eligibility is 10 years in respect of Central/ State Government servants entitled to superannuation pension under the respective service rules. Pension is calculated with reference to average emoluments, *i.e.* the average basic pay drawn by the Government servant during the last ten months of his service7. Full pension at 50 per cent of the average emoluments is payable for 33 years of qualifying service. For qualifying service less than 33 years, proportionate pension is payable. The minimum pension/family pension payable is Rs.1,275 per month. The maximum limit on pension is Rs.15,000 per month and on family pension it is restricted to Rs.9,000 per month8. Certain States have set lower limits for maximum pension/family pension payable.

The pension is indexed and adjustments to dearness allowance are made at half yearly intervals. A civil servant has the option to commute a portion of his/her basic pension, not exceeding 40 per cent, into a lump sum payment, with effect from January 1, 19999. Certain State Governments limit the commutation amount to one-third of the basic pension. No medical examination is required if the option is exercised within one year of retirement. If the option is exercised after the expiry of one year, he/she will have to undergo medical examination by the specified competent authority. The monthly pension will stand reduced by the portion commuted and the commuted portion will be restored on the expiry of 15 years from the date of receipt of the commuted value of pension10.

While all State Government employees are entitled to pensionary benefits, most States also extend such benefits to employees in grantsin- aid educational institutions; urban local bodies such as municipalities; panchayat raj institutions, *etc.* In the case of these institutions, there is, however, no uniformity among the States in respect of collections of contributions or in the payment of the quantum of pension. In a few States, the Government collect some contribution from these institutions, while in others no contribution is collected. The benefits also vary from State to State. Some States pay pension to the employees of these institutions on par with the Government servants and others provide a lower amount as pension.

10

Demand for One Rank One Pension by Defence Veterans

Retired defence personnel and war widows have been protesting for the implementation of One Rank One Pension for more than three decades. The agitation gained momentum in the last few months with a group starting protests at Delhi's Jantar mantar and some of then even going on fast-unto-death. There have been several round of meetings between the government and defence veterans but till now there is no solution.

THE DEMAND FOR ONE RANK ONE PENSION

Defence forces are the sword arm of a country and in India 85% soldiers have to retire between 35-37 years to maintain a youthful and fighting force. Defence personnel can also be discharged on account of disability.

Sepoys retiring before 1996 get 82% less pension than one retiring after 2006. An Indian Army Major and equivalent rank in the Indian Navy (Lieutenant Commander) and Indian Air Force (Squadron Leader) retiring before 1996 gets 53% less pension than a Major retiring after 2006.

Until 1973 officers drew 50% of their last drawn salary as pension and junior commissioned officers drew 70% of last drawn salary as pension. But the rule changed after Third Pay Commission's suggestions which was set up in April 1970 with

Justice Raghubir Dayal as chairman and gave its report in March 1973.

One Rank One Pension means

- Two military personnel who retired after equal length of service in same rank get equal pension.
- Payment of uniform pension to military personnel irrespective of date of retirement.
- Any hike in pension rates to be automatically passed on to past pensioners.

While the Central government wanted 2011 as base year for implementing OROP, the ex-servicemen wanted the base year as 2014. Now the government has agreed to take 2013-14 as the base year. While government wanted 2015 as the year of implementation, ex-servicemen wanted the OROP implemented from April 1, 2014. Now the government is willing to implement it from 2014.

Ex-servicemen want revision every year or at least once in two year but the government in in favour of doing it just once in 5 years. This is the biggest hurdle at present. Ex-servicemen have already compromised on some sticking points. They have agreed to a revision once in two years. Retired Havaldar of Army and equivalent ranks in the Navy and IAF, and lower ranks along with war widows will be given cash.

Personnel who retired as an officer will get bonds with 6% interest. The defence veterans can also accept relaxation of upto three months. The government has compromised on the base year and moved it from 2011 to 2013-14 while the year of implementation has been changed from 2015 to 2014. While the government started negotiation with once in 10 year revision clause and then offered it once in 5 years.

OROP RECENT DEVELOPMENTS

On 5 September 2015, the Modi government announced the acceptance of OROP, but the ex-servicemen on strike rejected the same. Defence Minister Manohar Parrikar said that the government has decided to implement OROP in which revision of pension would be done after every five years instead of two years. He also added that base year for this would be 2013 and ex-servicemen who had taken VRS would not be included in the same. On the contrary the ex-servicemen on strike have said that they will not agree for five year revision of salary and omission of VRS holders. They said they would continue their strike.

After not getting any timeline for OROP, on 17 August 2015, two protesting ex-servicemen launched a fast-unto-death at Jantar Mantar, New Delhi.

During his speech on the eve of Independence Day, PM Narendra Modi did not mention the timeline for the implementation of OROP but did refer to the same. He said that the talks are on and he expects a positive outcome from the same. He also added that his government ahs accepted OROP in principle.

According to government sources, the long-pending OROP scheme is likely to be rolled out ahead of the Bihar assembly polls.

On 15 June 2015, a group of about 55 ex-servicemen who belong to Jalandhar district began their relay-hunger strike at Jantar Mantar in New Delhi, demanding the government to announce a date to introduce the OROP policy.

On 10 June 2015, a group of ex-servicemen met Finance Minister Arun Jaitley and expressed their concerns regarding the delay in the OROP scheme which is likely to benefit as many as 22 lakh retired defence personnel.

On 3 June 2015, a group of ex-servicemen led by Maj Gen Satbir Singh (retd) met Dalbir Singh Suhag and discussed about the early implementation of 'one rank one pension' scheme.

ONE RANK, ONE PENSION : HISTORICAL BACKGROUND

One Rank One Pension (OROP), or "same pension, for same rank, for same length of service, irrespective of the date of retirement" is the basis for fixing the pension of Armed Forces since 2014. The implementation order for OROP scheme, however, was issued in November 2015, by the BJP Government, after five months of nation wide protests by veterans organization.

The OROP-2015, which was announced unilaterally, was greeted with dismay, disappointment, and disapproval by Indian Armed Forcesveteran organization and leaders of the OROP protest movement, who denounced the scheme and decided to continue with the protest.OROP 2015, veterans argue, does not conform to 'accepted' definition of OROP and is marred by several inconsistencies, and anomalies.

The causes of OROP demand, and OROP protest movement, are many, and not all are related to pensions issues. The event most often cited by OROP protesters and veterans to high light their sense of disenchantment, and as marker for the decline of the armed forces, is the expartedecision by the Indian National Congress (INC) led by Indira Gandhi Government in 1973, two years after the historic victory in the 1971 Bangladesh war, and shortly after Field Marshall SHFJ Manekshaw retired, to decrease the armed forces pension, by 20-40 percent, and increase civilian pension by 20 percent, without consultation with armed forces headquarters.

In 2008 the perceived slights were exacerbated by several decisions by Prime Minister Manmohan Singh led United Progressive Alliance (UPA) Government, that created radical asymmetries between armed forces and civil service and police pay grades: it created a system by which all civil servants and Indian Police Service(IPS) officers retire at the highest pay grade called the apex pay grade (Rs 80,000); ; it sanctioned 'non-functional financial up-gradation' which mandates all civil services including the Indian Police Service(IPS) are promoted and paid higher pay grades on a fixed time table ; it sanctioned hundred new posts of secretaries, special Secretaries, director general of police (DGP), all at the apex grade pay level, which made all police officers and civil servants eligible for highest pay, and pension, before retirement. For instance, scores of DG posts were authorized for Indian Police Service, with apex grade pay level, which ensured that all would in time retire at at the highest pension scale. These decision made all civilian and police officers eligible for apex scale OROP pensions. 'Non-functional financial up-gradation' (NFU) was not extended to Armed Forces, which had the effect of down grading armed forces pay grades , pension, and status.

These decisions widened the increasing the pay and pension gap between defence and civilian officials. It sharply downgraded time scale and highly selective Armed Forces pay grades and ranks across the board, most significantly, at the senior ranks of Colonel to Major General, and their equivalents in the Indian Navy and the Indian Air Force (IAF). For instance army officers with 13 years of service , who had historically been above IPS officers with similar number of service, were made junior in pay and grade to IPS officers, with similar number of years. Lt Colonel pay grades were fixed considerably below similar placed police and civil service officers.

Against the background Armed forces esteem and self worth continued to suffer. In the face of dismissive response of the Government to their concerns, armed forces veteran started a campaign, in the later half 2008, of nationwide public protests, which included hunger strikes. OROP protest, it appears, is a manifestation of a much larger malaise that afflicts the armed forces than their pensions. It is about what they call honor and izzat, an issue and concern that the UPA, and its successor BJP, Government have chosen to ignore, and is an important cause of the snowballing OROP protest movement.

In May 2014, the UPA Government was replaced by the National Democratic Alliance (NDA) Government led by the Bharatiya Janata Party (BJP), which like the Congress Party, had included implementation of OROP in its election manifesto but after it assumed office continued to make pledges, and promises, but did not implement OROP. The BJP ambivalence provoked nation wide protests by the veterans, starting 15 June 2015.

OROP: 2008-2014

Between 2008-14, during the tenure of the UPA Government led by Prime Minister Manmohan Singh, myriad Armed Forces grievances prompted by perceived inequities subsumed with OROP issue to make OROP a potent rallying call that resonated with all ranks.

The causes and grievances that inform OROP protesters and their high ranking supporters, in addition to failure of the government to implement OROP, are a string of contentious decision taken by UPA Government, in 2008-9, in the wake of Sixth Central Pay Commission (6 CPC), that sharply degraded Armed Forces pay grades and ranks. These decisions, discussed in following paragraphs, have had a radical impact on the armed forces sense of self esteem, honor, and izzat, and their trust in the government and security bureaucracy that had come to dominate policy under the UPA government.

Origin, causes and issues

Diminution of armed forces pensions

In 1973, the Indira Gandhi led Congress (I) Government, terminated 'One Rank One Pension' the basis for deciding pension of Indian Armed Forces Personnel 'which had been in vogue for 26 years since independence' through an ex parte administrative order. In addition, the Government, on the basis of the report of third Pay commission, from which Armed Forces representation was excluded, and which was dominated by bureaucrats, increased the pension of civilians, who retired at 58, by 20 percent, from 30 to 50 percent; and reduced the pension of soldier, Non Commissioned Officers (NCOs) and Junior commissioned Officers (JCOs), by 20 percent, from 70 to 50 percent of basic pay, with the caveat that for full pension the minimum service was 33 years. But as soldiers in 1973 retired after 15 years service, at the age of 33-36, they got less than 30 percent of the pay as pension. Soldiers pension was thus decreased not by 20 percent but 40 percent from 70 to 30 percent. In addition to down grading military pensions, the government inexplicably, and without assigning reason, down graded the status of soldier by equating "infantry soldier with less than three years' service" with a "semi-skilled/unskilled labour". These decisions were all the more galling for the armed forces as these were based on the recommendation, and endorsement of Defence Secretary K B Lall, ICS, whose job it was to ensure the well being of the armed forces. The decision was announced two months after Field Marshal Sam Manekshaw, who led the army in the the victorious 1971 war, retired from service. The reason for depressing the armed Forces pensions, which continues to rankles veterans and servings personnel, given by the Congress I government was that it wanted to ensure 'equivalence' of Armed Forces pensions with civilians.

WHY ARE THE VETERANS DEMANDING OROP?

One Rank One Pension provides for the same pension for the same length of service by personnel of the same rank, irrespective of the date of retirement. Any increments in pension rates are to be added onto the past pensioners' pay as well. This definition was accepted by the last committee to deliberate on the issue, the Koshyari Committee (2011). It will benefit over 20 lakh ex-servicemen and about six lakh war widows. In essence, this scheme, if implemented, would not discriminate among veterans, war widows etc. on the pesky premise of retirement date.

In this context, the organizers of the nation-wide war cry for the OROP have faced the brunt of numerous problems and justify their demands on several counts, like lack of parity with the civil services, inequity with the paramilitary forces and superseding powers of the bureaucracy.

What's The Tiff With The Bureaucracy?

The OROP, axed in 1973 during the authoritarian Indira regime to equalize civil and military pay, is hardly a new concept. Most of the dilly-dallying, as alleged by various organizations of ex-servicemen partaking in the demonstrations, can be attributed to the bureaucracy dragging its feet in this regard.

The non-functional upgrade (NFU) granted to the officers in all-India Group A services (IAS, IPS etc.) by the sixth Central Pay Commission (CPC) allows them higher pay than permissible for their rank during 'certain' conditions. This couteous gesture is limited to the bureaucracy, with no such additional aid being extended to the defence forces. Glaring disparities in field allowances of army special forces as against paramilitary commandos betrays the step-motherly attitude of the government towards the former. With limited prospects for career growth when compared to their contemporaries in the civil services, defence personnel deem themselves entitled for a hike in pay/pension to bridge the gap.

Even as the stalemate over OROP continues, the veterans accuse the civil servants of covertly sabotaging their efforts. This includes attempts to dilute the definition of the scheme and even suggesting alternative models such as the one proposed by the departments of the MoD, which seeks to implement OROP for those pensioners who retired prior to 2006. This exercise has been been dubbed as a design by the bureaucratic machinery to scale down the demands of ex-servicemen, and exercise its one-upmanship over the military.

Why Aren't Politicos Listening?

The politicians are equally culpable for the present scenario. A Supreme Court judgement, providing suffrage rights to serving defence personnel in their area of posting, compelled all political parties to extend piecemeal offers to appease them. The present government, in particular, vociferously supported the implementation of the OROP and its benevolence for the armed forces was evident by the appointment of ex-army officials like General V.K. Singh and Colonel Rajyavardhan Singh Rathore to key positions in various ministries. But when General V.K. Singh says- "*The Prime Minister has made a promise regarding OROP. It will be implemented. There is some delay because calculations are going on. Therefore it is taking time*", he is reiterating the government's position with little substantive effort to echo the sentiments of his defence brethren.

Road Ahead

The initial fervour now seems lacking, with the centre working on a fresh draft governmental letter (DGL) as opposed to the one forwarded by the defence services headquarters. Thus, the accepted definition of OROP is bound to be tinkered with. A highly disciplined section of our population had to take to the streets and sign petitions in blood in a mad dash attempt to jolt the authorities into action. The government, hiding behind technicalities, has propped feeble excuses like fund scarcity and inter-ministerial discord as its armour against the wrath of these betrayed citizens. The protesters, in their desperation, are even willing to set aside their pathological disagreement with the opposition and seek help from the Congress.

GOVT ACCEPTS ONE RANK, ONE PENSION; EX-SERVICEMEN CONTINUE AGITATION

Addressing a packed press conference here on Saturday, Defence Minister Manohar Parrikar announced the government had accepted 'one rank, one pension', or OROP. "The government respects its armed forces and ex-servicemen," Parrikar said. OROP would be implemented with effect from July 1, 2014, and would cost the government Rs 18,000-22,000 crore this year. The government has committed to pay Rs 10,000-12,000 crore as arrears, and another Rs 8,000-10,000 crore towards this year's enhanced pensions. With Budget 2015-16 allocating Rs 54,500 crore for military pensions this year, actual spending on defence pensions will now rise to Rs 72,500-76,500 crore.

"In simple terms, OROP implies uniform pension be paid to the armed forces personnel retiring in the same rank with the same length of service, regardless of their date of retirement. Future enhancements in the rates of pension would be automatically passed on to past pensioners," Parrikar said. However, former soldiers, sailors and airmen who have staged an almost three-month-long public agitation for their demand of OROP took just minutes to reject some of the government's offers, which failed to meet key demands.

Ex-servicemen agitation leaders in New Delhi expressed particular unhappiness about the exclusion from OROP of those who took premature retirement (PMR) before reaching the age of superannuation from service. When a delegation of agitation leaders conveyed this to Parrikar soon after his announcement, the defence minister quickly addressed their concern, providing an assurance that even soldiers who took PMR would be granted OROP.

Retired general Satbir Singh, who heads the Indian Ex-Servicemen Movement, agreed to withdraw the fast-unto-death of ex-servicemen, subject to the latest decision being given in writing. However, he said the larger agitation would continue until all the demands were met.

According to the government's OROP award, there will now be dynamic and continually rising pension scales for ex-servicemen, as pay commissions invariably raise military salaries and, therefore, pensions of the beneficiaries when they retire. "This implies bridging the gap between the rate of pension of current and past pensioners at periodic intervals," said Parrikar. "It has been decided that the gap between rate of pension of current pensioners and past pensioners will be bridged every five years."

Ex-servicemen groups have flatly rejected this. Satbir Singh told Business Standard pensioners couldn't wait five years for parity in pensions. Instead, pensions should be adjusted (equalised) every year, he said.

Indicating the ex-servicemen's vote bank had acquired a new salience, Parrikar issued a detailed critique of the United Progressive Alliance government, which, like other governments for the preceding four decades, had "remained ambivalent" on OROP. He said the complexity of OROP was the reason the National Democratic Alliance government had taken so long in announcing its implementation.

"In February 2014, the then government stated OROP would be implemented in 2014-15, but did not specify what OROP would be, how it would be implemented or how much it would cost. An estimated Rs 500 crore provided for OROP in the Budget presented in February 2014 was not based on any thorough analysis. It is pertinent to mention the then minister of state for defence in 2009 had, in reply to a question, informed Parliament that there were administrative, technical and financial difficulties in implementing OROP. It is for these reasons that the present government took some time to fulfil its promise."

Talking to Business Standard after the announcement, Minister of State for Defence Rao Inderjit Singh said, "The government has taken a decision that this is what we can give them (ex-servicemen). It will now be put to them and one can only hope saner elements among them will prevail."

OROP: MODI GOVERNMENT IS THE VICTIM OF PAST SINS

It's pathetically foolish for anyone to believe that that the NDA government will deceive the nation by not honouring its commitment to OROP. It's natural for the Pappu of our politics who has recently taken to social media to rave and rant about our Prime Minister having the money for his visits abroad but not for pensions to our veteran soldiers.

The real pity is that ex-servicemen, including some very senior officers, have been publicly expressing their anger on the issue. And some media people have naturally joined the word war to create yet another new item song for "Breaking News."

All of them, alas, are oblivious that what the Modi government is acing contempt of court proceedings as it inches to a happy solution for the long-term good of the servicemen and the country they serve so valiantly at all times, be it tremors of mother earth or the or the terrorists from across our borders.

All of them equally appear ignorant that on 18 February 2015, a Supreme Court bench of justices TS Thakur and AK Goel had directed the Centre to implement its six-year-old verdict of Justice Altamas Kabir 9 September 2008 to follow the one rank, one pension (OROP) principle for retired armed forces personnel.

Further it reminded the BJP government that it had promised to do so in the run-up to last year's Lok Sabha elections, and warned the government of contempt if it failed to keep its word within three months.

On 10 July this year, the Supreme Court gave the Centre six more weeks to comply with its 2008 judgment. The next hearing is scheduled for 25 August 2015.

The huge figure is not surprising considering that Indian Army alone has people of 17 ranks—from Sepoy to Field Marshal. With the National Pay Commission reworking salaries and pay scales every five years, utmost care is needed to ensure that the situation does not arise where another Major General S.P.S.Vains first files a writ petition challenging the scheme where a Brigadier gets a higher pension than him, wins against the Union government appeal and secures a historic verdict from the apex court on 9 September 2008 which, seven years later, is being hung over a one-year old government which, irony of ironies, warmly endorses that verdict which proclaimed the supremacy of Article 14 (Right Equality of Law) of our people, including those from the armed forces.

An important aside here is that a political party's election manifesto is being actually demanded to be implemented—by the apex court no less. This is a unique development in our democracy, and will make the political parties to be more cautious in making election promises in the future. For all you know, the Supreme Court may have opened the door for the Manifesto Bills I wrote about in my last commentary.

Another aside for the shouting brigade to note: does it really want the NDA government to announce its figures of OROP to the public first, even before it does so to the Supreme

Court which is hearing the matter? How and why did those ranting people forget the oft-touted phrase *sub judice*? Another overlooked possibility: instead of simply announcing the OROP figure, the government would be perfectly justified in putting forth a scheme that will reduce the number of pensioners over a period of time, thereby lessening the nation's pension burden.

In fact, the 142nd Report on OROP prepared by two BJP MPs in December 2011 and available in the Rajya Sabha Secretariat, advocated such a step strongly. It stated that the then existing ratio of pensioners to serving personnel in the military of 1.7 to 1 (as against 0.50 to 1 civil pensioners to civil work force) be decreased and the pension bill drastically reduced.

By the eminently sensible expedient of absorbing or laterally moving the Armed Forces personnel after the end of their military service into suitable government organisations and departments where their unique skills, training, disciple and strengths can be optimally used. Despite recommendations of the Parliament and Pay Commission to implement the lateral transfer of armed Forces personnel to civil departments, these proposals have yet to be implemented in a meaningful way, despite it being known that such measures are widespread the world over including in China, and in advanced economies like South Korea, Singapore, Israel, Switzerland, and the United States. This is mainly on account of want of energy and commitment by the MOD, and obstruction by the MHA.

Can you guess the savings that will result under the above scheme? Well, the Sixth Central Pay Commission's Report (March 2008) estimated that the "at the end of 13 years, the annual savings on this account will be to the tune of Rs. 7,800 crore at constant price index". Lateral transfer-absorption, if implemented, would in the longer term result in savings in the overall pension bill, and would more than off set projected expenditure on OROP. And guess what? The UPA government ignored this recommendation. Instead, seven Central Armed Police Forces, headed by officers from Indian Police Service (who have direct access to the Minister of Home Affairs),were elevated to apex pay grades, a grade higher than that of most

Lt Generals, including those in command of Corps of the Indian Army.

The Narendra Modi Government is truly suffering vicariously from the sins of omission and commission committed by the UPA government. First, the latter did nothing about the Supreme Court's OROP verdict of Justice Altamas Kabir of 9 September 2008. Then it did mere lip service to the Koshiyal Committee Report of 2011 recommending what is soon to be implemented—as promised by the present government.

GOVT ANNOUNCES DECISION TO IMPLEMENT OROP, VETERANS REJECT KEY PROVISIONS

When the defence minister, flanked by the service chiefs, announced the implementation of One Rank One Pension today, it was expected that it will bring the 83 day old protests by veterans to an end. But going by the response of the veterans and the mood at Jantar Mantar, the government has failed to satisfy the protesters.

Out of the seven points announced by the defence minister, the veterans have welcomed only one point: the implementation of OROP from 01 July 2014, with 2013 as the base year for calculation of pension. The veterans wanted equalization of pension every two years but the government has not budged from its stated position of equalization every five years.

The government has also said that it will fix the pension as the average of the maximum and minimum of the new retirees, while the veterans wanted it to be pegged to the maximum of the scale. The government has announced a one member judicial committee to look into the anomalies, if any, created during the implementation of OROP. The veterans have rejected it, because they wanted a five-member committee with three veterans as part of it. The government has given the judicial committee six months to submit its report while the veterans wanted the report within a month.

But what really seems to have irked the protesting veterans is a caveat inserted into the announcement at the last few days:

to keep military personnel who have taken premature retirement out of the ambit of OROP.

Due to the steep pyramidic structure of the armed forces, many deserving people choose to take premature retirement. As per extant rules, anyone who has served for a minimum of 20 years as an officer (and 15 years for jawans, NCOs and JCOs) is eligible for pension. As per veterans, this last minute clause will exclude 40 percent veterans from OROP. This is likely to be the biggest sticking point between the government and veterans, going forward.

The defence minister spoke of an additional financial burden of Rs 8,000-10,000 crore this year due to OROP. He also said this burden will continue to rise every year.

He mentioned that the previous UPA government had allocated only Rs 500 crore towards OROP, while omitting to mention that in its first full budget, Mr Jaitley had also allocated only Rs 1000 crore for OROP.

According to the defence minister, the arrears of OROP will cost another Rs 10,000-12,000 crore.

The government has budgeted Rs 54,500 crore for defence pensions this year. With the government committed to fiscal prudence, it is not going to be easy for Mr Parrikar to fully satisfy the veterans. Leave alone this announcement signalling the end of battle between the veterans and the government, it doesn't even bring a temporary ceasefire between the two sides.

OROP: MODI HAS NO CLUE WHAT INDIA'S ISSUES ARE OR HOW TO FIX THEM

Prime Minister Narendra Modi is learning first-hand, just how messed up this country is. Unfortunately for us, it is clear from his 2015 Independence Day address that he does not seem to have a measure of our problems, leave alone a schematic plan for resolving them.

There were some new buzzwords, a reiteration of some tired old ones, but little beyond that. Absent was the energy and expectations that marked his 2014 Independence Day address. But the most important failing was a measure of introspection of his term as the country's CEO in the past year, or the state of play of his key projects to make India into a major economic and industrial hub. A measure of the failure was the manner in which the occasion was derailed by the One Rank One Pension (OROP) issue. Governments, both the UPA and the NDA, have mishandled it to a point where we today have the military stepping dangerously close to the political ground, albeit through the ranks of its ex-service personnel. This is not a healthy development and we must reflect on this.

The real grouse

The retired service personnel have had a grouse which has been accentuated by the manner in which the other sections of the central government employees have been dealt with. Jawans retire at the age of 48 and officers from 54 onwards. Civil servants retire at the age of 60 and 62.

Over the years civil servants have expanded their power and pelf through direct and indirect means. An uncomfortably large number of central government employees make money through bribes and favours, and those who are relatively honest manage to use the network of regulatory and supervisory bodies that virtually guarantees a job for all senior retired government officers needing one. The military, by and large, is clean on this count and the soldier depends on his pension like no other in the government.

OROP can have dangerous fiscal implications, even though the claimed outgo at this juncture is Rs 8,000 crore. But it can only be resolved through a larger reform which equalises the remuneration of central government employees and deals with the cancer of corruption in the system. One way, suggested by the Fifth Pay Commission was to reduce the size of the government by 30 per cent. Another good suggestion was to have jawans serve for seven years and, thereafter, move them to the paramilitary forces where retirement age is between 57 to 60 years. Since the paramilitary serve till 58 to 60 years, the pension bill would come down and the paramilitary would have a set of well-trained recruits. But babus and politicians blocked these proposals.

The only rational way in which OROP can be implemented is if it is part of a wider reform of the central government employee system. We need not detain ourselves with the relative merits of the "brave veterans" versus "civilians". These are emotive terms, the fact is that India has a volunteer military and no one joins because they are especially dedicated nationalists or brave, but because it is like other central government jobs and provides good employment and social mobility.

The speech this year must also be looked at through the filter of performance. To be polite, this has been mixed. Instead of reform, we have a minister trying to undermine the IITs and place the RSS functionaries in several prestigious educational institutes; and others trying to stifle dissent. Modi may have declared that he will not tolerate casteism and communalism, but the facts on the ground are that communal violence has shown a dangerous uptick under his prime ministership.

Low-hanging fruit

The Modi government has picked up some of the low-hanging fruit - the scheme to give most Indians a bank account, the insurance schemes, the surrender of gas subsidies and the construction of toilets in most Indian schools - but not as completely as they would have us believe. Skill development and Make in India were the more important themes of his 2014 speech. And one of the more heartening sub-themes was the need to protect women and give their girl child her due. These have been largely marked by their absence this year.

New buzzwords

But we do have new buzzwords - "Team India", "Start-up India", and "Vikas ka pyramid". As for corruption, no charges may have surfaced at the top, but at all other levels it is business as usual and there is little that the Modi government is doing anything about it. It is difficult to avoid the impression that the Modi government has lost its mojo.

The main reason for this is that instead of overhauling a machine that had gone bust, it remains committed to using babus to keep that old machine going somehow or the other. So, the government has adopted a fire-fighting approach to douse the fires as they come up. The ex-servicemen have learnt this and have, therefore, taken to the streets to air their grievance.

PENSIONARY BENEFITS OF CIVILIAN EMPLOYEES

Retiral benefits available

Different retirement benefits available to civilian employees are discussed in the succeeding paragraphs.

Gratuity

Three different kind of gratuity is payable in Government:-

(i) Service gratuity is payable to a permanent employee retiring before completion of 10 years of qualifying service. It is payable at the rate of half month's emoluments for every six months of qualifying service. This gratuity is payable in addition to retirement gratuity

(ii) Retirement gratuity is payable to employees retiring after minimum 5 years of qualifying service. It is payable at the rate of 1/4th of emoluments for each six monthly period subject to a maximum of 16.5 times the emoluments (including DA) or Rs.3.5 lakh, whichever is less.

(iii) Death gratuity is payable in case of death in service. It is paid at the rate of twice the emoluments for service less than one year. In case of service between 1-5 years, it is payable at six times the emoluments. For service between 5 to 20 years, it is payable at twelve times the emoluments. In case the service exceeds 20 years, death gratuity is payable at the rate of half the emoluments for every six months period subject to a maximum of 33 times the emoluments (including Dearness Allowance) or Rs.3.5 lakh, whichever is less.

Encashment of leave

Presently in the Government, encashment of Earned Leave (EL) is allowed at the time of retirement as well as while availing LTC.

Limit of encashment of EL at retirement was increased from 180 days to 240 days by the Fourth CPC and to 300 days by the Fifth CPC.

No encashment while in service was allowed till Fifth CPC. Fifth CPC, apart from recommending increase in the maximum number of EL encashable at the time of retirement to 300 days, also allowed encashment of EL while in service. Encashment of EL upto 10 days on each occasion subject to a maximum of 60 days was allowed while availing LTC. EL encashed during service was to be deducted from the overall ceiling of 300 days.

Encashment of half pay leave is also allowed in case sufficient EL is not available. The extant formula reduces the half pay leave so encashed by the amount of pension payable. The Fifth CPC had observed that no real financial benefit accrued to the retiring Government employee on account of the deductions inherent in the formula.

The Fifth Pay Commission had, accordingly, recommended abolition of this formula for encashment of half pay leave and had proposed that Central Government employees be allowed to encash their accumulated half pay leave at the time of their retirement to the extent of the shortfall, if any, in the maximum earned leave that can be encashed by them. This recommendation of the Fifth CPC was, however, not accepted.

Family pension

Family pension is payable to the spouse of the deceased employee/pensioner or other eligible family members at the rate of 30% of the last pay drawn.

Family pension was first introduced under the Family Pension Scheme, 1950 which allowed 50% of the pension as family pension to employees rendering minimum 25 years of service. Family pension was admissible only for a period of 5 years and maximum family pension payable was Rs.150 p.m. The period of eligibility was reduced to 20 years and family pension made admissible for a period of 10 years w.e.f. 1/4/1957.

A revised Family pension scheme, 1964 was subsequently implemented. Under this scheme, all Government employees with one year of service or who had retired on pension were made eligible for family pension. Spouse and dependent children upto the age of 25 years were eligible. The quantum of family pension ranged from 30% of pay to 12% on a slab system. The scheme also envisaged payment of family pension at an enhanced rate (50% to 24%) for a period of 7 years or the age of superannuation, whichever was earlier.

The scheme of Family pension was liberalized subsequent to implementation of recommendations of the Third Central Pay Commission.

The pay limits under the slab system were enhanced. The benefit of family pension at enhanced rates was extended for a period of 7 years or till the employee/pensioner would have attained the age of 65 years, whichever was earlier.

The scheme of Family pension was earlier contributory and the retiring employee had to surrender two months gratuity in order to be eligible for grant of family pension on his demise. From 22/9/1977, the scheme was made non-contributory and the requirement of surrender of gratuity was dispensed with. The rules were liberalized to allow payment of family pension for life to handicapped children or till the time they became self-sufficient.

Subsequent to the Fourth Central Pay Commission, the minimum and maximum amount of family pension were revised to Rs.375 and Rs.1250 p.m. respectively. The slabs for paying family pension were also revised upwards and ranged from 30% to 15% of pay.

The condition of dependency for children of the deceased employee to be eligible for grant of family pension was removed in 1993. All children were made entitled for family pension upto the age of 25 years as against the age of 18 years prescribed in 1964 rules and the age of 21/24 years or till the time of their marriage, whichever earlier, for sons & daughters respectively prescribed by the Fourth CPC.

The scheme was liberalized further as per the recommendations made by the Fifth Central Pay Commission. Family pension was now payable at the rate of 30% of the pay last drawn in all cases. Maximum and minimum family pension was revised to Rs.9000 and Rs.1275 respectively. Family pension at enhanced rate of 50% of the pay last drawn was for a period of 7 years or till the employee/pensioner would have attained the age of 67 years, whichever is earlier. Married, widowed and divorced daughters were included for payment of family pension subject to the ceiling of 25 years.

The limit of 25 years was subsequently removed in respect of unmarried/divorced daughters.

Extraordinary pension

Extraordinary family pension is payable under the CCS (Extraordinary) Pension Rules, 1939 at the following rates:-

(i) In case of death or disability attributable to service or due to accidents in the performance of duty, extra-ordinary family pension is payable at 60% of the basic pay subject to a minimum of Rs.2500 per month.

(ii) In case of disability, normal pension and gratuity is payable along with disability pension equal to 30% of pay for 100% disability. The disability pension is reduced proportionately for reduced disability. This is subject to the condition that the aggregate of the service and disability elements are, in no case, less than 60% of the basic pay last drawn.

(iii) In case of death or disability due to acts of violence by terrorists, anti-social elements etc., whether in performance of duties or otherwise, extraordinary family pension equal to last pay drawn upto re-marriage or death is payable. After re- marriage, rules governing ordinary family pension are applicable. If the deceased employee has no widow but leaves behind only children, then all children together get 60% of basic pay subject to minimum of Rs.2500. In case of bachelors, family pension equal to 75% of pay last drawn is payable in case both the parents are alive. The pension is payable at the rate of 60% in case only one parent is alive, irrespective of their income.

Disability pension

If the Government employee is discharged from Government service on account of injuries sustained in specified operations as a result of either attack by or action against extremists, anti-social elements, etc. or in course of enemy action in international war or border skirmishes, he is entitled to a disability pension that comprises a service element and a disability element. The service element comprises the amount of the retiring pension plus gratuity counting service upto the date on which the employee would have retired in normal course. The disability element that is payable is equal to normal family pension for 100% disability with aggregate of service and disability element not being less than 80% of pay last drawn.

In case of death or disability attributable to attack by extremists, anti-social elements and enemy action, the following rates of extraordinary family pension are applicable:-

(i) family pension equal to last pay drawn upto re-marriage or death. After re-marriage, ordinary family pension is admissible. If there is no widow but only children, all children together get 60% of basic pay subject to the minimum of Rs.2500. In case of bachelors, family pension at the rate of 75% of pay last drawn is payable to parents or 60% in case only one parent is alive, irrespective of their income.

(ii) retiring pension plus gratuity counting service till normal age of retirement subject to the total amount not exceeding last pay drawn for 100% disability. Proportional reduction is made for lower disability.

Exgratia

Exgratia is also payable over and above the pension rules to families of Central Government employees who die in harness in the course of performance of their bonafide official duties. The rates of exgratia vary between Rs.5 lakh in cases of death occurring due to accidents in the course of performance of duty whether attributable to acts of violence by terrorists, anti-social elements etc. or otherwise to Rs.7.5 lakh in cases of death occurring due to enemy action in international war or border skirmishes or action against militants, terrorists, extremists, etc.

Changes made in the past in retiring pension

While considering the pension package for Central Government employees, the Commission has kept in view the various changes that have evolved in the pension benefits over the past decades.

The formula for computing pension has been substantially liberalized since the time of First Central Pay Commission. The pension was earlier payable at the rate of 30/80 (37.5%) of the average emoluments.

This was later revised to 41.25% (*33/80*). From 31/3/1979, a slab system for payment of pension was introduced, wherein pension was paid at various rates ranging from 50% to 42.86%. The formula was further liberalized by the Fourth Central Pay Commission and from 1/1/1986, the pension is payable at the rate of 50% of the average emoluments comprising basic pay, dearness pay, non-practicing allowance and stagnation increments.

From 1/1/1996, full neutralization of dearness relief has been allowed to all pensioners. This was in conformity with the recommendations made by the Fifth CPC extending 100% neutralization of the increase in the price index to all the serving Central Government employees.

Central Government employees are also allowed to commute part of their pension for a lump-sum payment which is the commuted value of that portion of the pension. The lump-sum payment is computed by multiplying the commutation factor by 12 and further multiplying the product by the amount of pension offered for commutation.

The commutation factor is taken from the commutation table with respect to the age next birthday. Originally, the amount of pension once commuted was not restored for life. However, pursuant to directions of the Supreme Court in writ petitions nos. 3958-61 of 1983, orders were issued allowing restoration of the commuted portion of pension both in case of civilian and defence pensioners after a period of 15 years on the ground that the commuted value of pension had to be restored once the lump-sum commutation paid and the interest thereon was fully adjusted.

The Fifth CPC had recommended an increase in the percentage of commutable pension from 33% to 40% of pension along with its restoration after 12 years.

The Commission had also considered the issue of revising the commutation table that has not been revised since March, 1971 and recommended that a detailed review of the commutation scheme based on current data should be carried out that would be more representative and closer to ground realities.

The Government accepted the recommendation regarding increase in the percentage of commutable pension without taking any action on the other two recommendations relating to restoration of the commuted pension and devising a new commutation scheme. The present position is, therefore, that a pensioner can commute upto 40% of the pension which would be restored after 15 years.

Demands- pension

Major demands on pension related issues made by the various staff associations and others sought the following relief:-

(i) Components for purpose of calculation of pension should also include deputation duty allowance dearness allowance and 75% of the running allowance in respect of railway running staff retired after 4.12.88.

(ii) Qualifying service for full pension should be fixed at 30 years

(iii) Full pension should be 60% of the emoluments of the last month or the 10 month average, whichever is higher.

(iv) Pension should be increased to 65% of the last pay drawn after age of 65 and by another 10% at age of 75.

(v) Minimum qualifying service should be reduced from 10 to 5 years

(vi) Minimum pension should be made equal to the minimum salary.

(vii) Full gratuity should be calculated on the basis of 25 days against 30 days in a month as admissible under the gratuity act. The ceiling of 16.5 months should be removed.

(viii) Full pension should be restored after 12 years, or on reaching 70 years of age, whichever is earlier.

Demands- family pension

Major demands relating to family pension are as under :

(i) The period of 7 years for grant of enhanced family pension should be raised to 10 years.

(ii) After the expiry of the above 10 years period, the family pension should be reduced to 75%.

(iii) The family pension should not be less than the minimum pension of Rs.10,000.

(iv) In the case of a son, the family pension may be allowed upto the age of 28 years because the recruitment age has been raised to 28 years. In the case of unmarried daughter, the age limit may be done away with.

Recommendations

The Commission has considered the various demands in light of the extant provisions, the need and justification of giving a proper deal to the pensioners and the capacity of the Government to bear additional burden on this account. Recommendations on various pension related issues have, accordingly, been made in the succeeding paragraphs.

Recommendations relating to quantum of pension

As regards the issue of raising the quantum of pension from the existing 50% of the average emoluments to a higher percentage (say 60%), is concerned, it is noted that this demand was also considered by the Fifth CPC who had recommended that a supplementary pension scheme that was contributory in nature could be a viable means of increasing post retirement incomes. It is observed that the new pension scheme that is mandatory for post 31/12/2003 entrants, also envisages a second tier where contributions can be made on a voluntary basis by the Government employees towards their future pension. This can perhaps be utilized by the employees who are desirous of increasing their post-retirement incomes. Consequently, the Commission does not recommend any change in the present rates of pension which is payable at 50% of emoluments on completion of minimum prescribed years of qualifying service. The Commission, however, is of the view that older pensioners require a better deal because their needs, especially those relating to health, increase with age. Accordingly, the Commission recommends that quantum of pension available to the old pensioners should be increased as follows:-

On attaining age of		Additional quantum of pension
80 years	-	20% of basic pension
85 years	-	30% of basic pension
90 years	-	40% of basic pension
95 years	-	50% of basic pension
100 years	-	100% of basic pension

Recommendations relating to qualifying service

Presently, full pension is payable only on completion of 33 years of qualifying service. The rules also allow grant of upto 5 years of additional qualifying service for purposes of computing pension subject to certain conditions. Hence, an employee presently has to put in a minimum 28 years of qualifying service to become eligible for full pension. This acts as a disincentive for many employees for leaving the Government at an early age even though they have reached a plateau in their career and are not satisfied with their job, because they want to complete the minimum years of qualifying service prescribed for being eligible for full pension. By the time they complete such minimum years of service, they are too old to look for an alternative career and continue in the Government without being motivated to make any significant contribution. This has an adverse effect on the efficiency of the machinery. At the same time, the concerned Government employee is also prevented from pursuing an alternative career. The Commission, accordingly, recommends that linkage of full pension with 33 years of qualifying service should be dispensed with.

Once an employee renders the minimum pensionable service of 20 years, pension should be paid at 50% of the average emoluments received during the past 10 months or the pay last drawn, whichever is more beneficial to the retiring employee. This will not work as a disincentive to the employees putting in longer years of service because their pay will increase along with the tenure that will have a direct bearing on the pension payable to them. With this, qualifying service will cease to have any relevance as full pension will be payable once minimum pensionable service is put in without any reference to qualifying service. Simultaneously, the extant benefit of adding years of qualifying service for purposes of computing pension/related benefits should be withdrawn as it would no longer be relevant.

Recommendations relating to commutation

Earlier, the amount of pension commuted was not restorable. Consequently, a pensioner was eligible to draw only the commuted amount of pension for the remainder of the retired life. The position changed with effect from April 1, 1985 on account of judgment passed in December, 1986 by the Supreme Court in Writ Petitions No. 3958-61 of 1983. In this judgment, the Supreme Court had directed restoration of the commuted value of pension once the commutation amount along with the interest element thereon was recovered fully. Accordingly, orders were issued for restoring the commuted amount of pension after 15 years. These orders were made effective retrospectively from April 1, 1985.

The Commission received many demands for reducing the period of restoring the full pension to 12 years. As mentioned earlier, the Fifth CPC had recommended such restoration after 12 years. The Fifth CPC had simultaneously recommended revision of the commutation table that was last revised in March, 1971. The commutation table is based on the mortality rates then extant amongst Government pensioners and a concessional rate of interest of 4.75% per annum. Department of Pension and Pensioners Welfare had considered the issue of revision of the current commutation table many times. These reviews revealed that whereas the mortality rates had not increased significantly, the rates of interest had become much higher. Another factor which has to be considered in any revision is that the commutation is now restored after a period of 15 years. Hence, any improvement in the age of life expectancy of Government pensioners beyond 15 years will cease to have any effect on computation of the commutation value. The present commutation table is more advantageous to the retiring employees and till the time, the commutation table is suitably revised to present the correct picture, there may not be any justification for decreasing the period of restoration. The Commission had commissioned the Centre for Economic Studies and Policy, Bangalore for evolving a new commutation table keeping in view all the relevant factors. This table is given in Annex 5.1.2 of the Report. The Government should modify the commutation table being used for purposes of commuting pension, accordingly. All future cases of commutation of pension should be considered as per the revised commutation table annexed to the Report which may be revised periodically by the Government keeping in view the interest rates and the mortality table.

Since the commutation under the proposed scheme will be in consonance with the prevailing market rates of interest and the mortality factor, it should be possible to outsource the entire process of making payment on this account. Accordingly, the Government may consider outsourcing the process of commutation of pension to any PSU Bank/Institution which would extend the commuted amount to the pensioners and get appropriate rate of interest on such amount. Government could extend an interest subsidy on the interest rate so charged, in case the same is found necessary.

Amount of commutation - Recommendations

In view of the aforesaid, the Commission does not propose any change in the maximum percentage of commutation allowed or in the period of restoration.

Recommendations relating to gratuity

Most of the Associations have demanded removal of the ceiling of Rs.3.5 lakh on retirement/death gratuity. The Fifth Central Pay Commission had recommended removal of ceiling on all kinds of gratuities keeping in view their recommendation to include dearness allowance in the definition of emoluments for calculation of gratuity.

They had observed that with the inclusion of DA in the definition of emoluments, the amount of gratuity receivable will change every six months and any ceiling thereon will become unrealistic. The Government accepted the recommendation regarding inclusion of DA in the definition of emoluments for purposes of computing the amount of gratuity receivable. However, they did not remove the ceiling on maximum amount of gratuity payable but increased this limit from Rs.2.5 lakh to Rs.3.5 lakh w.e.f. 1/1/1996. This has resulted in a situation where employees retiring with the average basic pay of more than Rs.11,687 as on 1/1/2006 get restricted by the maximum limit in so far as payment of gratuity is concerned. While prescribing a limit, it may be necessary to limit the expenditure on payment of gratuity. The existing limit will prevent many Group B and C employees from getting the full benefit of gratuity. Hence, the limit of gratuity has to be such that all employees barring those in the top grades are able to get full benefit of gratuity payable as per the given formula. This is justified as death-cum-retirement gratuity was, at its inception, carved out of pension payable which earlier was admissible at the rate of 30/60 of emoluments in the Liberalized Pension Rules, 1950.

The rate was reduced to 30/80 of emoluments when DCRG, at the rate of 9/20 of emoluments for each year of service subject to a limit of 15 times of the emoluments, was introduced. In view of this and the fact that there is a substantial revision of emoluments, the Commission recommends that the maximum pecuniary limit of Rs.3.5 lakh on payment of gratuity should be raised to Rs.10 lakh.

Recommendations relating to encashment of leave

The last two Pay Commissions had successively increased the limit in accumulation of Earned Leave and its encashment by 60 days which, therefore, increased from 180 days to 240 days pursuant to recommendations of the Fourth CPC and to 300 days as per the recommendations of the Fifth CPC. The last Pay Commission had also allowed encashment of leave while availing LTC but the number of leave so encashed was deductible from the maximum number of leave encashable at the time of leaving the Government.

The maximum number of EL that can be accumulated and encashed has substantially increased by 120 days in the last 3 decades. Consequently, no rationale for raising this limit any further exists.

However, it is not appropriate to deduct the number of EL encashed while in service from EL encashable at the time of leaving the service because the latter acts as a means for providing adequate resources to the retiring employee to meet the commitments at the start of the retired life.

The Commission recommends that while no change may be made in the maximum number of EL that can be accumulated and encashed, whether in service or at the time of retirement/ leaving the Government, however, the number of EL encashed while in service should be excluded from the overall ceiling of encashment of 300 days EL allowed at the time of retirement.

The present formula for making up the shortfall in the maximum amount of Earned Leave encashable at the time of retirement through encashment of Half Pay Leave (HPL) does not give any benefit. This is unjustified especially when leave salary equal to half the amount of leave salary on Earned Leave is payable during Half Pay Leave and the period spent on this leave is counted as qualifying service for purposes of pension. The Commission, therefore, recommends that both Earned Leave and Half Pay Leave should be considered for encashment of leave subject to the overall limit of 300 days. The provisions relating to encashment of Earned Leave shall continue unchanged. Half Pay Leave will be encashable at the rate equal to half the amount of leave salary payable during Earned Leave without any reduction being made on account of pension payable. To make up the shortfall in Earned Leave, no commutation of Half Pay Leave shall be permissible.

11

OROP and Premature Retirement

Defence Minister's decision to include the clause "Personnel who voluntarily retire will not be covered under the OROP scheme" in the OROP scheme announcement, on 5 September 2015, without warning the ex-servicemen, caused immediate outrage, and doubts about government intent amongst ex-servicemen.

Arguing against the exclusion clause the ex-servicemen have said that it was not a part of the discourse, and discussion between the ex-servicemen and the government; it was not an items on the discussion agenda on 5 September morning meeting between minister and ex-servicemen; voluntary retirement scheme(VRS) is a term used by Public Sector Units, and corporate sector, to retire their staff on mutually agreed package, which usually does not have a pension component; and that VRS is not applicable to the Armed Forces, as the Armed Forces does not have VRS.

Ex-servicemen have explained that the armed forces has premature retirement (PMR), which is different on many counts from VRS: to avail pension and PMR, Armed Forces officers must have completed 20 years of service, and soldiers 15 years service; and unlike VRS, PMR invariably has a reserve liability, i.e., they can be ordered back into service by the government if the national situation so demands. Ex-servicemen were surprised and disappointed that MOD, which oversees PMR, included, at the last minute, and without warning, the exclusion clause. They were also disappointed that the MOD conflated VRS and PMR in its announcement. Who was behind the confusion is unclear. The ex-servicemen have demanded an inquiry on how the offending caveat was slipped into the Ministers statement, and MOD press release. To defuse the ex-servicemen suspicion, distrust, and prevent further escalation, the Prime Minister, on 6 September, announced in Faridabad that all pensioners including those who took premature retirement will be covered by the OROP scheme. It is estimated that 46 per cent of all ex-servicemen are PMRs.

Judicial Commission

OROP is not a settled issue. It is, as MOD statement notes, 'a complex issue' and 'not an administrative matter alone', and therefore the MOD has decided to constitute "a One Member Judicial Committee", which will do a "thorough examination of interests of retirees of different periods and different ranks" and consider "inter-service issues of the three Forces".

The report was scheduled to be released in six months". Ex-servicemen rejected MOD decision to constitute a one-man committee headed by a retired Supreme Court justice.

Instead they urged the Government to constitute a committee of three military veterans, recommended by ex servicemen and an official, appointed by MOD, and that the committee be called upon to submit its report not in six but one month.

One of the main issues perceived as a limitation on the efficacy of the Judicial Committee, is the language of the Govt notification dated 14 December 2015.

It does not specify how affected veterans can approach the Committee for redressing anomalies in OROP implementation. The notification merely mentions how the Judicial Committee would make recommendations based on references received from the Government. The general perception is that as anomalies result from the manner in which OROP has been implemented by the Government, the Government itself is unlikely to view these as anomalies.

Veterans Response

Following the Manohar Parrikar statement on the decision to implement OROP, Major General (Retd) Satbir Singh said, "Out of the six demands that we made, the government has only agreed with one.

We want clarification on the premature retirement point in the OROP." On Government decision to revise pension every five years rather than every year he said, that this was not "in the spirit of One Rank, One Pension, it will be One Rank, Five Pensions," and therefore urged "the government to rethink it".

The ex servicemen dissatisfied with the OROP scheme announced by MOD, decided to call off the hunger strike, but continue with the protest till "all major demands are met". To press their demands a *maha-rally* was held on 12 September 2015.

Political response

A.K. Antony, former defence minister in UPA Government, on 5 September 2015, calling the BJP government OROP scheme "totally disappointing", said it "substantially diluted the provisions of the OROP announced by the UPA".

He said, it "ridiculed the ex-servicemen as well as the whole country." Refuting Manohar Parrikar's allegation that Congress Government was ambivalent on OROP, he said, "We had already accepted *in toto* the demand for OROP and were in the process of implementing it."

WHAT IS ONE RANK, ONE PENSION?

The 'one rank, one pension' rule means that retired soldiers of the same rank and length of service will receive the same pension, regardless of when they retire. As of now, the date of retirement determines the amount of pension. With each Pay

Commission coming up with its recommendations every 10 years, the military veterans who retire early, receive less pension as compared to those who retired later with the same rank and length of service. Under OROP, a sepoy who retired in 1995, for instance, would get the same amount of pension as the one who retired in 1996.

Who will benefit from OROP?

Ex-servicemen drawing pensions will benefit from the OROP scheme, especially those who retired before 2006. Why? Because at present, pensioners who retired before 2006 draw less pension than their counterparts and even their juniors. The scheme will benefit all three services — air force, navy and army.

How much will the OROP scheme cost the government?

The United Progressive Alliance government in their interim budget had announced an amount of Rs 500 crore for the scheme. However, NDA's Finance Minister Arun Jaitley in his Budget announcement allotted Rs 1,000 crore for the scheme.

Why has there been so much delay in implementing OROP?

Officials within the ministry of defence have been against the implementation of OROP, citing financial, administrative and legal impediments. In 2011, the Department of Ex-Servicemen Welfare of the MoD pointed out to a parliamentary committee that OROP was not feasible to implement since documents of military personnel are weeded out after 25 years — which is not true.

In reality, the Pension Payment Orders of pensioners, which contain all relevant details such as the rank last held and the length of service, are retained during the lifetime of each pensioner and then during the lifetime of the family pensioner in case of his demise. Further, all these details are available in a document called 'Long Roll' which is maintained in perpetuity in terms of Regulation 592 of the Regulations for the Army. Another reason given by those opposing the scheme was that "other employees" would also start demanding OROP.

When did OROP become a reality?

After several protests and demands, the Manmohan Singh government towards its fag-end agreed in principle to clear the scheme in 2013.

Realising the importance of correcting the wrong, the Narendra Modi government and the prime minister himself gave renewed hope to the veterans by announcing the implementation of the OROP scheme "as soon as possible".

On April 9, Defence Minister Manohar Parrikar said, "All hurdles, including a political clearance on its financial implications, have been removed. Now the actual calculation and administrative details are being worked out. We are sure to get the scheme rolling in the next few weeks."

OROP: GOVT CLEARS PAYMENT PLAN BUT VETERANS SAY SOME ISSUES REMAIN UNRESOLVED

The government also issued OROP tables which said that the arrears from July 1, 2014 to December 31, 2015 would be approximately Rs 10,900 crore. 86 per cent of the total expenditure on account of OROP will benefit the Junior Commissioned Officers and other ranks.

However, military veterans are not satisfied with government's announcement and have said that they will continue their protest. The veterans body has said that anomalies remain in the OROP scheme announced by the government. The main complaint with OROP tables is that instead of giving the highest pension at one rank, government has decided on giving the average pension of a rank which 'nullifies' the meaning and definition of OROP. Is the government's claim that it has fulfilled its promises premature?

Big questions

1. Has the government delivered OROP as it was promised?
2. Will the long agitation come to an end?
3. Will OROP implementation solve the dispute?

4. Why are some veterans still unhappy?
5. What else can be done to implement OROP?
6. Will the government and veterans find a common ground?
7. Why is government silent on equalisation of pension?
8. OROP delivered or only pensions enhanced?
9. How will government remove pay 'anomalies'from OROP?
10. Does government's scheme nullify the meaning of OROP?

Speaking on the show To The Point, former Deputy Army Chief Lt. Gen. (retired) Raj Kadyan said that though the release of OROP tables is a welcome development, some issues are yet to be resolved.

"The recommendation of the 7th pay commission, if they are accepted by the government, then civilians get OROP totally and their is no restriction of VRS in their case, so qualitatively also we will be discriminated," Lt. Gen. Kadyan said. Speaking on the issue, former Army Chief General Ved Prakash Malik stressed that pre-mature retirement (PMR) was not in the interest of armed forces and therefore this clause must go.

"There are very large number of people, who can not go up the ladder because there are no vacancies. And therefore to hold on to officers who have not been able to go up and they remain static in their rank....I think we are just unnecessarily carrying dead wood and also blocking promotion avenues of young people," General Malik said.

Malik added that he feels that if Defence Minister and Finance Minister are made to understand that some things are not in favour of the veterans then they will definetly take some action to resolve the issues.

Former Secretary, Ministry of Defence, Ajay Prasad pointed out that it is in the interest of the Army to see that people who are not interested in serving the Army for various reasons should be encouraged to leave so that more motivated, energetic and keen people continue in the officer cadre.

ORÓP IS A SUB-OPTIMAL SOLUTION

Prime Minister Narendra Modi meant well when he promised veterans of the armed forces an early implementation of one-rank-one-pension (OROP).

Like most Indians, Modi wanted to acknowledge the immense contribution the brave men and women of the armed forces make to keep the country secure, doing work and battle in some of the toughest conditions in the world.

The fact is that as a nation, we haven't done enough to recognise those who risk their lives so that the rest of us are safe. We pay our armed forces less than their civilian counterparts, we haven't built proper war memorials, the list can go on.

However, one-rank-one-pension is a terribly flawed concept and notwithstanding their own demand for it, a poor way to compensate the men and women of the armed forces.

My objection to OROP is not at all related to the huge cost involved, though that seems to be the only reason the government is dithering.

The problem lies elsewhere. In principle, pension is always linked to the last salary received by an individual while in service (contributions are of course made throughout service). That is so across the government, which has a most generous system of pensions, something those who work in the private sector can only envy.

Needless to say, pensions are index-linked, so inflation is accounted for by periodic raises.

But under this system there will be a difference in the pension received by a colonel who retired 30 years ago and a colonel who retires next month — the salary scales would have been revised in the interim.

OROP would grant the colonel who retired 30 years ago the same pension as the one who retires in 2015, even though the latter would have made higher contributions to his pension fund because of his higher salary.

That isn't the biggest problem. Once the principle of OROP is accepted for the armed forces, how will the government prevent it from being extended to all government services and cadres from top to bottom?

Why shouldn't all those who, say retired as joint secretary, get the same pension? If that happens, the cost implications will become really serious and probably unaffordable.

Remember also, that basically pension is a subsidy from the working population to those who can no longer work. Essentially, it is an unproductive spending. At its stage of development, India needs more people to be in work for longer than out of it.

However, in the armed forces, because of a sharply pyramidical structure, personnel begin to retire in their 30s and 40s (unlike their civilian counterparts including those in uniform who retire at 60).

Their dependence on pension from a younger age is perhaps what makes the demand for OROP (basically a demand for a higher pension over time) very strong.

What the government must seriously consider, instead of an unviable and unproductive OROP, is ways to keep the personnel of the armed forces engaged in gainful employment until they are at least 60.

It is a waste of a trained and disciplined workforce to send a majority into retirement when they can still be working. If the forces have no place for them, the government should see if they can be engaged in other civilian departments.

More importantly, if the government has the resources to spend, it should set up institutions where the men and women of the armed forces can be retrained (in skills, or degrees) to get jobs in the private sector.

An armed forces background is considered an asset in many private sector companies, but those at the lower rungs (say non-commissioned officers or jawans) may not have the requisite qualifications to be employed. The government could also fund specialised placement cells in each of the forces to help retiring personnel find jobs.

Politically, it may now be difficult for PM Modi's government to deny OROP. It risks losing an important constituency of support.

However, even if it goes ahead with OROP, it should continue to find ways to encourage and help retired armed forces personnel to stay in work. It is the right thing to do and it comes with the dignity that the brave personnel of the armed forces deserve. After all, a working wage will always be much higher than any pension.

OROP EXPLAINED: EMOTIVE ISSUE FOR VETERANS AND SOLDIERS, BUT REASONS FOR CAUTION

One rank one pension (OROP) for military veterans was one of the first public promises made by Narendra Modi in September 2013 after being declared the BJP's prime ministerial candidate.

Although Congress party followed with its promise of implementing the OROP, Modi's announcement at Rewari immediately won him the support of the majority of 2.8 million veterans in the country. The UPA government even allotted Rs 500 crore for OROP in the interim budget last year but not many trusted its intentions by then.

Despite many assurances by various BJP ministers over past one year, the government has still not issued orders for implementation of OROP.

Based on off the record briefings from senior ministers, most veterans expected PM Modi to formally announce it during the first anniversary rally at Mathura last week.

His silence on OROP has caused much anguish among the veterans. The emotions are running high as some war heroes refused to attend a function at Pune on Thursday where the defence minister felicitated the veterans. An ex-servicemen organisation has announced a public protest rally, including a hunger strike, in Delhi on 14 June.

Put simply, OROP means that every soldier who retires in the same rank gets the same pension, irrespective of his date of retirement.

As of now, soldiers who retired more recently receive more pension than those who did earlier, because pensions are dependent on the last salary drawn — and successive pay commissions have hiked salaries.

Parliamentary Standing Committee on Defence and Rajya Sabha Committee on petitions have recommended holistic implementation of OROP. In his first full budget last July, Finance Minister Arun Jaitley reaffirmed his party's commitment by allotting Rs 1,000 crore towards OROP. That allotment has lapsed and no such allotment was made in this year's budget.

After taking over as the defence minister, Manohar Parrikar spoke of 80 percent satisfaction levels for pensioners with his model of OROP. The debate over what constitutes OROP – and the formula to fix the OROP pension – has exercised the defence services and defence ministry. Even soldiers who retire in the same rank do not usually draw the same last salary. This is because one Brigadier could spend more time in the rank of Brigadier while another Brigadier may take longer to get promoted, thus getting less pay as Brigadier — or one could reach retirement age earlier than the other.

The formula prepared by the defence ministry, with the concurrence of the three defence services, overcame the problem of variations in rank and last pay drawn by creating standardised slabs for each rank with a certain length of service. This proposal was sent to the finance ministry for approval.

ONE RANK ONE PENSION: PM MODI PROMISES SOLUTION

This government will find a solution to the the One Rank One Pension issue, Prime Minister Narendra Modi promised the defence forces this morning in his monthly radio address Mann ki Baat.

"You have been patient for 40 years, wait for some more time. This is a complex issue... I promise we will hold discussions and resolve it," he said. "Is it not true that the issue has remained unresolved for 40 years? Every government talked about this, but did nothing?"

"I am not talking as the Prime Minister, I wish to address our forces as an individual, from the heart," he said.

This was the second time PM Modi promised action on the issue that had pushed two decorated war veterans to boycott an event attended by Defence Minister Manohar Parrikar last week.

PM Modi was widely expected to announce the scheme last Monday when he addressed a rally in Mathura in Uttar Pradesh, but he had not.

Wing Commander SD Karnik, a 1971 war veteran, had said he was disillusioned by the non-implementation of the scheme, which is meant to ensure that defence personnel who retire at the same rank and with the same length of service get equal pension, irrespective of when they retired.

Mr Parrikar has said the scheme was "on its way" but he could not promise a date for its implementation.

"Two or three steps remain so can't give you a specific time," he had said. What made it more difficult was that it involved various departments. Sources told NDTV that the file is shuttling between the finance and defence ministries.

Six years ago, the Supreme Court had directed the government to implement the scheme. In February, the court gave three more months to the government, saying non implementation by the end of it will amount to contempt of court. The time limit ends in May. The Congress criticised PM Modi for saying the issue was a "vexed" one.

"Unfortunately, he (PM Modi) did not touch upon even a single of these issues. Rather, he chose to further compound the problem and confuse the entire issue by saying that OROP is a very complex issue," senior Congress leader Ajay Maken told reporters.

MODI PROMISES SOLUTION TO 'ONE RANK, ONE PENSION' ISSUE

Vowing to address the "vexed" issue of 'one rank, one pension' (OROP), Prime Minister Narendra Modi today asked the ex-servicemen to give him some time as he targeted the previous governments, saying they had only "played" with the sentiments of the armed forces for 40 years without doing anything on the matter.

He attacked those indulging in politics over the matter and said "problems" have been added to the issue over the years and effort was underway to simplify it and make it acceptable to all.

In his monthly 'Mann Ki Baat' programme on radio, Modi said he has directed various departments in the government to look for solutions to the issue. "For 40 years, you have been patient. Give me some time. "Allow me to work on this. We will together find a solution to the problems," he told the ex-servicemen who are agitated over the delay in implementation of OROP.

"I want to tell one thing, not as the Prime Minister but as a human being with full sincerity, especially to the soldiers who are engaged in protecting the country as well as those who have retired from the armed forces and those who have made sacrifices. "Is it not a fact that the question of 'one rank, one pension' has not been hanging for the last 40 years? Is it not a fact that all the previous governments only talked but did nothing," he said.

"I assure you. I have made a promise in the midst of ex-servicemen that my government will implement one rank, one pension. We do not shun our responsibility," he said, adding that soon after his government was formed, various departments have been working on this.

Modi said the issue is not as simple as he had thought but much more "vexed" as "problems" have been added to it over the years. Apparently referring to the impatience that is being exhibited on the OROP issue, the Prime Minister said "there is no need to give step-by-step information to the media. There can be no running commentary on this".

He repeatedly assured the ex-servicemen that "this government" will resolve the one rank, one pension issue. "You (armed forces) have importance in the ideology from which we have come and the principles on which we are moving ahead. For me, to help you (armed forces) is not any government programme or political agenda, but a matter of service to the nation," Modi said.

He said those trying to get political mileage out of the issue have been "playing with you" for 40 years. "That path is not acceptable to me and neither do I want to take any such step which will complicate the issue.

You keep faith in me. "Rest, those who want to rake up the issue, do politics over it, let them do. I am determined to do whatever I can for those who are ready to die for the country. I am confident that my 'Mann ki Baat', which has only been sincerity, will reach you," he said.

Completing one year in office, Modi said the 'manthan' (debate) about the performance of his government is good for democracy as it would help him know what was "lacking".

He said the entire nation has conducted analysis of the first year of his government and there has been "criticism" even while "many gave distinction to us".

"In a democracy, this 'manthan' (debate) is necessary. Views, for and against, are important. It is very essential to know what was lacking.

The good things have their own benefits," he said. Contending that he feels for the poor, he specially mentioned three social security schemes—PM Insurance Scheme, the Jeevan Jyoti Bima Yojana and Atal Pension Scheme, for the benefit of the downtrodden people.

He said these schemes had become a hit within 20 days as 8.52 crore people had enrolled for them. "I feel for the poor... These schemes are a very important step for social security... These will ensure that the poor are not dependent on anybody and are empowered," Modi said. "I want to create an army from among the poor to fight poverty and defeat it so that the burden of poverty that the nation is carrying for years is removed. For ridding the nation of poverty, we will continue to make efforts and succeed," he said.

Talking about the 'Kisan TV channel' launched recently, the Prime Minister said it will help the farmers as well as fishermen to learn the best practices and improve productivity. In this context, he emphasised the need for better nurturing of milk-bearing animals to improve production as he observed that India was far behind in terms of milk production per animal. He pressed for use of scientific technology in this regard.

Modi also mentioned about June 21 which is being celebrated as the International Yoga Day and asked Indians, within the country and abroad, to participate enthusiastically to make it a success. He said the declaration of June 21 as International Yoga Day by the United Nations is a matter of pride for every Indian. Yoga, besides helping the body and soul, can be a catalyst to unite the world and help remove tensions.

He also talked about the heat wave that has gripped the nation and asked people to take care of themselves as well as animals and birds. The just-declared results of board examinations were also mentioned by the Prime Minister who gave a pep talk to the students, asking those who failed not to be disheartened but take it as an opportunity to do better in life.

In this context, he cited the example of renowned scientist and former President A P J Abdul Kalam, saying he had written in his book that he wanted to be a pilot but failed in the test for it. "There is ray of hope even in failure," Modi said, highlighting how Kalam, after failing to be a pilot, became such a famous scientist and then the President of India.

He also asked parents of those students who had failed not to treat it as the end of the world and support them.

SMALL SAVINGS AND RETIREMENT PLANNING

The objective of savings is to cater to future needs. The small savings schemes introduced by the Government of India help people develop the habit of savings to finance their future needs. The concept of retirement planning in India is still at a nascent stage.

This could be attributed to the low income levels and the lack of awareness about the importance of retirement planning early in life. There are different types of small savings schemes and they differ from one another on parameters like investment limits, maturity period, liquidity and returns, interest rates offered to the depositors and tax concessions, if any.

When individuals have small amounts of money at their disposal, the best option for investment is the small savings schemes.

The pension plans can be categorized under compulsory, voluntary, and social assistance schemes. The compulsory schemes include the employee provident fund, employee pension fund, civil service pension scheme, group superannuation plan, etc. Pensions under the voluntary category include products offered by private banks, the post office, insurance, and mutual fund companies.

The targeted social assistance programs are meant for a specific target group, usually from the economically weaker sections of the society. They include the National Old Age Pension Scheme (NOAPS) and National Family Benefit Scheme (NFBS) under the center. Pricing of the small savings schemes is not rational in the sense that different savings schemes have differing interest rates, maturity terms, liquidity, and returns. Most of the savings schemes were launched by the government as a social security measure and to mop up funds for social development. The determination of the cost of a retirement plan is a difficult task.

The cost of a retirement plan is the difference of the assets (the sum of investment returns and the contributions made to the pension plan) and liabilities (benefits to be paid as per the pension plan and the administration expenses) possessed by the retirement solutions marketer.

These components of the cost system are measured and estimated by the complex process of actuarial valuation.

Promotions are very important in marketing small savings schemes and retirement products. They are used by both the public as well as the private sector.

Advertising in the small savings category makes effective use of radio and print ads. The media strategy of retirement solution providers includes greater emphasis on television advertising supported by radio (FM radio) and print advertising.

Various appeals used by marketers for advertising include emotional, fear-evoking, and zealous appeals. The sales promotion activities with regard to the small savings are managed by the National Savings Institute (NSI). These promotional activities include contests, special campaigns, and sweepstake offers.

Sales promotions are restricted in retirement products, especially pension plans of insurance marketers as there are certain restrictions imposed on offering gifts and conducting contests.

The public relation activities of small savings marketers include distribution of pamphlets, hoardings, conducting dramas in villages, exhibition, handbills, seminars, press release, etc. The PR activities of marketers of retirement products primarily focus on two objectives - increasing consumer awareness and improving brand receptivity among customers.

Increasing awareness is preferred by the government and branding is the focus of private players. The PR activities include conducting seminars on retirement solutions, distributing retirement planners, and providing retirement calculators. Distribution for small savings as well as retirement products is through direct and indirect channels. The direct distribution is through the personal selling. Personal selling is done by the agents who are categorized based on the type of the scheme and the target group.

The agents are crucial in the mobilization of savings. There are generally three types of agents, viz., Standard Agency System, Mahila Pradhan Kshetriya Bachat Yojana (MPKBY), and the Public Provident Fund Agency. Indirect distribution makes use of channels like post offices, and the branch network of public and private banks. The distribution of retirement products is also done through the direct sales force and agents (direct distribution) and through the bancasssurance route and Direct Selling Agents (indirect distribution).

Bibliography

Adami, Roberta and Orla Gough: *Pension Reforms and Saving for Retirement: Comparing the United Kingdom and Italy.* Policy Studies, 2008.

Ajey Lele: *Strategic Technologies for the Military : Breaking New Frontiers,* Sage, Delhi, 2009.

Anderson, Karen M.: *Pension Politics in Three Small States: Denmark, Sweden and the Netherlands.* Canadian Journal of Sociology, 2004.

Archie, Anthony: *A Small Step Toward Public Pension Reform.* Pacific Research 2006.

Ascah, Louis: *Recent Retirement Income System Reforms: Employer Plans, Public Plans and Tax Assisted Savings.* The Canadian Journal of Economics, 1996.

Banks, J., Blundell, R., & Emmerson, C.: *The Balance Between Defined Benefit, Defined Contribution, and State Provision.* Delhi, 2005.

Barr, Nicholas: *Reforming Pensions: Myths, Truths, and Policy Choices.* International Social Security Review. 2002.

Barrientos, Armando: *Pension Reform and Pension Coverage in Chile.* Bulletin of Latin American, 1998.

Bellamy, C.: Knights in White Armour: The New Art of War and Peace, London, Random House, 1997.

Benoit, E.: *Defence and Economic Growth in Developing Countries,* Lexington MA: Lexington Books, 1973.

Bhaskara Rao: *Military Conversion : Impact on Science and Technology,* Discovery, Delhi, 2003.

Bryant, Bunyan: *Environmental Justice: Issues, Policies, and Solutions,* Washington, DC, Island Press, 1995.

Burch, William R. Jr.: *Human Ecology: An Environmental Approach,* Belmont, Duxbury Press, 1994.

Cathy Solheim: *Military Economics: Issues, Policies, and Solutions,* Washington, D.C., Island Press, 1995.

Charles E. Faupel: *Environmentalism and Civil Rights in Sumter County*, Colorado, Westview Press, 1992.

Cocco, Joao F. and Paula Lopez: *An Empirical Study of Pension Reforms*. London Business School, London School of Economics. London. 2004.

Crabbe, R.J.W. and Poyser, C.A.: *Pension and Widows' and Orphans' Funds*, Cambridge, 1953.

Dearing, Charles L.: *Industrial pensions*, Brookings Institution (USA), 1954.

Dixit, Prabla: *Defence Budget: A Struggle for Power*, New Delhi, Orient Longman, 1981.

Dunlop, Rev. A. Iain: *The Scottish Ministers' Widows' Fund 1745-1993*, Saint Andrew Press, Edinburgh, 1992.

Dunne, J. P. and Brauer, J.: *Arms Trade and Economic Development: Theory, Policy*, Routledge, London, 2004.

Fehr, Hans: *Pension Reform During the Demographic Transition*. Scandinavian Journal of Economics. 2000..

Friedman, G.: *The Future of War: Power, Technology and American World Dominance in the 21st Century*, N.Y., Random House, 1996.

Galtung, Johan: *Pax Pacifica: Terrorism, the Pacific Hemisphere, Globalisation and Peace Studies*. London: Pluto Press, 2005.

Goel, Suresh : *International Encyclopaedia of Military, Security and Intelligence Agencies*, MD Publications, Delhi, 2009.

Gupta, Asha: *Military Rule and Democratization : Changing Perspectives*, Deep & Deep, Delhi, 2003.

Heimanson, Rudolph: *Dictionary of Economics*, N.Y.: Oceana Publications, 1967.

Huntington, S.P.: *The China Modernisation Military and the State*, N.Y., Vintage Books, 1964.

Jones, W.H.: *Government and Politics of India Military Budget*, London, Hutchinson, 1971.

Leena Parmar: *Military Budgeting: Global Perspectives*, Rawat, Delhi, 1999.

Logan, Sir Douglas: *The Birth of a Pension Scheme*, 1985. A history of the Universities' Superannuation Scheme.

Radhakrishna: *Military Ethics: Guidelines for Peace and War*, Sumit Enterprises, Delhi, 2009.

Raj Kumar: *Weapons and Military Technology*, Sumit Enterprises, Delhi, 2009.

Raphael, Marios: *Pensions and Public Servants: A Study of the Origins of the British System*, Mouton, 1964.

Rhodes, G. *Public sector pensions*, 1965.

Rhodes, Richard, *The Making of the Atomic Bomb*, New York: Simon and Schuster, 1988.

Rita Raj: *Global Encyclopaedia of Military Education and Training*, Global Vision, Delhi, 2010.

Robert M Cassidy: *Counterinsurgency and the Global War on Terror: Military Culture and Irregular War*, Pentagon Press, Delhi, 2008.

Rosen, P.: *Societies and Military Power: India and its Armies*, Ithaca, Cornell University Press, 1996.

Sali, M L : *Military Geography*, Manas, Delhi, 2009.

Samuel P. Huntington: *The Soldier and the State : The Theory and Politics of Civil-Military Relations*, Natraj Pub, Delhi, 2005.

Sharma, G.K. and M.S. Jaswal: *Study and Practice of Military Law*, Deep and Deep, Delhi, 2006.

Simon, D. : *Public Administration and Policy of Indian Military*, New York, Knopf, 1950.

Singh, R.S.N. : *Asian Strategic and Military Perspective*, Lancer, Delhi, 2005.

Singhal, D. P.: *India and Afghanistan: 1876-1907. A Study in Diplomatic Relations*, St. Lucia, University of Queensland, 1963.

Strange, Susan: *The Retreat of the State: The Diffusion of Power in the World Economy*, Cambridge: Cambridge University, 1996.

Sutton, J., *Technology and Defence Market Structure*, MIT Press, Delhi, 1998.

Index

❑❑❑